JAILHOUSE

COOKBOOK

D1617224

Praise for Artie Cuisine's

JAILHOUSE COOKBOOK:
THE PRISONER'S RECIPE BIBLE

"A MUST-READ FOR A UNIQUE AUDIENCE"

Chef Artie Cuisine's "Jailhouse Cookbook" is an excellent and truly useful "how to" book that could ease and enhance the lives of any of the hundreds of thousands of inmates that populate U.S. federal and state prison systems. I say this from the perspective of spending the last 40 years as a criminal defense lawyer who has both observed and discussed prison conditions with numerous clients throughout the United States. The book is highly informative with a myriad of practical suggestions and recipes that can be adapted by the user to the available ingredients and specific conditions at the location of his or her incarceration. Even if the inmate lacks access to a formal kitchen, it provides insights into what creative uses can be made of things that are often available in a prison environment. Given the author's education and substantial experience as a trained chef, the recipes are also well worth trying even in a non-prison environment. It also might provide inspiration to the reader for a viable career on the "outside". **APC , CA**

"I HIGHLY RECOMMEND THIS AMAZING BOOK"!

I sent this book to a friend in prison who was desperately looking for recipes after he learned he could cook there. HE LOVED IT!!! It seems the author went out of his way to make this book not just about cooking in prison and other places with limited resources, but also about the challenge of having something positive to look forward to every day. This book is very cleverly written. I enjoyed the story before each recipe, Artie's great wit and positive attitude made what must have been a difficult experience seem easy. **Sunshine, NY**

"JAILHOUSE COOKBOOK ROCKS"

Talk about turning lemons into lemonade. New York chef Artie Cuisine spends his time doing time creating amazing dishes you'll want to try. With a minimum of fancy ingredients and cooking equipment, he serves up a multitude of recipes, including just the right amount of instruction and a large dollop of humor. **BDG, NY**

"I LOVE THIS BOOK"

I really enjoyed this book. It is written by a trained, New York professional chef, who really knows his business. The introduction to each recipe is fascinating, with descriptions of what inspired them. It is amazing that such gourmet meals can be cooked in prison. The instructions are very clear and easy to follow. I have a very small kitchen with very few utensils, and I made the Won Tons and the dipping sauce and they were delicious. **Alho, NY**

"FABULOUSLY ENTERTAINING"

I hope when I'm in lockup I'll be there with Artie! This book is filled with great recipes and fabulous entertainment. **John T. Carter, NY**

"HIGHLY CREATIVE"

One of the best ways to pass time - especially in prison - is to be highly creative with limited resources. Food takes on a special position in these circumstances and this book "Jailhouse Cookbook" shows a wonderful creativity being put to good use. What one can do with limited supplies and ingredients is amazing. Great cooks can't be confined. **Time to Read, FL**

"GREATEST COOKBOOK"

Jailhouse Cookbook is a fascinating read, amazingly poignant insight into Chef's extraordinary life. Cleverly written, humorous, innovative, I couldn't put it down. How to do the most with what you have! And amazing recipes too! Can't wait for Book No. 2. **Lana, CA**

"FASCINATING"

This cook book is amazing! I love reading cook books, but I have never read one with such detailed explanations of each cooking process. The humorous, down to earth descriptions of each culinary accomplishment is entertaining reading. **Florida Foodie, FL**

"WORTHWHILE"

We really enjoyed this very unusual book. It is well written and informative. The recipes look very tempting although we haven't tried them yet. We recommend the book. **JKK, CT**

JAILHOUSE COOKBOOK

THE PRISONER'S RECIPE BIBLE

by

ARTIE CUISINE
CHEF

GoodReadBooks™, Inc.
"Reading Is Time Well Spent"

AUTHOR'S NOTES:
1. Except that I changed some names, everything written here is true.
2.While incarcerated in the New York Prison System, I prepared and cooked all the recipes in this book, using the ingredients and methods described.

AC

GoodReadBooks™, Inc.
"Reading Is Time Well Spent"

JAILHOUSE COOKBOOK - THE PRISONER'S RECIPE BIBLE.
Copyright© 2006 by GoodReadBooks™, Inc. All rights reserved. Printed in the United States of America. No part of this book may be used or reproduced in any manner whatsoever without written permission except in the case of brief quotations embodied in critical articles and reviews. For information, contact:
Service@GoodReadBooks.com

At the publisher's discretion, GRB's books may be purchased at a discount for educational, business, or sales promotional use. For information please write to
Service@GoodReadBooks.com

Published New York City, NY, USA
Library of Congress Cataloging-in-Publication Data
Cuisine, A.
   Jailhouse Cookbook: The Prisoner's Recipe Bible /
   A. Cuisine.

ISBN 978-0-615-41927-5 (trade paper)
1. Cuisine, A. 2. Cooks - Food - Cooking Biography - Chef - 3. Prison - Jail
4. New York (State) - New York.
1. Title.

LCCN: 2011924618

6 5 4 3 2 1

For my Mother on her birthday.
I dedicate this book to you,
Through all the bullshit,
Through all the hardship,
Through all the crazy times,
Through the teenage years,
Through the trial,
Through sickness and in health,
You were always there.

I love you very much.

Contents

RECIPE CHAPTERS

x The Jailhouse Cookbook

PREFACE & AUTHOR'S NOTE

Dear Food Lovers,

As a chef, I can tell you that this **Jailhouse Cookbook** – *The Prisoner's Recipe Bible,* can be considered a primer ... if you can master these recipes, for sure you will be able to get a job on the street as a cook or apprentice chef. It's true that the initial pay isn't much, just enough to survive on, BUT restaurant owners notice talented, hard workers, so if you work hard and are prepared to put in the time, YOU could become a professional chef with a rewarding job. Oh, and as my mother said to me, "You'll never be hungry"!

How do you cook in a cell without a kitchen? How can you bake two and three layer cakes without an oven? Well, here's the inside information! The recipes in this book can be cooked not only in prison but also in school dormitories, apartments with kitchenettes (no ovens), RV's, and anywhere else you happen to be. After you've mastered this Jailhouse Cookbook, you will be amazed at how many recipes you'll create on your own.

I've found myself in many places where my professional culinary knowledge was utterly useless and I've had to apply the basic Marine Credo: 'Improvise, Adapt, Overcome', as this was the only way to end up with a decent meal. Sure, in the winter if you don't have a refrigerator you can put your sodas out on the window sill until they get cold, but baking cakes and pizzas in a dorm or room without an oven, or making a grilled cheese sandwich in a maximum security prison cell using only a tin foil juice lid and a half pint milk carton, are a bit more of a challenge. However, for obvious reasons I'm not including *that* recipe here ...

ABOUT THE AUTHOR

Cooking has always been my life, and the kitchen my home. I have never felt uncomfortable cooking anywhere, unless some head chef was smacking me around.

At the age of eleven I found myself working a sauté station for a friend's father at his health food restaurant. I used to stand on an upside-down plastic milk crate so I could reach the stove. At 13 I worked in a pizzeria and sold gelati from a cart on the street.

Loving bars and clubs I took a bartending course and did some bartending. After high school it was cooking school, and I was off to the races.

After graduating from Peter Kump's Professional Cooking School Program in New York City, (now ICE, Institute of Culinary Education), I was proficient in preparing both modern and classical cuisines.

Next I worked and trained in some of New York's most prestigious restaurants, and furthered my culinary education by studying at culinary schools in New Orleans, Hong Kong and Bangkok. I also attended the prestigious International School for Confectionery Arts in Maryland and studied under renowned pâtissier and chocolatier Ewald Notter, learning chocolate work, sugar casting and sugar sculpting.

I founded a culinary consulting firm which provided menu and food design, food quality improvement, and cost reduction advice to the restaurant industry. I was a food stylist for food magazine film shoots; I provided food preparation and technique demonstrations at food festivals and department stores; and also provided banquet service for 100 to 2,000 at charity functions. Oh, and I had a television cooking show - Yeah, I was one of those TV chefs.

To launch New York's Summer Restaurant Week one year, with a ribbon cutting by New York's Mayor Bloomberg, I built a giant cake, six feet round by four feet high. It weighed approximately 300 pounds ... well, actually only one-eighth of it was edible yellow sponge cake -- but the whole cake was covered in chocolate butter cream frosting and fresh flowers -- no mean feat considering the event was outside in the middle of the summer with no overhead cover.

I spent the next ten years or so cooking in all sorts of fine dining restaurants all over New York City. When I was asked what my specialty was I would say "Progressive American Cuisine with Global Influences", that always shocked anyone who asked. I never really found having to be creative with food a challenge, it came naturally. Until now!

Now, there are no more truffles, no more *foie gras*, no more flavored oils, no more fancy equipment, and I definitely don't have to worry if my meat and fish are fresh, because there aren't any ... I now reside at a New York State Department of Corrections facility. My kitchen consists solely of four electric burners, a toaster and a microwave. My footlocker - which doubles as my pantry - (ha ha) - is well stocked, but with foodstuff I have to think more than twice about before trying to prepare a meal. Although I am Jewish I did not grow up cooking Jewish food, and if I were kosher now I would starve. I asked my mother to look on the Internet and see if there were any jailhouse cookbooks or recipes I could check out for reference. All she could find were recipes for very weird concoctions that frankly, I wouldn't feed my dog.

When I arrived at my correctional facility and entered the kitchen in my dorm, I couldn't believe how good it smelled. A guy was cooking up a storm, breading canned fish, making sauce, tossing vegetables and cooking yellow rice. I had to get to know this guy. Besides wanting to meet someone who enjoyed cooking, I didn't have any pots or pans. When I finally got to the commissary store I found myself with pasta but no pot to boil it in, canned sauce but no sauce pot, you get the picture.

What we cook now can only be referred to as jailhouse cooking. Sure our backgrounds influence us, but what we have to work with is so limited that we really have to be very creative to make meals interesting.

So I decided to write this cookbook with all of you who are incarcerated in mind, in the hope that with my help you will never have to eat another "spread" (*See Glossary*) unless you want to.

None of the obvious obstacles have stopped me from putting down a white sheet for a tablecloth so we can eat like humans. I even put cups of fresh garlic bread sticks on our tables as a nice centerpiece when we eat Italian.

I try to be as civilized as possible, I despise eating out of one large Viking bowl, so I don't!

I haven't included appetizers here, but any of these recipes can be cut down to appetizer size. Inmates rarely eat in courses, and only those who eat with me actually have a salad course. Guys walk past our bounty and come up to me later and want to know how they can "get down" (join the team).

I wrote home:

> *"Hi Mom & Pop:*
> *"My culinary ability has reached far beyond what I would have thought possible given my circumstances and limited resources. Tonight I made five of us a two-course meal that if I'd had garnishes, I would have given at least two stars. Two of the guys agreed that they had never eaten anything like that before. I toasted bread in the toaster and had my newly-appointed sous chef carefully remove the crusts. I drained two cans of mushrooms then sautéed them in oil until they were slightly crispy. I added a package of chicken seasoning from a soup packet to the mushroom juice and enough water to make some chix stock. I added some chix stock to the mushrooms, and then added the butter, knob by knob, agitating the pot to emulsify it into a sauce, called a "beurre monte". I nuked three cans of sardines in mustard sauce. I seasoned the 'shrooms with oregano and garlic powder and S&P TT (salt & pepper to taste) then I was ready to plate it. I placed a little sauce on one piece of toast, then stacked another piece of toast on top of that - you know how I love to stack! - I spooned some of the 'shrooms and more sauce on top of that, topped that with some of the sardines and drizzled some of the mustard sauce around the plate. Then of course I had to do a 'BAM'! That got a good laugh, I didn't know if anyone here would get the reference, then I sprinkled a little more oregano on the plates. I finished*

the meal with spaghetti in a creamy white clam sauce that also came out great".

So, inside this book I've included a list of foods they sell at my commissary store; a list of the foods we are allowed to receive by mail in packages from outside; typical (and approved) foods I asked my mother to send me; a list of cooking utensils that will make your cooking life easier, various cooking tips; and obviously my well-tried recipes. All these recipes are easy to follow and proven tasty. Once you try them, I bet you will even be cooking them when you get home.

Just a reminder, it is essential to read a recipe all the way through before starting to make it, that way you'll know what you need and get my hard-earned tips under your belt before you start.

Good luck, be well and God Bless.

Oh yeah, and enjoy!

Chef Artie Cuisine

Note: *We hope you enjoy this book and find it helpful. Send your comments to Editor@GoodReadBooks.com and let us know what's on your mind.*

AC

EQUIPMENT TO MAKE
YOUR COOKING LIFE EASIER

You do what you gotta do to get by, but the following cooking utensils will certainly make your cooking life easier while you are *"A Guest of The Government"*.

Cans, empty and clean, from beans or soup, etc., to use *for measuring.*

Cans, empty and clean, size of your choice, to use as *a cookie shaper/cookie puncher.* Dust the edges with flour to prevent sticking, and punch out disks of dough for biscuits and cookies.

Cans, large sardine and ham cans, empty and clean, to use as *ring molds.* Remove the top and the bottom so you can fill them with cake mix, or soft foods which you want to set into a round molded shape, such as puddings and Jellos.

Cans, largest possible, to use as *risers/heat deflectors for pots.* Two types, both easy to make. A riser is placed on the burner, under a pot to deflect the heat, allowing slower cooking and preventing burning. So, you can use the ring mold described above, OR you can punch holes in both ends of a can large enough to support your heavy pot. You place the riser on the heat and put your cooking pot on top of it.

Soda can, full, to use as *a rolling pin.*

Soda can, empty, to use *for measuring.*

Cardboard Pieces, to use as *hot plates,* for putting hot dishes and pots on, also good for *draining fried foods.*

Cook Pot: IMUSA aluminum cooking pot. Heavy, with non-removable handles on each side. These IMUSA brand pots have no forbidden screws or bolts, come in several sizes, and are priced right. Before having one sent to you, check with the CO in charge of your package room to find out what specific size pots are allowed at your facility. Between my two cooking partners and myself, we had all the sizes they made! Of course a cooking pot is your most essential item, you'll use it to *make stews and fry stuff, even make cheesecakes and pies in it,* and if you look after your cooking pots they'll last a long time.

Frying pan, non-stick, (remember no screws or bolts).

Lids from juice containers.

Milk cartons, empty.

Paper bags, used to *drain oil from fried foods, and to put finished pies on.*

Paper cups.

Paper towels.

Plastic bags, large, like garbage bags, *to cover the surface of a table or locker so you can work on it.* Slightly dampen the surface you want to work on, or even better dampen a towel or paper towel and place it on your surface, so when you spread the garbage bag on top of it, it will stick and *give you a nice rolling surface.*

Plastic bowls, *for mixing and eating.*

Plastic food containers, (like Tupperware) with lids to *store your leftovers.*

Plastic forks, (sorry no knives allowed).

Plastic plates.

Plastic spatulas.

Plastic spoons.

Plastic stirring and serving spoons.

Rice pot, made specially for making rice. Not essential, you can use your IMUSA pot if you don't have a rice pot.

Tin foil/aluminum foil, (useful, but not essential).

Toilet paper 'doughnut' ring. 35 to 40 turns of paper towel *to use as a pot holder and hand protector.*

Note: *See 'Glossary of Terms' for further explanations.*

FOOD ITEMS SOLD
AT 'MY' COMMISSARY

Nobody cooks alone here, it's always three or four guys chipping in. Nobody has all the ingredients they need, so pooling is necessary. Prison commissaries across the board generally carry the same stuff, so I'm told. I think this trip will be the extent of my research, so I'll take people's word for it! If you're in jail and have my book, and you want to make something out of ingredients not available at your commissary, someone in your pool can try and get it sent in. If I can have it sent in so can you, and of course you can substitute.

Canned Meats & Seafood:

Canned chunk chicken
Beef stew
Corned beef
Roast beef
Luncheon meat
Vienna sausage
Pink salmon
Clams
Kipper snacks
Sardines
Tuna
Mackerel
Calamari
Octopus
Chili

Rice/Pasta/Soups:

Macaroni & cheese
Chicken Rice-A-Roni
Rice
Elbow macaroni
Spaghetti
Rigatoni
Cream of mushroom soup
Soup Beef Ramen
Soup Chicken Ramen
Soup Shrimp Ramen

Sauces/Canned Vegetables & Fruits:

Peaches
Fruit cocktail
Pineapple
Tomato paste
Tomato sauce
Crushed tomatoes

Whole kernel corn
Chickpeas
Red kidney beans
Mixed vegetables
Mushrooms
Potatoes
Pigeon peas
Spaghetti sauce
White clam sauce

Milk/Sugar:

Honey
Maple syrup
Powdered milk
Coffee creamer
Canned milk
Sugar

Candy:

Assorted Candy
Peppermints
Tootsie Pops
Life Savers
Almond Joy
M&M's with peanuts
Kit Kat
Milky Way
Hershey's with almonds

Cookies/Pastries/Bread/Snacks:

Oatmeal cookies
Honey buns
Swiss Rolls
Vanilla cream cookies
Peanut butter cookies
Pop tarts

Chocolate chip cookies
Doughnut Stix
Chocolate Chip Granola
  Bars
Donuts
Cheese Curls
Potato chips, plain
English muffins
French bread
Italian sliced bread
Granola bar, raisin
Bagels, cinnamon
Bagels, plain
Snack crackers
Saltine crackers
Microwave popcorn
Corn chips
Potato chips /BBQ flavor
Potato chips /Sour Cream
  flavor

Condiments:

Mustard
Ketchup
Hot sauce
Mayonnaise
Real lemon juice
Sazon
Garlic powder
Peanut butter
Strawberry preserves
Grape jelly
Adobo seasoning
Oregano
Cooking oil
Onions
Hot peppers

Kosher pickles
Salad dressing
Salt

Lunch Meat/Cheeses/ Frozen Foods:

Margarine
Cream cheese
American cheese
Mozzarella cheese
Parmesan cheese
Beef franks
Beef sausage
Pepperoni
Sliced pastrami
Sliced turkey
Chicken wings
Banquet-So-Fried-Chicken

Breakfast/Baking Products:

Instant oatmeal
Grits
Pancake flour
Flour
Yellow cake mix
Chocolate frosting
Egg Beaters
Orange juice

Ice Cream:

Vanilla
Butter Almond
Cookies & Cream
Ice Cream Sandwiches

Coffee/Tea/Cocoa/ Drinks:

Taster's Choice coffee
Decaf coffee
Instant coffee
Tea
Cocoa mix
Iced tea
Kool-Aid cherry
Kool-Aid punch
Kool-Aid grape
Orange drink

Soda:

Pepsi
Welch's Grape
Cherry Coke
Mountain Dew
Classic Coke
Sprite
Diet Pepsi

FOOD & UTENSILS 'MY' FACILITIES
ALLOWED SENT IN FROM OUTSIDE

The food and utensils listed on the next page may be received by inmates through the Package Room at "my" correctional facility, ... *subject to the following restrictions and qualifications:*

No glass containers.

Fresh fruit, vegetables and food products must be received commercially packaged, in airtight, hermetically sealed containers, impervious to external influence.

No home bakery, restaurant, or delicatessen prepared foods.

No alcoholic contents or ingredients.

Inmates may receive two packages per month containing foodstuffs, the combined weight of which shall not exceed 35 lbs.

This package list does NOT contain all rules and procedures for the receipt of articles in packages.

Everything is subject to the restrictions and qualifications of Directive 4911 and/or individual facility memoranda which should be reviewed for complete information. If in doubt, you can send a message to the Package Room Officer.

Ultimately, what's allowed in is at the Superintendent's discretion!

Food Items:

Beverages - including dried beverage mix (no plastic soda/liquid drink containers)

Bread (*in double-sealed package, no twist ties*)

Canned food, no larger than 16 oz each

Candy, no alcohol filling

Cheese, sliced or chunk, must *not* require refrigeration

Coffee, not over 16 oz can

Cold cuts

Dried coffee cream

Fruit, no dried fruit, except one 2 oz package of raisins per food package

Meats, cooked only. Meat requiring refrigeration after opening is allowed.

Frozen meat, and meat requiring refrigeration prior to opening is not allowed

Pastry

Seafood (*cooked only, including smoked*)

Snacks, potato chips, pretzels, cheese twists, crackers, cookies and other similar items, no peel backs.

Tea, no loose tea (herbal and flavored tea allowed)

Vegetables

Utensils, plastic:

Bowls

Cups & saucers

Food storage containers, 2 quart maximum each

Plates

Spoons & forks, pliable only

Drinking container, not to exceed 16 oz

Utensils, metal:

Non-electric pot, 6 quart max.

1 Fry pan, 12" max., no removable handle, no cast iron, permit item.

Pots and pans:

With removable screws *not* allowed

Cast iron, *not* allowed

TYPICAL FOODS
I REQUESTED FROM HOME

Each month, the authorities allowed 35 pounds of food to be sent in from the street, in two individual packages, each weighing no more than 17.5 pounds each. I told my mother what I wanted and after a while, using my requests and the prison list as a guide, she typed up and sent me a monthly list of items I could choose from. I knew pretty much what I needed as I prepared my menus well in advance, and I checked those items off on the list and mailed it back to her so she could shop for the next package.

Here's a list of foods I typically asked for. Remember (1) fresh breads must be double-wrapped at the source, no twist ties allowed, (2) fresh fruits and vegetables must be individually Saran-wrapped, and (3) cans can weigh no more than 16 oz. each.

I always reminded my mother to buy whatever was cheapest, on special offer, or on sale, and not to buy something on my list if it was expensive. Items like three bean salad were excellent because they came in vinegar which I poured off and used to make salad dressings and sweet & sour sauces. I specified how many of each item I wanted, for example: three onions and one green pepper. By being precise, I got exactly what I needed.

TYPICAL FOODS
I REQUESTED FROM HOME

Fresh Produce:

Green peppers, sweet
Red peppers, sweet
Chilli peppers, assorted
Head of lettuce, Iceberg
Hard tomatoes
Cucumbers:
. Large English, whole/half
. Small Kirby's or other
Radishes
Onions, yellow
Potatoes
Broccoli
Apples
Pears
Bananas, Spanish, Green
Oranges
Grapefruit
Cranberries *(for holidays)*
Celery
Carrots large/small
Cabbage, half/whole
Mushrooms
Garlic, whole heads
Garlic peeled
Cheese, without "*Keep Refrigerated*" on label
Green beans
Other fruits & vegetables in season.

Meats & Fish, Canned & Packaged: *(cans 16oz maximum weight)*:

Jerky
Jerky Bites
Jack Links ready cooked ground beef:
. Italian flavor
. Mexican flavor
. Regular flavor, lightly seasoned
Salami
Ham
White chicken
Salmon
Sardines in sauce
Tuna
Mussels
Squid
Oysters, regular/smoked

Milk, Canned & Packaged:

Milk
. Evaporated
. Condensed
. Coconut milk, small/large
. Creamer powdered

Fruits Canned:

Tangerines/oranges
Pears
Fruit cocktail
Pineapple
Other fruits, well priced

Vegetables, Canned:

Corn
Beets *(w/without vinegar)*
Green beans
Peas
Chinese mixed vegetables
Chinese stir fry vegetables
Chinese bamboo shoots
Chinese water chestnuts
Artichokes
Three bean salad, in vinegar
Pinto beans
Chick peas
Tomatoes/plum, other
Chipottles

Condiments, Canned:

Curry paste Indian
Curry paste, hot oriental
*(No curry powder or dried
spices allowed.)*
Pizza sauce
Spaghetti sauce
Sloppy Joe sauce
Enchilada sauce

Pie Fillings & Frostings, Canned:

Fruit
Lemon

Peanut butter/frosting
Chocolate, baking
Coconut
Cherry
Blueberry
Pumpkin *(for holidays, with
& without spices*

Other Canned/Packaged Products:

Coffee, powder/granules
Sugar
Tea in bags:/plain/flavored)
(no loose tea allowed)
Seltzer/soda water
Drink mixes, powdered:
. Tang/orange flavor
Bread, whole wheat/sliced
Muffins (6 per pack)
*(All bread products double
sealed package, no twist ties)*

Chapter 1

BREAKFAST ITEMS

Sausage, Egg & Cheese Biscuits
Spicy Egg & Potato Frittata
Breakfast Wrap
French Toast Pockets
Cracker Brie Omelet

SAUSAGE, EGG & CHEESE BISCUITS
For 6 - 8 Sandwiches

When was the last time you had a good breakfast sandwich? Unless you're at home or reading this on the train on your way to work, it might have been a while. Manhattan's Midtown is famous for 'delivery'. At 4 o'clock in the morning I can get a six-pack of beer, a pack of cigarettes, and an Egg McMuffin delivered to my door in less than five minutes. Oh, you don't believe me? Where I live McDonald's delivers. Not some company playing middleman so you get soggy cold fries and nasty burgers, Mickey D delivers, it used to be 777-FAST. Well, due to my recent incarceration I thought I would have to settle for EggBeaters on toast. Not so, check out this recipe.

The only special equipment you're gonna need is four ring molds (*see Glossary*). Now ring molds can be made almost the same way you make risers for your pots, but the edges must be smooth and clean. You can't just hack the bottoms off the cans, they must come off clean. If your commissary tuna fish cans have rounded bottoms like mine, you might have to search for a few days as I did. Someone had some chunk chicken cans from the street that have thin flat edges on both sides, so when I took a can opener to them I got both sides off quite easily. Zap, now I had four ring molds. This search only has to be conducted once, clean them and re-use them. Perfect ring molds will be multifunctional, you can also use them as flame deflectors under your pots, and inside pots as risers for your water-bath (*see glossary*) needs. OK, now you have ring molds and we're going to place them in a buttered rice pot, line them with pastry dough, fill them with EggBeaters and sliced cooked, sausage (you can use any meat - bacon, turkey-bacon, ham, pastrami), sliced cheese, and another layer of pastry dough.

When this biscuit dough is lightly browned on top, you're going to remove it from the pot with a spatula, pop off the ring mold, and BAM! Sausage-Egg-and-cheese-biscuit-pastry-sandwich things!   I don't really know what to call them, but they are good!

Ingredients:

1½ Cups flour
2 Tablespoons pancake flour mix
½ Teaspoon salt
1 Stick butter, chilled (8 tablespoons = 1 stick)
10-12 Tablespoons cold water.

Step 1: In a large enough bowl mix all your dry ingredients (salt, flour and pancake mix).

Step 2: Cut the butter into very small pieces and chill until firm. If the butter is already very cold and hard, simply cut it into little pieces. Add the butter pieces to the flour one tablespoon at a time.

Step 3: Using a thick plastic fork mash each cut-up tablespoon of butter into the flour mix. The idea here is to mash and stir each tablespoon of butter until it is mixed into the flour-mix so well that you no longer see any butter. Lots of people like to incorporate their butter until the mashed butter resembles little peas. Not here. We want this flour-mix to look like sand, so keep mashing.

Step 4: When all the butter has been incorporated and your mix looks like sand, start adding the cold water, about two tablespoons at a time. At this point discard the plastic fork and start kneading with your hand. With one hand squeeze the dough gently as if you were giving a massage. With the other hand, drizzle in the cold water. Don't use all the water if you don't need to. (Remember, the tablespoon measure you are using is actually a large plastic teaspoon, it's not really a teaspoon measure, but it's not a tablespoon measure either). When the dough comes easily and cleanly away from the sides of the bowl, stop adding water.

Step 5: Let dough rest for at least 15 minutes, preferably covered with a damp cloth or paper towel. It isn't necessary to refrigerate it, but if you do, remember to let it come back to room temperature before you use it.

> **Note:** *If you need to refrigerate your dough for more than an hour or overnight, omit the damp cloth or paper towels, and instead cover it tightly with either plastic wrap, or tie it tightly in two plastic bags.*

Step 6: Flour the edge of your ring molds to prevent your dough from sticking to them.

Step 7: To make the tops: after the dough has rested, roll it out to ⅛ of an inch thickness, and use one of the ring molds to punch out six to eight circles. The number of sandwiches you can make will depend on the size of your ring molds. After punching out your tops, set them aside.

Step 8: Put all your scraps and leftover dough back together and roll it out again to ⅛ of an inch thickness. This second batch of circles you punch out are going to be larger and will be the bottoms.

Step 9: For the bottoms: place a ring mold on the rolled out dough, but don't press it down because this time you want to cut an extra large circle by cutting the circle one inch away from the edge of the ring mold. This will leave you with six to eight pastry circles that are two inches larger than the first batch you cut for the tops.

Step 10: Butter and flour a heavy-bottomed rice pot. Also butter and flour the insides of your ring molds, and shake out the excess flour. I wouldn't bake more than four at a time. If you're making six sandwiches, bake only three at a time.

Step 11: Place the ring molds in the pot. Place the larger pastry circles inside the ring molds, press them flat against the bottom of the pot and up the sides of the ring mold. Don't squish the dough, press it lightly against the sides of the mold.

Step 12: First sear off your chosen meat product on both sides. In this recipe each sandwich gets three thin slices of Beef Summer Sausage. The same goes for any meat, bacon etc., cook it first, then gently place it inside the pastry ring.

Step 13: Pour 2 oz of EggBeaters on top of the sausage. Use a real egg if you have one (wouldn't that be nice?) Season with a pinch of salt.

Step 14: Float one slice of American cheese on top of the eggs.

Step 15: Now place the smaller pastry circles - which are exactly the same size as the ring molds - on top of the cheese.

Step 16: Using a fork, press the edges down gently, sealing the top pastry circle to the bottom pastry circle. Get it?

> **Note:** *If you want the tops to be shiny and brown, brush them with a little egg before baking. I don't like them au-natural!*

Step 17: Cover the pot but do not place the pot lid completely on the pot. Leave it a little off to the side (only a little) so steam can escape.

Step 18: Place the pot on low heat for about 25 minutes or until the top of the biscuit is hard.

Voila! Breakfast is served. Hooch Mimosas anyone?

SPICY EGG & POTATO FRITATA

Everyone should have a good egg dish under their belts. Gee, how many reasons can I think of? A lot actually, most of them really apply to the street, but there's no reason you can't practice some dishes here to perfect them, then make them when you get out. How about impressing your wife or your girlfriend with breakfast in bed the next morning. Add a glass of juice, a couple of pieces of toast, some coffee, and maybe a flower? Yeah, she'll be back. Want a more pressing reason? Hmm ... how about weird hot cereals five days a week? Gross. Personally I don't care for Farina, Wheatina, oatmeal, corn meal and whatever other warm larval concoctions they seem to love to feed us in the mess hall. I understand it must be cheap, but swallowing gooey matter just ain't my style.

As always, this dish doesn't have to be spicy, simply omit the

Jalapeno and the hot sauce if you want to. A non-spicy version will work just fine. Any vegetables will be good. Frittatas are basically just large, thick, round omelets, so whatever you like in your omelets you will like in your frittata. Here is what I made mine with, because it's what I had at the time (what's new?). This frittata will give you four nice size wedges, but if you're starving you might need two. One of my buddies had some turkey-bacon, and another had English muffins, and so on, by the time we all got our breakfast stuff together we had so much food to accompany our frittatas, that one slice each was plenty.

Ingredients:

1-15 oz Can potatoes, drained, dried and diced small
2 Tablespoons butter or margarine
½ Jalapeno, chopped small
1 oz EggBeaters
½ Small onion, diced small
⅓ Green bell pepper, diced small
3 Tablespoons cooking oil
A good pinch of salt
2 Shakes of Tabasco (or any hot sauce).

For best results use a small non-stick frying pan or an omelet pan, but any small skillet will work.

Step 1: Place half the oil in a hot pan with the diced onion. Cook until tender (3-4 minutes).

Step 2: Add the rest of the oil, the peppers and the potato and cook, stirring occasionally, until the potatoes start to brown (3-4 minutes)

Step 3: Place butter into the mix and let melt, about 1 minute.

Step 4: Last, add the Jalapeno, the salt, the EggBeaters, and the hot sauce. Turn the heat down to medium (about 4). Stir well until everything is incorporated. Let stand in the pan for about another 3 minutes. Using a spatula, carefully flip the frittata upside down and lightly brown the other side.

If you're worried about flipping the frittata, I have an-other technique for you. In the real world we could just place the pan under the broiler for a minute or two until the frittata browns, or we could simply place the whole pan in the oven, assuming the pan doesn't have a plastic handle. Here's a quick fix: place a large lid or plastic plate on top of the frittata and pan, and flip both over (basically turning it upside down) so the plate is on the bottom and the pan is on the top. Gently lift off the pan, place it back on the stove and slide the frittata back into the pan, brown side up. This will enable you to cook the other side for another minute or two.

Step 5: Place your lid or plastic plate on top of the frittata again and flip it out just as before. Slice and serve. That's it.

BREAKFAST WRAPS

I've mentioned this idea elsewhere in the book, but I thought I'd make it a headliner. Unless it's your day off or you're lucky enough not to have any 'programming', I wouldn't start making these from scratch. When you make any kind of dough, I recommend you save some (patty dough, pizza dough, stromboli dough, they are all basically the same combination of flour and pancake mix). When I make a recipe for dinner that uses dough, I save a nice chunk and put it in the refrigerator. I've never kept dough in the fridge longer than a week so I don't know how long it will last, but it will definitely keep refrigerated for a week. So save some dough.

I got moved again, I couldn't believe it. This time to an R-SAT (Residential Substance Abuse Treatment) dorm. Just another dorm, with different rules. My first day in R-SAT I walked into the kitchen to put away my fridge and freezer bags, and people were making pancakes and breakfast stuff. After I started getting packages from home and my commissary money caught up with me from Rykers Island, I vowed to never, ever eat breakfast in the mess hall again, I won't go into detail here ... Seeing everyone cooking, and not yet having had anything to eat, I was instantly starved. I remembered I had a nice size ball of dough in the refrigerator, left over from gyros

I'd made a few nights before. I pulled out the dough, a container of EggBeaters, a couple of cheese slices and half a sausage, and it was on.

Ingredients for the dough:

2 Bean-cans of flour, plus extra for rolling out the dough
1 Bean-can filled with pancake mix
3 Teaspoons salt
2 Teaspoons garlic powder (if you have it)
1 Teaspoon Adobo seasoning
2 Teaspoons dried oregano (if you have it)
About ¾ of a bean-can of cold water.

Step 1: In a large pot mix 2 bean-cans of flour, the salt, pancake mix, oregano, Adobe seasoning and the garlic powder. Mix well.

Step 2: Add half the water, and (wearing a glove if you can get one) mix with your hand. Keep adding water a little at a time and mixing until the dough comes together. If you don't need all the water don't use it. When you can pick up the dough ball in one large piece and there is no flour mix left on the sides of the pot, you have added enough water.

Step 3: Lift the dough out of the pot and sprinkle just a little of the leftover half-can of flour on the bottom of the pot. Replace dough on top of the flour, then lightly dust the top of the dough with more flour. Press the dough down until it is spread out evenly into a large disk touching all sides of the pot. Fold the dough in half, then in half again, forming a sort of triangle. Press dough down into a large disk again, then lift it out and dust the bottom of the pot with more flour, sprinkle more flour on top, and fold again. Repeat this process about 8 times or until you have a smooth soft dough and it isn't at all tacky. Set the dough aside.

My first egg sandwich in E-dorm was simply scrambled eggs, sausage and cheese. After I had made them on request, for stamps of course, I started filling them with such ingredients as tomato omelets, potatoes, sautéed onions and fried bacon. Here's how:

Ingredients for the filling:

Scrambled eggs
Cheese
Any meat product (cooked or heated)
Potatoes
Sautéed onions
Whatever else you like...

Step 1: Scramble the eggs.

Step 2: Heat or fry meat product.

Step 3: Sautee onions and/or vegetables.

Step 4: Wrap eggs, meat and cheese in the dough.

Step 5: Put your breakfast wrap in the pan and sear it off.

Eat it right away. It's just like having eggs, cheese, sausage or bacon and toast, except all in one.

How about an egg pizza roll? Yeah, we get egg pizza here once a month or so, it's not very good. So, an egg pizza roll? Try wrapping some scrambled eggs in your stromboli dough (see recipe for strombolis), with a little spaghetti sauce (or pizza sauce if you have it), and some sliced pepperoni and cheese. Bangin' egg pizza rolls! Like green peppers? Got some? Use 'em. Add your favorite pizza toppings to the roll, whatever they are. Just remember, if they're raw vegetables like peppers and onions, saute' them first until just turning tender, and season them.

FRENCH TOAST POCKETS

My favorite French toast pockets are stuffed with peanut butter and jelly. I must say that of all the different kinds of cheesecakes I make, peanut butter and jelly by far outsell my other varieties. So of all the stuffings I could use between my slices of French toast, it seems only natural that PB&J would be at the top of my list. I find that if I flavor my egg batter well, with almost anything sweet so that enough flavor is infused into the actual French toast, only a small amount of mix needs to be packed between the slices for a surprise center.

You can use anything here as a stuffing, like I always say "be creative". Use what you have and like. I recommend not using more than two tablespoons of your favorite mix when making these sandwiches. The idea is that with just enough filling, leaving about an inch of the perimeter without mix, the edges will adhere to each other when the egg mix cooks. Lots of combinations work well. What do you like? How about mashing some bananas and putting some chocolate pieces in? Snickers, M&Ms and peanut butter?

Oh yeah baby.

Whenever someone in my dorm gets something interesting sent in from the street, we try it. My PB&J version is what I'm going to map out for you here, but you can use Twix bars, honey, Kit Kats or fruit puree, really anything that is thick will work.

Ingredients for 4 pockets:

8 Slices of bread, left out overnight
4 Tablespoons jelly (any kind)
4 Tablespoons peanut butter
1/2 Container EggBeaters (or two eggs)
1/2 Can evaporated milk (about 2 oz)
2 Tablespoons honey
2 Tablespoons sugar
Pinch of salt
Pinch of cinnamon (if you have it)
Butter or oil for frying.

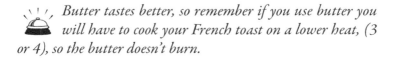 *Butter tastes better, so remember if you use butter you will have to cook your French toast on a lower heat, (3 or 4), so the butter doesn't burn.*

Step 1: Let the bread slices sit out overnight or until dry and firm. You can place them in a paper bag with a napkin if you're concerned about hygiene, but they do need to dry out.

Step 2: Mix the eggs, sugar, salt, honey, milk and cinnamon (if you have it) together in a bowl deep enough to allow you to submerge your sandwiches.

Step 3: Place one tablespoon of jelly and one tablespoon of peanut butter right in the center between two slices of bread. This way when you press the slices together, the filling will stay in the middle leaving the edges bare. Press the slices together gently so you don't break the hardened bread. Repeat this with the other three sandwiches.

Step 4: Give your egg mix a good stir, making sure all the sugar and salt have dissolved. As you submerge your sandwiches in the egg mix air bubbles will start rising out of the mix. When there are no more bubbles you have soaked each sandwich for long enough. Just under five seconds should be sufficient, depending on how thick and dry your slices of bread are. The last sandwich won't be submergible so flip it over to absorb the rest of the egg mixture.

Step 5: Fry both sides of the sandwiches in a skillet with either butter or oil, over medium heat until golden brown.

Serve with pancake syrup, or for a nice twist try chocolate syrup, or even make your own chocolate sauce, (*see index for chocolate sauce recipe*). An extra shake of sugar and/or cinnamon is also a great idea if you don't have any syrup or sauces. Try topping them with fresh or canned fruit or whipped cream and that chocolate sauce.
Wow!

CRACKER BRIE OMELET
Good for 4 portions

This simple egg dish is my jailhouse rendition of a dish my mother used to make for me when I was a kid. Matzo is a Jewish bread, an unleavened cracker sold in huge six inch square sheets. This traditionally Jewish preparation of eggs and matzo is known as Matzo Brie (pronounced bry). My mother is European so she prepared it the European way, savory. She used to sauté onions and mushrooms with the matzo and eggs. Sometimes it even got topped with cheese and finished in the oven. But I always smothered it in ketchup. The American or Western version of matzo brie is served sweet like a pancake with lots of powdered sugar and/or maple syrup. Both ways are delicious, I guess it just depends on your mood. I can only imagine that the original concept of soaking matzo in milk or water before adding it to beaten eggs was to stretch the eggs. It comes out sort of like a cross between an egg frittata and a quiche. In fact, a frittata is the Spanish version of matzo brie, one stretches the omelet-like dish with potatoes, and the other with matzo.

Well, one morning four of our crew were hungry and we only had 20 minutes before we had to go to our respective programs. The mess hall that day was serving something unappetizing, so we opted to throw breakfast together ourselves. Sometimes we made pancakes or eggs with bagels or muffins, but we rarely (being nocturnal) had time between waking up and getting out to do much in the way of breakfast stuff, except on weekends. Our Monday through Friday gig was more like coffee and go.

Well this just kinda happened. I didn't want to start cutting and cooking vegetables with only a 20-minute window. So, one huge non-veggie matzo brie omelet coming up. Of course I didn't have matzo, but I did have Saltine crackers. I went for it, and just like old times I slapped on some ketchup and we all chowed down. Toast, coffee and a huge cracker omelet, what more could you want? Oh yeah, steak and eggs, soooooon, real soon!

With toast, bagels or muffins this cracker brie omelet will feed four people.

Ingredients:

12 oz EggBeaters, or six eggs
1 Sleeve Saltine crackers
6 oz Milk or water
3 Slices white American cheese (any cheese will work)
½ Teaspoon salt
2 Tablespoons butter or margarine
½ A beef sausage (about 5 oz), cubed small.

Step 1: Break the crackers into large pieces (not crumbs) and soak them in the milk or water. Let stand for at least five minutes.

Step 2: While the crackers are soaking, scramble (beat) your eggs or pour your EggBeaters into a large bowl.

Step 3: Place the butter and the cubed sausage in a large frying pan, 10 -12 inches in diameter (non-stick works best). Sauté sausage 3 - 4 minutes, or until just starting to crisp around the edges.

Step 4: Drain off any excess liquid from the soaking crackers (don't squeeze them, just pour off the excess). Add crackers and salt to the eggs and stir for one minute. Tear the cheese slices and add to the mix, then pour egg mixture into the hot pan with the sausage.

Step 5: Let egg mixture cook 3 - 4 minutes until it starts to firm up. Using a plastic knife or the handle of a plastic fork or spoon, gently go around the entire edge making sure it will come free from the pan. Place a plate on top of the cracker brie, turn the pan upside down so the cracker brie slides onto the plate. Slide the cracker brie back into the pan with the un-browned side down, so you can cook the other side. If you have an oven (and your pan doesn't have a plastic handle) you can just put the whole pan in the oven for a minute, I don't, but you could.

Step 6: Cook the other side for another two minutes or so, until firm.

Step 7: Slide cracker brie out onto a plate, cut and serve with ketchup and your favorite toasted bread product.

Chapter 2

SOUPS & ENTREES

I rarely left the dorm to go to chow during the winter ... it was very cold, and I had to walk almost a mile in each direction to and from the mess hall ... so I cooked and had the sense to create lots of hot dishes for those cold, frigid days. I've included some of my favorite winter weather soup and casserole recipes to warm you up.

Sopa de Pescau
Ghetto Onion Soup
Mexican Black Bean Soup
Spicy Salmon Cakes
Jamaican Beef & Cheese Patties
Chilled Tuna Casserole
Surf & Turf (Tuna Sausage Cakes)
Gyros
Chicken Dijonaise
Yum Yum's Roast Beef Slammers & Sauce
141st Street Tuna Mayo
New Age Shepherd's Pie
Jack Mack 11 Different Ways
Black Fish Stew
Chicken & Turkey Pot Pie
Beef & Kidney Bean Stew
Chicken Tenders

SOPA DE PESCAU (FISH SOUP)
Makes 5 Healthy Servings

Pronounced just the way it's spelled, it sounds much nicer than 'fish soup'. It's really more of a stew than a soup, it's thick, and delicious over any kind of rice. One of the Spanish guys in my dorm prides himself on his culinary abilities and likes to show off by giving me tastes when he cooks. This stew recipe became more of a base for me to work with than a dish that I liked to frequent. The simple concept of this base can be easily modified to imitate foods from many different cultures. Sauté in some fresh ginger, use lime juice and a little cilantro, and it becomes a Thai dish. Add a couple of teaspoons of curry paste, and depending on the type of curry paste you use, this dish becomes Indian, West Indian, or even Jamaican. I had a shock when I received a can of *Maesri brand Leang Curry Paste*, a product of Thailand, it smelled and tasted awful, no surprise considering the ingredients included 40% snakehead... say what? Yes, snakehead. No, I checked it out and snakehead is a popular fish in Thailand. Nonetheless, it was really bad.

Anyway, be creative here, use any of your favorite vegetables or whatever you have at your disposal, canned or fresh. Mushrooms, tomatoes, potatoes, plantains, yucca, squash, almost anything will work. I kept this stew inexpensive using the all-popular Jack Mack as my fish. If you happen to have shrimp and scallops, use 'em. If you have cans of roast beef in gravy, use them instead of fish. Fried chicken? Of course, take it off the bone and use the skin for crackling. Do you get my point? This stew can become almost any kind of dish you want with minimal effort and ingenuity.

Ingredients for 5 healthy servings:

2-15 oz Cans Jack Mack, cleaned, with juice
1-4 oz Can mushrooms in water
3 oz Tomato paste
3 oz Tomato paste (half a 6 oz can))
1-14 oz Can coconut milk
1 Medium onion, sliced
4 Tablespoons lemon juice

1 Teaspoon garlic powder
1 Teaspoon Adobo seasoning
1 Packet Sazon seasoning
3 Tablespoons cooking oil
4 oz Water
2 Teaspoons sugar
Salt to taste

Step 1: In a large sauce pot, over medium heat (3-4), place the oil, onion, garlic powder, Sazon, Adobo and the tomato paste. Let simmer uncovered until onions are soft, (4–5 minutes).

Step 2: Clean the Jack Mack but reserve the juice. Try to pour the juice out of the can slowly, and carefully using your fingers, stop any large pieces of skin or bone passing out.

Step 3: When the onions are tender, add all other ingredients except the fish, and bring to a boil.

Step 4: Lower your stew to a simmer and check the seasoning for salt. If you like it more tomato tasting add more tomato paste, if you want it spicy hit it with a Jalapeno, etc.

Step 5: When you are happy with the flavor, turn off the stove. Gently break the cleaned Jack Mack into bite-sized pieces and add it to the pot. Don't let the fish sit in a simmering pot of stew because the fillets will break into tiny pieces, and your beautiful stew will become a mush pie filling.

Serve over rice, delicious! This tastes especially good over rice with Sazon and a little coconut.

GHETTO ONION SOUP
Makes 4 large bowls

Not too many people bother making soup here, but this recipe came out so good and was so easy I had to include it. I have made French onion soup in fine-dining restaurants in New York City, and unbelievably this version came out just as good, if not better. All the onion soup recipes I've encountered have been slightly different, but they were all the same in one respect, they contained some amount of alcohol. A light splash of cognac or sherry are very common, as is pouring red wine over caramelized onions and letting it reduce. You know what? All that liquor is going to waste, it's totally uncalled for. I think the strength and the flavor of the beef stock, or even vegetable stock, are what is going to make this a delicious soup. Just as important is the cheese, it should be neither too bland nor over-powerful when we use it to top off the soup at the end.

For my beef stock I used the packets of seasonings that come with the beef ramen noodle soups. Of course use whatever cheese you have, if it's mozzarella, so be it. I had a block of extra sharp cheddar, so I chopped it up to a grated cheese consistency and it came out great. The Hellava Good brand of sharp Cheddar isn't overly sharp, it's just right. You can try using grated Parmesan, but I don't recommend it. Real grated Parmesan, like Parmigiano Regiano (Parmesan) would probably work, however the fake, processed Parmesan they sell at my commissary won't melt, it gets powdery and weird. It's okay for pasta because it kind of dissolves, but for melting, forget it. Use real cheese. Do what you gotta do to get American cheese, it will make a big difference. Also, some chefs swear by using expensive onions at their peak of freshness, such as sweet Vidalias. As far as I am concerned, this is another myth, like using liquor. I say use the cheapest onions you can find. In fact this is a great recipe for using up onions that are going bad. Peel off any discolored layers and forge ahead. When we cook these onions on a medium heat, they are going to release their natural sugars, which aids in their caramelizing. Also, we are going to add a tablespoon of sugar, so use any onions you've got.

Ingredients:

5 Small onions, sliced thin (4 cups) (fine to use old onions here)
3 Tablespoons oil
3 Packets beef seasoning, from three ramen noodle soups
4 Cups water
1 Tablespoon sugar
1 ½ Teaspoons salt
4 Slices bread
Enough grated cheese to cover 4 slices of bread.

Step 1: Place the oil and the onions in a medium pot, over a medium heat. Sauté them, stirring constantly until they turn a nice brown. This is called caramelizing.

Step 2: Keep the water nearby, ready to go, so when the onions are evenly browned, "caramelized", but not too dark, you can add the water immediately, which will stop them from continuing to brown further.

Step 3: Bring the water to a simmer and add the beef seasoning packets, the salt and the sugar.

Step 4: Let simmer for ten minutes, uncovered, skimming (removing) any foam that rises to the top.

Step 5: Turn your stove down to the lowest heat possible, place the lid on tight, and let simmer for another ten minutes.

Step 6: While the soup is simmering toast the four slices of bread well. Set your toaster to dark. Don't burn your bread, but get it dark. It is mess hall bread and free, right? So, if it gets too dark, just toast some more.

Step 7: Place a good amount of your grated (chopped up) cheese of choice on each slice of toast.

Step 8: Taste the soup, it should be really good.

Step 9: Ladle the soup evenly into four small bowls that have lids. The commissary cereal bowls are what I use, they're only 98 cents for two bowls with lids, they're perfect.

Step 10: Place the cheese-covered toasts on top of the soups, then tightly affix all four lids.

Step 11: Lastly, place the bowls in the microwave for 30 seconds. Let stand covered for a minute or two after you take them out, or until the cheese is all nice and melt-y.

Step 12: Remove lids and eat soup!

MEXICAN BLACK BEAN SOUP

One night a couple of new guys transferred into our dorm. It was interesting how whenever someone new came in who belonged to some clique, although there wasn't a free cubicle near the rest of their crew, one would magically free up. I thought maybe the guards figured if they stick a Latin over on the other side of the dorm smack in the middle of Chinatown, there might be problems, so they let them segregate. It was of course more interesting to imagine inmates telling guards to move people around. So being that these two new inductees into D dorm were Mexican, two inmates bordering the Latin Quarter of the dorm -- where I was -- were moved, and in came the new guys. These two "Esays" could have been brothers, they looked exactly the same to me. Perhaps it was the same light skin tone, the uniform, and the haircut.

I was one of two Jews whose cube was in the *Jewish Quarter,* which was smack in the middle of the *Latin Quarter* and *Little Italy,* between the Italian area and the Lower East Side, just like the layout of New York City. So one of the new Mexicans starts talking to me in pretty quick Spanish because he saw my LK tattoo -- which stands for Little Kitty -- but he immediately mistook me for a Latin King.

I couldn't understand half of what he said, but I got the gist of it, he wanted to trade stamps for food. I laid one of my lines of broken Spanish on him: "Hablo solamente Español para la cocina y para el amor, la conversación normal es más difícil." That made 'em smile. Then off we went and had some soup, fish and rice. This was one of my first attempts at making Mexican food inside, but these two guys loved the soup so much I had to include the recipe for it.

Ingredients:

1/4 Cup water

2 Cans black beans, (approximately 15.5 oz, or 16 oz, sometimes cans are 19 oz, all are good.)

1/2 Lemon or lime

2 Tablespoons Soffrito (1/4 onion, 1/4 red pepper -- you can use green or orange pepper, and 1 garlic clove, directions how to make soffrito below)

10 Dorito chips, original flavor, crushed
1 Tablespoon olive oil.

Step 1: Soffrito ... All the Spanish guys who cooked in my dorm started off their soups and stews with Soffrito. It is a combination of onions, red bell pepper and garlic, diced small, and cooked in a little oil until just starting to become tender. If you have a ready-made soffrito, heat a small sauce pot on a low flame and add the oil and soffrito to just get it hot. If you don't have soffrito ready made, small dice the 1/4 small onion, 1/4 red pepper (green or orange pepper will work too), and garlic clove and saute til tender.

Step 2: Add all the other ingredients and let it simmer slowly, mashing with a fork until the Doritos are dissolved.

That's it, if you like it spicy add a few shots of hot sauce. Mexican soup recipes often use tortillas as a thickening agent so I tried Doritos, Wow, did they add flavor! I think I used Doritos "Cool Ranch", but any Doritos flavor will work.

Lastly, to make my black bean soup Michelin star worthy, I pressed it through a small-holed strainer. Now I had a smooth black bean soup. That's not necessary, nor was writing the inmate's name on top with thinned-down sour cream, and perching a large cilantro sprig to one side, but I did it anyway cuz I love the "oohs" and "aahs".

Viva Mexico!

SPICY SALMON CAKES
This makes 22 nice-size cakes

These cakes are part of the first meal I cooked in jail.

One of the guys had his wife send him a couple of cans of crab meat and I saw him making crab cakes. I won't mention any names but his crab cakes weren't very good. I thought, what a waste of crab. However, after seeing them and trying one I wanted to make some of my own. Three of us contributed enough canned salmon to make 22 nice size cakes.

This recipe is so easy and so good you'll make these salmon cakes over and over again. Try serving them over a nice seasoned rice, we ate them with vermicelli.

Ingredients:

3 Cans octopus, drained and diced small
5 Cans pink salmon drained (reserve the liquid)
3 Jalapeños, small dice
2 Medium onions, small dice
½ Cup flour
1 Sleeve crackers, crushed
1 Teaspoon garlic powder
1 Teaspoon oregano
1 Teaspoon Adobo seasoning
Oil for frying.

Step 1: Cook the diced onions in 2 tablespoons of the oil until tender, about 2 minutes. Set aside to cool.

Step 2: Mix together the salmon and the Jalapeños, onion, octopus, flour, seasonings, and 4 tablespoons of the crushed crackers. If the mix is dry add a little of the liquid from the salmon. Mix by hand and form into patties.

Step 3: Put the remaining crushed crackers in a bowl.

Step 4: I like my patties to look like hockey pucks, but a little smaller. Pack your cakes by throwing small handfuls into your palm as if you were throwing a baseball into a mitt.

Step 5: Using your finger rub a little bit of the salmon liquid on all sides of the cakes, then one at a time, place them into the bowl with the remaining crushed crackers to coat them. The salmon liquid will help the crushed crackers stick. Swirl the bowl around until each cake is covered with crackers.

> **Note:** *You can make a batter, or use eggs to help the crackers adhere, but I don't.*

Step 6: Heat enough oil in a pan so it rises up about a ¼ inch, and make sure it's really hot. Fry cakes as many at a time as you can handle, until they are dark brown and crispy but not burnt. Using a spatula make sure to check the bottoms frequently.

Step 7: Drain them on paper towels or a paper bag, then serve.

These cakes can be eaten right away or refrigerated or frozen for later - they also microwave well. Enjoy!

I didn't have any fresh peppers, but if you do, use half of a medium-sized red, green or yellow pepper, dice it small and cook it with the onion. Of course, fresh garlic would be a plus, so if you've got it, use it. You can substitute 1 teaspoon of minced, fresh garlic for the powdered garlic.

JAMAICAN BEEF & CHEESE PATTIES
Recipe for 12 Patties

I always wondered what made Jamaican beef patties yellow. Now I know. It's these little packets of a seasoning called Sazon. It has a yellow dye in it, and everyone in jail seems to like to put in almost everything. On the Sazon packet, listed under ingredients, it says "con azafran". Azafran is Spanish for saffron, which is yellow. Saffron is the most expensive spice in the world and is even listed on the Stock Exchange, so I doubt there is very much Saffron in each packet, it's got to be all yellow dye number whatever.

We didn't have any ground beef or the traditional seasonings, but our patties came out pretty darn close to authentic, and then we added cheese. Try substituting chicken for the beef in this recipe or making your own seafood mix. Vegetarians can even cook some veggies with a little tomato puree (sort of a ratatouille), and use that. Once you have mastered this dough, you can fill your patties with anything.

Dough Ingredients for 12 Patties:

1 Cup pancake mix
4 Cups all-purpose flour
2 Cups warm water
1 Packet Sazon seasoning
2 Teaspoons garlic powder
2 Teaspoons Adobo seasoning
1 Teaspoon salt

Step 1: Reserve 6 tablespoons of the flour for dusting your work surface. Place the rest of the flour and all the other dry ingredients into a large bowl or pot and mix well.

Step 2: Add about two-thirds of the warm water to the dry ingredients and mix gently with your fingertips. Over-working this dough by using a spoon, or over-kneading with your hand, will result in a tough dough and it will be hard to roll out. Add more water a little at a time, continuing to gently work with your fingertips, and flipping the dough over until all of the flour has come together into a soft ball of dough.

Step 3: Let the dough rest for at least 20 minutes in a warm spot, (like on top of the microwave or by the stove), preferably covered.

While the dough is resting make your filling.

Note: *If you refrigerate your dough for longer than an hour, like overnight, cover lightly with plastic wrap or tie tightly in two plastic bags.*

Filling Ingredients for 12 Beef Patties:

1 Can roast beef, (don't wash off the gravy)
1 Can corned beef
6 Slices American cheese
2 Small onions, sliced
2 Garlic cloves, minced
1 Can mushrooms, drained
3 Tablespoons oil, plus oil for frying
1 Teaspoon Adobo seasoning
1 Teaspoon garlic powder
1 Teaspoon oregano
2 Jalapenos, diced small

Step 4: Add the 3 tablespoons of oil to your pan and sauté the onions, garlic and the Jalapenos until tender, about 3 minutes. Add the drained mushrooms and cook for another 2 - 3 minutes, or until any excess moisture has evaporated.

Step 5: To the same pot add the corned beef and the roast beef. Don't wash the gravy off the roast beef. Add two tablespoons of the roast beef gravy to the pot, then add the dry seasonings and cook for 2 more minutes on medium to low heat. Check the seasoning. Set aside to cool.

Step 6: By now the dough has rested and is ready to be rolled out.

I've found that the best way to make a good rolling surface is to cover a counter with a clean garbage bag. Rip off a large piece of the bag, don't try to work with a whole garbage bag. Sprinkle a little water on the table or counter and spread it around, basically dampening the area to be covered. Place the piece of garbage bag on the damp surface, then using a dry towel smooth out the bag, pressing out any air pockets. The bag will stick, I promise. If it doesn't stick, you have either too much water under the bag or not enough, you'll get it. Of course if you have lots of tape, you can just tape the bag down well, but water is free and I believe it works the best.

Step 7: When rolling out the dough always work with small pieces, because any excess dough you end up with each time you roll one out, will end up getting over-worked when you roll it out again. So, break off a small piece of dough and roll it out to about a thickness of ⅛ of an inch. Using a small cereal bowl or the lid of a coffee can as a guide, cut out 12 circles of dough. Continue to sprinkle the extra flour on your dough and work surface so it doesn't stick.

Step 8: Divide the meat filling (or whatever filling you are using) among the dough circles, 2 - 3 tablespoons of filling placed right in the center should be about right.

Step 9: Using your finger and the water dampen half of the edge of each circle closest to you. Envision a smiley face. Now fold the circle over into a half moon shape, pressing the edges together like a large ravioli. Crimp the edges using a fork, making sure they're sealed well.

They look just like the ones in the pizzeria don't they?

Step 10: To cook, place about a ¼ inch of oil in a frying pan on medium heat (4 - 6). Cook both sides of the patties until they're golden brown and crispy. If the large straight edge is not cooked, stand the patties up on their sides so all the dough including the edges, gets cooked.

Serve immediately. If they sit for too long, or are placed in a bowl with a lid they will steam and get soft.

> **Note:** *Use a full soda can for a rolling pin, regular cans have extended edges that can cut into the dough. Keep one full can of soda in your locker that you never drink and you will always have a rolling pin. All the other items you could use for a rolling pin, such as a piece of a broom handle or an empty plastic-wrap tube, are all fine and dandy until you get caught! Remember 'Standards of Inmate Behavior Rules and Regulations Outlines and Procedures for New York State', (where I am) says: '106.10 Obeying Rules', '113.11 Possessing Contraband', '113.13 Illegal Exchange', '113.18 Tools', '113.22 Unauthorized Articles', '114.10 Smuggling', and a whole slew of rules under '116' concerning 'destruction and tampering' with items. Then turn your attention to the 'Miscellaneous Rules'. I won't go on. Just use a soda can!*

The Jack Links company sells pre-cooked ground beef, it's vacuum packed and doesn't need refrigeration. It's allowed in facilities and can be purchased at WalMart Superstores. It comes in Mexican Style, great for tacos and burritos; Italian Style, great for sauces; and Regular. They will all work for patties. They're expensive but they're much better than corned beef. If you can get a few packs sent to you in your next food package, do it!

CHILLED TUNA CASSEROLE
Makes about 6 regular sized sandwiches

At first I thought this dish was going to be too similar to my other tuna fish recipe, and I wasn't going to add it to the book. However, after trying it, I couldn't leave it out. I can't help but wonder if the origin of this dish has something to do with inexpensively stretching tuna fish. Ramen noodles only cost 10 cents, and each packet of those noodles more than doubles the volume of a can of tuna. As I said, after tasting this recipe I realized it is so good I had to pass it on.

Ingredients:

1 Small onion, fine dice
2 Cans tuna fish, drained
1 Packet Shrimp Ramen Noodles with seasoning
6 Tablespoons mayo
5 Tablespoons French's mustard
4 Tablespoons honey
Salt to taste.

Step 1: Break up the noodles and boil until tender, (3 - 4 minutes). Microwaving works fine. Drain out all the water, then rinse under cold water and drain again.

Step 2: Drain all the water from the two cans of tuna. Add all ingredients to noodles including the packet of seasoning that comes with the shrimp ramen.

Step 3: Chill for 20 minutes

That's it.

Serve on bread. It doesn't get much easier than that. I always spread mayonnaise on both slices of bread when I make sandwiches, of course that's is up to you.

SURF & TURF
Makes 10 nice Tuna Sausage cakes

Yeah, I know you saw surf and turf in the index and thought you'd check it out anyway, right? Well, it's not fillet mignon and lobster tail, sorry. I've heard stories about wise guys doing Fed. time at places like Louisburg Federal Penitentiary, where there are steaks and whole provolones. I'm sorry to disappoint you, but at this little old CF, surf and turf is tuna cakes with diced Summer Sausage. Don't fret, there's a reason why this recipe is here.

When my neighbor in 19 Cube gave me one of his tuna cakes to try, I was extremely impressed at how light and delicious it was.

Since I already have salmon cakes in this book, I thought it might be redundant to have another fish cake style recipe, but they really are so good I couldn't hold back. Like the salmon cakes and many of my other recipes, you can basically add anything you like to these cakes. It's the technique here that makes them stand out. To my surprise, he (who shall remain anonymous) used pancake flour in place of regular flour. The leavening agents in pancake flour (various types of leavening sodium) are why his cakes were so light and sweet. Pancake flour has corn syrup in it. At first I couldn't believe that he only used pancake flour and didn't cut it with regular flour. I wasn't going to call him a liar (for obvious reasons) but you know I got him to make them with me. The ones he gave me to try originally didn't have sausage in and came out sweeter than this recipe with the sausage. I was pleasantly surprised that these cakes were light and fluffy, but not at all pancake-y, which I had expected them to be. If you want light and fluffy tuna cakes without the slightly salty sausage, just leave it out. You can really use anything you like here, try mushrooms, bell peppers, hard fruits, roast beef, literally anything.

Everyone makes these cakes different sizes, so for argument's sake divide the finished mix into ten even balls and it will make ten cakes. The balls should be bigger than a golf ball but smaller than a handball. Press them flat and now you have cakes. Since we put meat and fish in this batch I coined them Surf & Turf Cakes.

 Try them with either Demon Cave Hot Sauce or Tangy BBQ Sauce, see the index for both recipes.

Ingredients:

2-5 oz Cans tuna fish, drained well
1-4 oz Can octopus, drained well and diced small
Half a 15 oz Can of corn, drained
1 Large Jalapeno, chopped small
1 Medium onion, diced small
5 oz or Half a Summer Sausage, diced small
4 oz Pancake flour mix
1 Tablespoon Adobo seasoning
1 Teaspoon garlic powder

3 Tablespoons grated Parmesan
Oil for frying.

Step 1: Mix all ingredients together

Step 2: Form into cakes

Step 3: Fry each cake until golden brown on both sides.

GYROS
Makes 6 to 8 Gyros

When was the last time you had a Gyro? How about the last time you had a home-made gyro? Probably never, right? I can't really speak for other parts of the country, but in New York City you can probably find gyros being sold every few blocks, in some type of deli or pizzeria, or on the street by vendors. Gyros are very common where I live, and even though most of them are nothing more than beef cubes in pita bread, they're still really good. Authentic gyros are made from lamb that's been sliced very thin. Needless to say we don't have lamb or rotating spits for roasting here, but we can make something very close. You might want to plan ahead when you decide to make gyros, so you can acquire some fresh veggies for toppings. Lettuce, cucumber, onion, and tomatoes work the best, but feel free to use anything you have. There are a couple of guys in my dorm who don't eat meat and they asked me if I could make theirs with Jack Mack. At first it didn't seem too appetizing, but after giving it a little more thought I figured why not Jack Mack gyros? They came out awesome. Just another example of how we can be creative with Jack Mac when we put our minds to it.

I am going to keep this very simple, but you can elaborate with additional seasonings or sauces. For example, whether I use beef cubes from a can of roast beef in gravy or Jack Mackerel as my pita filling, I add only a little salt to the flour before coating them. Sure I could add garlic powder, Sazon, or any other spices, but it isn't necessary as I'm going to smother them with my secret white gyro sauce (no longer a secret, see Sauces section), and either home-made or store-bought hot sauce, and any BBQ sauce I happen to have. I use all three together when I have them. So using lots of spices during flouring would just be overkill and a waste of my spices.

What? You don't have any pita bread? No surprise there, fear not, we are going to make our own, none of this is complicated or labor intensive. Once you try one of these gyros you're going to want them all the time, you'll see. Even a strict vegetarian could enjoy this concept, pitas filled with sautéed vegetables and sauce would still be good. Now thinking about it, since our jailhouse gyros are so fresh and the pita is still warm and soft right out of the pan, they're better than almost all of the gyros I ever had on the street. This recipe for the pita bread will make 6 - 8 pitas, each about 6 - 8 inches across. They don't necessarily have to be round, if your pitas come out some odd amoeba shape, who cares? They're gonna get stuffed and folded in half anyway, so why go to the trouble of meticulously shaping them? If you don't want to make the white sauce for your gyros, you can just go with the hot sauce or BBQ sauce. I suppose if you are a die-hard Italian you could put meatballs in them with tomato sauce, but that would be weird. Let's stick to a basic gyro.

Ingredients for 6 - 8 fresh pitas for the Gyros:

2 Cups flour
1 Cup pancake mix
2 Teaspoons salt
Water for binding
Oil for frying.

Step 1: Mix the dry ingredients together, then gently mix in enough water to form a soft dough. Don't overwork your dough or it will get tough and overly elastic. Less is more here. When it comes together in a dough ball, leave it covered somewhere warm until you're ready to roll it out.

Step 2: Roll out pieces of dough as thin as possible and as large as will fit into whatever size pan you have for frying them.

Step 3: Place about ⅛ of an inch of oil in your pan on medium heat, about #4 on an electric range.

Step 4: Place your flat pita dough in the hot oil for about a minute or until lightly browned. If you overcook the pita bread it will get hard and crack in half when you try to fold it later, so "light" brown is the key. Flip the pita over and again cook just until it turns light brown on the other side. If the pita starts to form air pockets, press it down gently with your spatula.

Step 5: Set your pitas aside on something that will absorb the excess oil, paper bags, towels, etc.

About the filling ingredients:

For beef Gyros here in jail, without fresh beef or lamb, the next best thing is cans of roast beef in gravy. I never rinse off the gravy from the roast beef, no matter what I'm making, so neither should you, it adds flavor. I recommend removing the meat from the can carefully so you are left with nice large chunks. Gently wipe off any excess gravy with a towel, but don't rinse them off. The little gravy left on the meat will help the flour to adhere. Also, I don't throw away the leftover gravy, I jar it and freeze it. Believe it or not, that gooey gravy is good for lots of stuff, it's like having a nice reduced beef stock (sort of).

Three 12-ounce cans of roast beef should be enough to fill your pitas. Remember, you only need a little meat as your first layer. Trust me, after you top the meat with shredded lettuce and other veggies, they will all be stuffed full.

Ingredients for filling 6 - 8 Beef Gyros:

3-12 oz Cans roast beef in gravy
6 oz Flour
1 Teaspoon salt
Oil for frying.

Step 1: Mix flour and salt well.

Step 2: Remove beef from the can, wipe off excess gravy and coat it with the salt and flour mix.

Step 3: Place only a couple of tablespoons of oil at a time in your pan. We don't want to deep fry here, we want to sear the beef cubes on all sides until they are nice and brown. Don't overcrowd your pan or the beef will steam and you won't get a nice sear. Take the extra few minutes of cooking time needed to do it in a few batches. This will yield you the nicest product.

If you are using Jack Mack, just flour and fry it like you normally would. Be creative, got a can of scallops? Scallop gyros, why not?

To Assemble:

Place your fried meat or fish inside or on top of your pita bread. Top with the sliced lettuce, tomato, onions, cucumbers, or whatever you like, then smother with gyro sauce (see index) and hot sauce, and/or BBQ sauce (see index). Fold over or roll up. You won't be able to eat just one, you'll see.

How about some rice on the side? Check out the index, you and your crew will be very happy.

CHICKEN DIJONAISE

Yeah, I know this dish sounds all French, but we're going to Americanize it. Let's call it "Chicken Dijon", okay? Again, trying to broaden my creativity and looking for a challenge, I got friendly with a guy I'll call Tony Burger. As I was now into my third dorm change, I was kinda learning what the do's and don'ts are in jail. I learned what seemed to be the appropriate protocol for approaching others with a view to collaborating without getting myself in trouble, (which was very easy), and/or ending up cooking for ten people a night.

Tony Burger and I spent a few minutes in the kitchen my first day in G-dorm, and we chatted about doughs as I admired his pies. I told him I was trying to get a cookbook together, and the next day, when I was making my extra crispy barbecued Jack Mack and white rice, he wanted to get down. He cleaned his own Mack, gave it to me and off I went. He was pleasantly surprised, never having seen anyone bread their Jack Mack with uncooked soup noodles before. He liked my sauce, and the next day he came up to me again. Half hungry, and I think half joking, he said: "Here's a can of salmon, see what you can come up with for your book."

Well, I took the 16 oz can of salmon, opened it and out slid a log of salmon the exact shape and size of the can. I thought I would get a little creative, seeing the log reminded me of days when I used to tie roasts and loins, and I decided to tie it off like fresh salmon steaks. I went up to the bubble (the C.O.s enclosed, see-through office) and asked the CO on duty for a length of string. It just so happens that the string we use in jail for clothes lines in our cubes is (probably unbeknownst to them) butchers' twine. The state actually buys cooking string for inmates to hang their clothes on, how funny is that? Anyway, I cut three smaller lengths of string out of the one the CO gave me and tied the log of salmon in three evenly spaced places. Next I took the lid from the salmon can, and carefully spinning the log I cut it into three even size steaks, each now neatly tied. I couldn't believe they didn't fall apart. All I had to do next was make some rice and a sauce. This might seem like a little much but let's face it, at this point cooking had become my rec.

The sauce I made came out almost like a classic Dijonaise (without the wine of course). Tony Burger and I liked the sauce so much we decided to make it again. However, we never found another can of salmon that wasn't flaky like canned tuna fish. Hey, isn't this Dijon sauce classically served with chicken? Why, yes it is. So here is my jailhouse version of Chicken Dijon.

The canned chicken-in-water they sell here at this correctional facility seems to be hit or miss. Sometimes it's nice chunks, and sometimes it's like cat food and only good for chicken salad or some type of filling. If you are getting your chicken sent in from the street, you want to ask for Hormel brand premium chunks in water. The premium chunks come in a can with a green label, that's the one you want, they always have nice big chunks and can be used just like real chicken breast (which is what it is). This recipe is really easy and shouldn't take you more than 15 minutes from start to finish.

If you're going to make rice or pasta to go with this dish, prepare it first. Rice only takes about 25 minutes to cook, so if you get the rice going before even collecting your ingredients for the Chicken Dijon, they will probably be ready at the same time.

Ingredients for two portions of Chicken Dijonaise:

3-6 oz Cans premium chicken chunks in water
2-5 oz Cans evaporated milk
5 Tablespoons yellow mustard, or ten packets of mustard
2 Tablespoons lemon juice
½ Teaspoon Adobo seasoning
1 Medium onion, diced small
2 Tablespoons butter or margarine
1 Packet chicken seasoning from a ramen soup
¼ Cup flour to coat the chicken
4 Tablespoons oil for searing.

Step 1: Remove the chicken chunks from their water and reserve the water.

Step 2: Dredge the chicken chunks in the flour.

Step 3: Sear the chicken in the oil on medium heat until all sides are golden brown. Set aside on paper towels to absorb the excess oil.

Step 4: Wipe out the pan and add the butter and the onion, cook on a low heat with the lid on until onions are tender (this is called sweating the onions).

Step 5: Add all the other ingredients, including the reserved water from the chicken, and bring to a simmer.

Step 6: Add the chicken chunks to the sauce to reheat them.

Taste the sauce, if it is too thick or tastes too powerful, add a little water. If you want your sauce to be stronger or have more mustard flavor, add a little more mustard.

Step 7: Serve on rice or any small pasta like little shells or ditillini.

That's it. Enjoy.

YUM YUM'S ROAST BEEF SLAMMERS
& SAUCE
Makes 8 sandwiches

One day a guy they call Yum Yum moved into our dorm. He had been at this facility a lot longer than me and had just been kicked out of the honor dorm, apparently for picking dandelions. What he was going to do with the flowers I don't know, but this at least 300-pound guy they called Yum Yum was definitely no pansy. We hit it off and at a glance you could tell he liked to eat so we swapped some recipes. This, he says, is his favorite jailhouse sandwich. Yum Yum recommended eating it with what we're calling an international sauce. It's a cross between Russian and French dressings. Without the sauce they were like his version of a Philly cheese steak. With the sauce they tasted like a Big Mac without the lettuce and tomato. Yum Yum made us four sandwiches each but after eating only two I had to stop. He ate all of his and I could see how he got to be so big.

This recipe makes eight sandwiches, so if there are only two of you, unless you're starving, you might only want to make half the recipe. They re-heat alright in the microwave, but obviously fresh out the pan they are better. The microwave leaves them a little soft for my taste.

Ingredients for 8 sandwiches:

3 Garlic cloves, minced
4 Small onions, sliced thin
5 Small pickled Jalapeños, chopped
2-12 oz Cans roast beef in gravy
8 Tablespoons hot sauce
4 oz Water
8 Slices American cheese
16 Slices bread
2 Teaspoons oregano
2 Teaspoons Adobo seasoning
2 Tablespoons garlic powder
1 Stick margarine.

Step 1: Take the beef chunks out of the gravy, (reserve and freeze the gravy for another time, it freezes well). Rinse the beef under cold water to remove any more gravy. Using your hands shred the beef into little strands resembling "pulled beef".

Step 2: In a small pot, add the sliced onions, the hot sauce, the water, Adobo seasoning, the minced garlic and the oregano. Bring the mixture to a gentle simmer on low heat, just until the onions are cooked but not too soft, (2 - 3 minutes).

Step 3: Strain out all the garlic and onions and set aside. Add the pulled beef to the pot with the hot sauce liquid and add the garlic powder. Stir gently just to heat through or until about half the liquid has boiled off.

Step 4: Place the chopped Jalapeños and the stick of margarine in a bowl and microwave for 30 seconds. Stir well then let stand.

Step 5: Assembling the sandwiches is easy. Place 8 slices of bread on a garbage bag-covered counter. Top the eight slices with even amounts of onions, pulled beef, the Jalapeños without the margarine, and one slice each of American cheese. Place the other 8 slices of bread on top to form 8 closed sandwiches.

Step 6: In a pan, heat the reserved melted Jalapeno-flavored margarine, and sear off both sides of the sandwiches, just like a grilled cheese.

Step 7: Use the International Dipping Sauce listed in the index under Sauces.

Dunk and enjoy!

141ST STREET TUNA MAYO
Makes 6 thick sandwiches

How could it possibly be that the best tuna fish I have ever eaten has been in jail? I never worked in a deli or a coffee shop, I worked in fine dining restaurants. The only time I ever made tuna fish was for the restaurant staff and that was out of fresh tuna, which I grilled and which tastes nothing at all like the canned tuna.

I have found two major differences between the types of tuna the inmates make here and what I have eaten on the street. The first major difference is that in jail the tuna fish never tastes fishy. When these guys open cans of tuna they press down on the lid so hard that all the liquid is drained off and the fish that's left is almost a dry paste. I bet there's no-one on the street working in a deli with muscles like these guys.

Anyway, perhaps they're lazy on the street or don't know the difference. It might also be a cost factor because the less liquid you drain from the can, the less mayonnaise you need to add to make a moist tuna mayo, so my guess is they don't know and/or don't think twice about it. Trust the boys on the inside for this one, don't just drain canned tuna for a tuna mayo, press out all of that liquid. Removing all the fishy water leaves a clean taste and using more mayo replenishes the moistness. The second reason I found the tuna here better is that everyone adds diced canned octopus which gives this dish a really nice consistency, and they also add celery and onion to add a little crunch. This recipe originated from an ex-con on 141st Street in Harlem, who new how to do it right. Tabasco and a little honey, oooh baby. This truly is the best tasting canned tuna fish I have ever eaten. I never met the guy from 141st Street, but whoever you are, your tuna is the best.

Ingredients:

3 Cans tuna, well drained
1 Can octopus, well drained, diced small
1 Small onion, diced small
½ Packet Sazon seasoning
12 Tablespoons mayonnaise
2 Tablespoons honey
2 Tablespoons Adobo seasoning
1 Teaspoon garlic powder
4 Good shakes Tabasco.

Step 1: Open the 3 cans of tuna fish and the octopus. Using the lids, press the fish down as hard as you can, removing all the water or oil.

Step 2: Using one of the tuna fish can lids, dice your onion and your octopus into very small pieces.

Step 3: Mix all of the ingredients together, and serve on bread or crackers.

NEW AGE SHEPHERDS' PIE
For two 9 inch pies

What's going on here? Another shocker. I can't believe that not one of the guys in my dorm has ever heard of Shepherd's Pie. I went to school in Spanish Harlem in uptown Manhattan, and it's just like the rest of Manhattan, there are Irish pubs, bars and diners that serve this classic dish. It's just seasoned minced meat cooked with vegetables, topped with mashed potatoes, and heated in the oven. When the Shepherd's Pie is hot all the way through it's placed under a broiler to brown the top of the mashed potatoes, sounds good, right?

Well, as usual, I've twisted this traditional dish into my own jailhouse adaptation. What's new, right? No oven, no broiler, hey, no chopped meat, so what the heck am I doing making a Shepherd's pie you ask. Try it, my new age jailhouse version is wonderful, it's more like a chicken pot pie with corned beef, a meat pie if you will. In fact, my first thought was to call it a meat pie, but that sounds so unappetizing and caveman-esque. More meat pie, ugh, I don't think so. It came out too good to give it such a simple, bland name, so New Age Shepherds' Pie it is.

Ingredients for the filling:

3 Small carrots, sliced small
2 Ribs celery, split in half length-wise then sliced small
2 Medium potatoes, diced small
4 Cloves garlic, minced
1 Medium onion, diced small
1 Medium green pepper, diced small
1-12 oz Can roast beef in gravy
2-12 oz Cans corned beef
1 Package beef seasoning from a ramen noodle soup

½ Teaspoon each salt, garlic powder, Adobo seasoning, oregano, and sugar
Oil for sautéing.

Step 1: In a large pot sauté the onion in two tablespoons of oil until tender, (3 - 4 minutes).

Step 2: Add the garlic and continue cooking until the garlic is lightly browned.

Step 3: Add 3 more tablespoons of oil and the rest of the vegetables. Reduce the heat to low and place the lid on top. Sweat these vegetables until just lightly softened, stirring frequently.

Step 4: Add all the seasonings and all the meat with its gravy, stir well and replace the lid. Cook everything for only about ten minutes and remove pot from the stove.

> **Note:** *Don't worry if some of the vegetables, such as the potatoes, aren't cooked yet, because they're going to cook for about another 45 minutes in the pie shell.*

Ingredients for the pie dough:

3 Cups flour
1 Teaspoon salt
1 Cup butter
Cold water.

Step 5: Follow the instructions for the pie dough in the Chicken and Turkey Pot Pie recipe, see index.

Step 6: Fill the pie shell with the meat and vegetable mix, and cook according to the instructions for the Chicken and Turkey Pot Pie.

Step 7: Let cool for at least ten minutes, then slice and serve.

JACK MACK 11 DIFFERENT WAYS

I've got some ideas on how you can eat Jack Mack more frequently without getting burnt out on it. If you tried the BBQ Mack with the crushed ramen noodles, hopefully that will give you some faith in my not-so-conventional creativity. Variety, they say, is the spice of life, so why should we just flour and fry our Mack?

Most of the guys I've seen breading Jack Mack start by battering their mackerel fillets in a flour and water mix, then rolling them in something crunchy like crushed crackers, Doritos, Cheese Doodles, or something similar. I've even seen different breakfast cereals used to crust Mack, and some guys don't use any batter at all. It would seem that the list of possible ingredients that we can use for crusting fish is endless. As long as the outside of the fish is crunchy and the inside is nice and juicy, I don't really care what it's crusted with.

This is one of my jailhouse cooking pet peeves. 98% of those who fry Jack Mack in jail overcook it to death until it's very dry and chewy like rubber. This is because they don't get the oil hot enough. Frying on each side in very hot oil for a maximum of a minute and a half, should be more than sufficient to crisp the outside of your Mack and heat it through.

Peep this: canned fish is already cooked, all you need to do is to cook the batter and the crust. If the frying oil isn't hot enough the food sits in it, absorbing oil and getting overcooked. One of the fundamentals of high heat cooking is the concept that frying or searing quickly, on a high temperature, will crust the outside of the food while sealing in all its natural juices. If your fish doesn't get brown after a minute and a half, your oil is too cold.

Also peep this: often people place one small piece of fish or chicken in their oil to test its temperature and that's great. However, what often happens is that they then fill their pans with cold chicken or fish, which immediately lowers the oil temperature. Unless they're using a huge vat of oil like they do in a restaurant, this is a no-no. The solution: don't overcrowd your pan, fry a few pieces at a time. Simple, right?

MACK 1
SWEET & SOUR CRISPY MACK
See Asian Corner

This recipe made me think of my corner Chinese restaurant.

MACK 2
TANGY BBQ MACK

Follow Steps 1 - 6 in Mack 1, Sweet & Sour Crispy Mack, Asian Corner, (see index), and for Step 7 substitute the Tangy BBQ Sauce recipe, (see index).

MACK 3
HONEY-BACON-WRAPPED MACK

After cleaning your Jack Mack carefully so that you end up with nice large fillets and not little fish sticks, try this:

Spread a little honey on both sides of your fish then roll each fillet in a piece of bacon. We have turkey bacon in the commissary here and it works great. Roll them tightly, then sear them in a frying pan with only a little oil. Fry the flap side down first and the bacon will adhere to itself. When they're nice and brown flip them over and sear the other sides. Honey bacon wrapped Mack, how about that?

Serve with whatever else you like.

MACK 4
JACK MACK PARMESAN

Like Italian food? After breading your Mack in your favorite seasonings and/or a batter, try this:

Spread a little tomato sauce on each fillet of mackerel, then top it with mozzarella and sprinkle with Parmesan cheese.

Place fillets back in a dry pan on a low flame to reheat them and melt the cheese. Jack Mack Parmesan!

I would serve this one with pasta just to keep with the Italian theme .

MACK 5

JACK MACK GYROS
(Greek Sandwich)

I was making my jailhouse version of Beef Gyros and someone asked me if I could use Mack instead of beef. I said: "Sure, why not?" He breaded and fried his Mack and gave it to me. I put the Mack inside the fresh pita bread wraps, topped them with hot sauce, white sauce, lettuce and onion. They were bangin'. Jack Mack gyros, the only thing missing was a tomato. (Check index for Gyros).

MACK 6

MACK & PEPPERS

Sounds crazy, right? Sausage and Peppers doesn't sound so weird, right? So try another Italian inspired dish. This time we want small pieces and you can cut them up either before or after you fry them. Cutting them after will make less work when you batter or flour and fry. Set your fried Mack aside then sauté some fresh garlic with onions and fresh bell peppers -- yellow, green, red. Just as your onion and pepper mix starts to get soft and wilted, add enough water to make as much sauce as you want, then season with your favorite ramen soup seasoning packet. Use shrimp flavor to stick with the fish idea, or use a little beef seasoning for a more authentic sausage and pepper taste. You don't want soup so only add a little water and just enough of a seasoning packet to add some flavor. You might not need a whole pack.

If you want your sauce thick, take a teaspoon of flour and add just enough cold water to it to make a paste. Drizzle that into your mixture and when it comes to a boil it will be nice and thick. You don't really have to make a sauce at all, just season your onion and pepper mix. Serve in hot dog buns or rolls, or wrap the mix in stromboli dough. (See index).

MACK 7
PHILLY CHEESE MACK

Speaking of stromboli dough, hmm. Do you like Philly cheese steaks but don't have any steak? Even if you don't eat meat and have never had one, take the stromboli dough (see index) and wrap the fried Mack with sautéed, seasoned onions and a slice of cheese. You guessed it, Philly Cheese Mack, or in my case, NYC Cheese Mack.

ABOUT MACK & PASTA SAUCES

I saw some Spanish guys fry Mack then submerge it in tomato sauce. I tried it, it was pretty good, sort of like a fried Mack stew, and they served it over rice. This little taste I was given instantly inspired me to think in terms of pasta sauces. After giving this idea only about five minutes to sink in, I realized you could add fried Jack Mack to almost any pasta sauce. The options are limitless. I don't want to write pages of pasta sauces, so I'll give you a few to get your creative juices flowing, then it'll be up to you.

MACK 8
JACK MACK CARBONARA

Carbonara sauce on the street is a cream reduction with chunks of bacon and peas. There are a few ways we could replicate this, chop up some bacon, onions and garlic and sauté them in a little bit of oil until just turning brown. Add some mushrooms and some evaporated milk, season with your favorite ramen soup seasoning and let reduce until thick. Add some fried Jack Mack pieces and a little Parmesan cheese and you're done. You don't need the peas, and in all actuality you don't need the bacon either. You can sauté onions and garlic then use a can of cream of mushroom soup, an old Betty Crocker staple. Cut the soup with some water until it's a consistency you're happy with, add some Parmesan and for all intents and purposes we'll call this a carbanara. If you have some peas add them at the last second so they keep whatever color they have left. Serve over linguini or other pasta.

MACK 9
JACK MACK & VEGETABLES/
JACK MACK IN PIZZAOLA SAUCE

This is a no-brainer and really good. We used to make this sauce for pizza as a special on the weekends at a restaurant I worked at in midtown Manhattan. If you want to make a nice red sauce, go ahead. If you want to open a can of store-bought spaghetti sauce, fine. Got some leftover sauce in the fridge to use up? Even better. Sauté any vegetables you have, canned or fresh, add peppers if you have them, chunks of onion, large pieces of mushrooms and some fresh garlic. Add your tomato sauce to the veggie mix and let simmer for a few minutes. Last, of course, add your fried Jack Mack pieces, serve over Rigatoni or your favorite pasta. Fried Jack Mack Pizzaola!

MACK 10
JACK MACK PAELLA

See Index for Hearty Paella recipe.

MACK 11
JACK MACK A LA PUTANESCA

How exotic do you want to get? Mash some capers with their juice. Chop up some anchovies in oil. Slice some olives (any kind). Now the trick to this sauce is to add a tomato sauce to the anchovy, caper and olive mix not the other way round. Keep adding tomato sauce until it balances the saltiness of the mix. Last, add your fried Jack Mack pieces and a small squeeze of lemon juice and BAM! It's Jack Mack Putanesca. Serve over thin spaghetti or angel hair pasta, they go the best.

Like I said, I'm not going to overload you with pasta sauces, just try adding fried Mack to your favorite pasta sauce and I bet it will work.

BLACK FISH STEW
Serves 6 human or 3 Viking portions

You think the Iron Chefs are under pressure? Try cooking for half a dozen linebackers in prison every day. Imagine if they don't like the food!!! If the idea of just sitting around as the world goes by, while you read, eat, drink and play cards sounds like heaven to you, you would love it here! Just kidding.

I don't know if this type of recipe is really Spanish, but as some of my Spanish buddies were making their versions of this dish, I'm kinda guessing it is. I'm not the only one whose creative around here, as I've said before prisoners are some of the most creative people in the world, essentially because we're forced to do what we can with what we've got. So the true background of this recipe - if there is one - is unbeknownst to me. Another interesting question is whether this is a stew, it could just as easily be construed a sauce.

"Freeway" - my Spanish homey, who I was in transit with for six days from the SHOCK incarceration facility to Demon Cave, New York - and I now lock in the same dorm. Needless to say, Freeway and I bonded. It was common for us to make each other bowls of food and try each other's cooking. When Freeway gave me a small bowl of his 'black fish' over rice I liked it enough to run with the ball and come up with my own concoction. I added a can of black beans to my version, which made it more hearty and made me feel more comfortable calling it a stew. Lastly, and perhaps most importantly, this dish does not contain any black fish. It's octopus, Jack Mack and calamari with its ink. It comes out black, hence the name. I suppose a traditionalist would have named it "dirty fish" or something to that effect, but how appealing does that sound? "Dirty rice" for some reason sounds fine, but dirty seafood stew just doesn't work, so "Black Fish Stew" it is.

This recipe will serve a decent size portion to six humans, or three Viking bowls. Serve it over your favorite rice or pasta.

Ingredients:

2–4 oz Cans octopus with their oil
1–4 oz Can calamari with its ink

1–16 oz Can Jack Mackerel, cleaned
1-16 oz Can black beans with their liquid
1–4 oz Can mushroom pieces with their water
2 Small onions, medium dice
1 Large celery rib, medium dice
2 Packets Sazon seasoning
1 Packet shrimp seasoning from a ramen soup
3 Tablespoons lemon juice
3 Tablespoons hot sauce (optional)
1 Teaspoon salt
1 Teaspoon oregano
1 Teaspoon garlic powder, or 3 cloves minced garlic
Half a green pepper, medium dice
2 Fresh chili peppers, or 4 pickled (optional)
4 oz Water
4 Tablespoons oil.

This is basically a one-pot deal, except of course for the rice or pasta you serve with it.

Step 1: Place the oil from both cans of octopus in a medium-sized pot over medium heat (3 - 4).

Step 2: To the oil add the celery, half the onion and the green pepper, and sauté for 3 - 5 minutes, or until onion becomes just soft. If you are using fresh garlic, add it now.

Step 3: Add everything else except for the rest of the onion and the Jack Mack. If the octopus pieces are very large cut them in half. Bring your stew to a simmer then turn down the heat to low, and place the lid on the pot for 15 minutes. This sort of acts like a pressure-cooker.

Step 4: Remove the lid and add the rest of the onion and the cleaned Jack Mack, and let simmer uncovered for another 5 - 10 minutes.

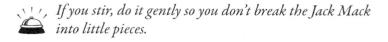 *If you stir, do it gently so you don't break the Jack Mack into little pieces.*

If it gets too thick, add a little water, if it's too thin, let it simmer a little longer.

That's it, check the seasoning.

Serve hot over rice or your favorite pasta.

As usual, if spicy foods aren't your cup of tea, leave out the chili peppers and the hot sauce. If you go this route, you may need a little sugar or vinegar, or just a dab more salt. Check it.

CHICKEN & TURKEY POT PIE

When I moved to G-dorm with all the other guys who work in inside grounds, the first place I checked out was my new kitchen. The kitchen in G-dorm is on one side of a large day room, not enclosed, just off to one side. An open kitchen, excellent. Guess what I saw on my first day. Give up? This guy Tony Burger was making apple pies, a dozen of them, all different sizes, and he had pie tins. Hooray, pie tins. I had met Tony Burger before in the gym so we knew each other, but only as acquaintances. After saying hello, I just stood nearby, quietly observing. He had the cardboard tube from a mess hall roll of plastic wrap, which still had some plastic wrap on it, and was using it as a rolling pin, much better than my soda can. But the pie tins, wow! After about five minutes of just watching, Tony Burger looked up at me and said "What's up? Wanna buy a pie?" Pointing at the three different sizes he was making, he said "5, 12 and 15 stamps." I just smiled and told him I had mastered making my apple pot pie without pie tins, he was instantly intrigued.

After swapping pie dough recipes and techniques it was obvious I had found my first culinary cohort in G-dorm. Tony Burger told me that his pies took between 45 minutes and an hour and ten minutes to bake, so I asked him if he had ever made and tried selling cheesecakes. He said "Yeah, but they're more like ..." I raised my hand cutting him off because I had seen how people made cheesecakes here, and I knew what he was going to say, so I said "Whoa, my cheesecakes are just like New York style cheese cakes, not like frozen puddings. They can be made any flavor and they take between 15 and 25 minutes to cook." Tony Burger's eyes almost popped out of his head as he screeched "Fifteen minutes!" That's all it took, and as they say "it was on".

We made three cheesecakes and they were sold for 12 stamps each even before they were done cooking. Suddenly we had more orders than we could fill and up went the prices. Peanut butter and Jelly cheesecakes 12 stamps; chocolate 13 stamps; strawberry and other fruits 15 stamps. So I had my new cooking buddy and about three nights a week we started cooking dinner together. Well, on this particular night, knowing I liked to experiment with recipes for my cookbook, Tony Burger gave me three pieces of fried chicken and three onions which were just beginning to rot and said "OK, let's see what you can make out of these."

After taking inventory of both our lockers I pulled out a few cans here, and some flour there, and using his pie tins here's what I came up with. The only things missing were a can of peas and some mashed potatoes on the side. This recipe makes two large pies, so just divide it in half for one large 9 inch pie. We had leftover filling but that was no problem, the next day I served the leftover filling over rice and we basically had Chicken a la King. You could make patties with the leftover filling too, you can always be creative with your leftovers.

Ingredients: Filling for 2 large 9 inch pies

1-15 oz Can corn chowder
1-10 oz Can cream of mushroom soup
1-4 oz Can mushroom pieces
1-12 oz Can turkey spam, diced
3 Pieces fried chicken, skin discarded and picked into small pieces
2 Cloves garlic, minced
2 Medium onions, diced small
1-15 oz Can potatoes, diced small
8 oz Water
1 Teaspoon Adobo seasoning
1 Teaspoon garlic powder
Salt to taste.

Step 1: Sautee the diced onions on high heat for 4 - 5 minutes until soft. Add the minced garlic and cook just until the onions start to turn brown.

Step 2: Place the sauteed onions and all other ingredients in a pot on a low heat (2). Cover and cook for 20 minutes, stirring frequently. Check seasoning for salt. That's your pie filling.

Ingredients for pie dough:

1 Egg, beaten lightly
3 Cups all purpose flour and more for dusting your work surface
    and the pot
1 Teaspoon salt
2 Sticks (16 tablespoons) butter, plus two tablespoons more for
    greasing
24 Tablespoons cold water.

Step 3: In a large enough bowl mix salt and flour.

Step 4: If the butter is very cold and hard, simply cut it into little pieces and add it to the flour one tablespoon at a time, (remember, 8 tablespoons equals one stick). If the butter is not very cold, cut it into very small pieces and chill until firm, then proceed to add it to the flour.

Step 5: Using a thick plastic fork mash each cut-up tablespoon of butter into the flour mix. The idea here is to mash and stir each tablespoon until it is mixed into the flour so well that you no longer see any butter. Lots of people like to incorporate their butter until the mashed butter resembles little peas. Not here. We want this flour-mix to look like sand, so keep mashing.

Step 6: When all 16 tablespoons (2 sticks) of butter have been incorporated and your mix looks like sand, start adding the cold water, about two tablespoons at a time. At this point discard the plastic fork and start kneading with your hand. With one hand squeeze the dough gently as if you were giving a massage. With the other hand drizzle in the cold water. Don't use all the water if you don't need to. (Remember the tablespoon measure is actually a large plastic teaspoon, it's not a real teaspoon measure but it's not a tablespoon measure either). When the dough comes cleanly and easily away from the sides of the bowl, stop adding water.

Step 7: Let dough rest for at least 15 minutes, preferably covered with a cloth.

Step 8: When your dough is ready, roll out a large enough circle, an eighth of an inch thick, to cover whatever size pie tin you have. Press the dough into the sides, leaving enough to just overlap the edge.

Step 9: Place half the mix in the pie shell.

Step 10: Brush all the way around the edge with the beaten egg or EggBeaters.

Step 11: Roll out another piece of dough for the top, again an eighth of an inch thick, and place it on top.

Step 12: Pinch the dough edges together all the way round to seal them.

Step 13: Brush the whole top with the beaten egg or EggBeaters, then poke a hole in the center to let out steam when it bakes.

Step 14: Place a large rice pot on a can with the top and bottom removed, for a riser, (the DAK ham cans work the best).

Step 15: Place two well-washed, empty octopus cans or calamari cans inside the pot.

Step 16: Place the pie on top of the small cans inside the pot and cover the pot.

Step 17: Bake on a high heat (6 or higher) until the top of the pie is nice and brown, about 45 minutes to an hour.

Step 18: Let cool slightly, slice and serve.

Tony Burger had two rice pots, one of them was strictly for baking and is no longer nice and shiny. This type of dry baking (Dutch oven) tends to discolor the pots a little, so don't borrow your friends' pots, use your own. If you like to bake a lot and it's possible, buy another pot just for baking. You can buy IMUSA pots, they're under $20 and you'll make that back in stamps your first day selling pies!

BEEF & KIDNEY BEAN STEW
Makes 6 regular or 3 Viking servings

I love winter food. It happened to be December when I made this stew, but I would eat it any time of year. It's a good thing I used a large pot to make this stew as there was a lot of it. Although only three of us ate it we had seconds and leftovers for the next day, so I would say this recipe will make six normal servings or three Viking bowls of food.

My crew was out of potatoes when I made this or I probably would have added some. Serving this stew over mashed potatoes would be really good too. I find that canned potatoes are almost as good as fresh potatoes after they're heated, and you don't have to peel, chop or boil them. So you can use whatever you have. Bring a can of potatoes to a boil, drain them, add some soft butter and a little evaporated (canned) milk, season, and BAM! Mashed potatoes. Anyway, as none of us had potatoes this stew got served over Jalapeno rice, (see index).

The next day we had the leftover stew tossed with a box of cooked rigatoni. As you can see this dish is pretty versatile, so eat it however you enjoy eating stews. How about ladled over biscuits? (See index for biscuit recipe). If you don't want leftovers and there are only three or four of you, make half this recipe. I didn't add any hot spices to this because I served it over spicy rice, but feel free to add Tabasco, Jalapenos or red pepper flakes, they will all be good.

Ingredients:

2-12 oz Cans roast beef in gravy
2-16 oz Cans kidney beans with their liquid
1-4 oz Can mushrooms with their water
1-6 oz Can tomato paste
1-8 oz Can tomato sauce
2 Ribs celery, split lengthwise and diced small
2 Medium carrots, diced small
1 Medium onion, diced small
1 Green or red pepper, diced small
4 Cloves garlic, sliced thin

6-8 oz Beef sausage or salami, peeled, cut in half lengthwise, and
    sliced thin into half moons
½ Teaspoon garlic powder
½ Teaspoon Adobo seasoning
½ Teaspoon salt
½ Teaspoon oregano
1 Packet Sazon
4 Tablespoons sugar
4 Tablespoons oil
Water as needed.

Step 1: Place the garlic and the oil in a large pot and cook on medium to low heat until the garlic just starts to turn brown.

Step 2: Quickly add the rest of the vegetables and the sausage or salami, which will stop the garlic cooking. Stir well, reduce the heat to low, and cook covered for 4 - 5 minutes or until the onion is just starting to wilt, this is called "sweating".

Step 3: Add the tomato paste, the tomato sauce, the mushrooms and their water, all the seasonings, all the gravy (not the meat) from both cans of roast beef (reserve the roast beef meat itself until later), and 2 - 3 cups water to start.

Step 4: Stir gently and bring to a simmer. If there's still tomato paste or sauce or roast beef gravy on the sides and bottom of the cans, pour some of the simmered hot liquid into the cans and swish it around to get every last drop of the contents.

Step 5: Let simmer for 30 minutes while you prepare your side dish of rice, pasta, potatoes or biscuits.

Step 6: Add the two cans of beans and the meat from the roast beef cans and stir very gently so as not to break up the roast beef, you want to have nice large chunks when you're done. Simmer for about another 20 minutes.

Step 7: Check seasoning and if necessary, adjust to your liking. If you find your stew has reduced and is too thick for you, add some more water.

That's it, fill your Viking bowls with your favorite starch, then top them with the stew and feast!

CHICKEN TENDERS

I really wanted to make some sort of chicken fingers with a dipping sauce. I get those 10 oz cans of premium chunk breast of chicken in water from the street and they are really good. The canned chicken they sell at my commissary looks like cat food by comparison, but will work just fine for this dish. The premium chunks are really great, it's just like fresh chicken breast. I dry off the chicken, flour it, fry it, then add it to so many dishes, like Chinese food and gyros.

Anyway, I started off with these beautiful chunks of chicken and ended up (after adding some pancake flour) with compressed molded chicken tenders and realized that I could have used an inexpensive canned chicken for this dish. Admittedly for chicken fingers they were weird, you really need whole chicken breasts, but for chicken tenders they were great.

I happened to have a papaya and half a cucumber, so after a few minutes of product searching in my dorm, I made a nice spicy papaya salsa with onions, Jalapenos, honey and lemon juice. Amazing what we can do when we put our minds to something, right? When you make sauces and glazes like BBQ and sweet citrus, make a lot. For example, when I make BBQ sauce I usually make enough to fill a 24 oz ketchup bottle. It keeps just fine in my locker, un-refrigerated.

My point is, I usually have a few different sauces around to choose from for times when I want to dip. I recommend you do the same. If you want BBQ chicken, half the work is done, as your dipping sauce is already made. Stock up on your condiments.

Ingredients for 20 chicken McNugget-sized chicken tenders:

2-10 oz Cans premium chunk chicken, or the equivalent weight of
   any canned chicken
7 Tablespoons pancake flour
½ Teaspoon garlic powder
½ Teaspoon salt
½ Teaspoon Adobo seasoning

4 oz EggBeaters, or 2 eggs beaten
½ Sleeve crackers, crushed
Oil for frying.

Step 1: Mix together very well, the chicken, pancake flour and all the seasonings.

Step 2: Mold chicken by hand into 1 oz flat skinny tenders. Imagine a "McNugget" as a guide.

Step 3: Dip them one at a time in the EggBeaters or beaten eggs, and then in the crushed crackers.

Step 4: Fry them on a medium heat halfway submerged in oil. Flip them, then fry the other side. This will give them an even color on both sides. If you don't use enough oil a white stripe seems to magically appear around the sides.

When both sides are crispy and golden brown, remove from pan, and dip in sauce and 'mange'.

Chapter 3

TASTE OF SPAIN

Guiso de Verrano (Summer Stew)
Hearty Paella
Tortillas & Quesadillas
Chilliquillas (Mexican Lasagna or Flautas)
Fast & Easy Bake Burritos
Spicy Jalapeno Rice
Beans in Red Sauce

GUISO DE VERRANO (SUMMER STEW)

This is an easy-style stew that really takes minimal effort. If I had my choice I would eat winter foods all year round. I love stews, pot pies, casseroles, gravies. They're my comfort food. There's nothing like a thick veal sauce made with a good port wine reduction on mashed potatoes any time of year.

This mellow sausage and red kidney bean stew is good over just plain rice, however, you can season your rice to your liking and have it with vegetables or whatever you have. I wish we had a huge plate of buttery-garlic-mashed potatoes, but the only potatoes we had at our commissary were canned and I don't know how many cans of potatoes it would have taken to feed us. As we had rice, and rice is inexpensive, rice is what we ate. This stew was light enough to eat in June, when we made it. It has a heavy ratio of beans, which gives it sort of a Spanish flare, so I gave it a Spanish name, Guiso de Verano, or Summer stew.

Ingredients:

1 Large onion, sliced
2-16 oz Cans red kidney beans
8 Tablespoons oil
1 oz Summer Sausage
10 Tablespoons flour
3 Tablespoons garlic powder
2 Tablespoons Adobo seasoning
2 Tablespoons oregano
3 Garlic cloves, sliced
2 Tablespoons salt
3 Cups water
1 Tablespoon honey.

Step 1: In a pan with oil, on low to medium heat (2 - 3), sauté garlic, onions, sausage, garlic powder, oregano and Adobo seasoning. Cook partially covered for about 10 minutes or until the onions are tender and you can smell the aroma of the cooked seasonings. Stir every minute or so making sure not to let it burn.

Step 2: Add the flour and stir until the flour becomes light brown, 3 - 5 minutes, scraping the bottom of the pot and making sure the flour doesn't stick and burn.

Step 3: Add the beans, the water, the tomato paste and the honey, and let simmer on the lowest heat possible for about twenty minutes.

Step 4: Serve over your favorite rice.

HEARTY PAELLA
Makes 3 nice portions or two Viking-sized bowls.

Paella, is an extremely popular dish in Spain. I incorrectly equated Spain with all "Spanish-speaking" lands. Obviously Mexicans, Puerto Ricans and Dominicans are not from Spain, but surely I thought, people from those parts of the world would know what paella is. Well I was wrong. When I made this paella all of the "Spanish" guys I was cooking for turned their noses up at the concept of mixing fish, meat and rice together. I couldn't believe none of them had ever heard of paella. Of course once they tasted it they loved it, and wanted me to make it again and again, so I added the recipe to the book.

Traditionally, paella is rice, saffron, oil and seafood or meat. Depending where in Spain you're eating it, you'll find it contains different ingredients; the closer you are to the ocean the more seafood you will find in your paella. This dish is usually prepared in one pot, but I find it difficult to get the rice to cook perfectly and fluffy with all the other ingredients I add, so I use a rice pot and a frying pan.

Simply, we're going to cook some ingredients with the rice, and sauté other ingredients separately, and we'll mix all the ingredients together later. When I cook rice, I use a 16 oz bean can as a measuring cup for the water. Remember, one level 16 oz bean can filled with rice equals a one-pound bag of rice. For perfect rice every time, I use one and two-thirds bean cans of water per one pound bag of rice or per one level bean can of rice. For two pounds of rice, use 3 ½ cans of water. I season my water and bring it to a boil, add the rice, bring the water back to a boil, stir well and reduce the heat to low, and cover the pot. I don't stir it, check it, or mess with it at all.

I don't use risers either which I see a lot of guys doing, no paper towels or plastic bags, nothing weird. I leave it covered on low for 20 minutes before I check it. It should need another 10 to 15 minutes sitting off the stove, covered, to steam until done. It doesn't stick to the bottom or burn, it comes out perfect consistently. We are going to follow the same cooking method here for our paella. Of course if you have perfected your own method of making rice and wish to go that route, go ahead, season it really well and then follow my other directions to turn it into paella.

Now the recipe I am laying out for you here is how I make it, and it's great. However, be open- minded. Use any ingredients you like, remember the basics are rice, saffron, and oil, all of which we have, right? Sazon seasoning is saffron with salt, and that's what makes everything turn yellow. Once you have a nice yellow rice, you can gently fold in any seafood, chicken or meat. What we are allowed to have at this facility is so limited it seems ridiculous, as I'm told that at other facilities I could have jumbo shrimp sent in, and meat, and a slew of other things I don't want to think about until I get out. OK, ready? Try this.

Ingredients for two Viking size bowls of rice:

1 Pound rice
1-8 oz Can tomato sauce
1 Packet Sazon seasoning
1 Tablespoon garlic powder
1-4 oz Can octopus, half drained
1-4 oz Can calamari, cleaned
1 Teaspoon oregano
3 Cloves garlic, minced
Water
1-16 oz Can black beans, rinsed
Salt to taste.

Ingredients for the rest of the paella:

2 Pieces of fried chicken
1-15 oz Can Jack Mackerel
½ an 11 oz Summer Sausage (5.5 oz), sliced small
½ a 5 oz Pepperoni (2.5 oz), sliced small
1 Medium green pepper, large dice
1 Medium onion, large dice
¼ Cup flour
1 Teaspoon each salt and garlic powder
Oil to fry the Mack.

First, the rice:

Step 1: Put the octopus and half the oil from the octopus can in a rice-pot, and place the pot on medium to high heat. If the octopus pieces are really large, cut them in half. Discard the remainder of the oil from the can.

Step 2: Rinse off the calamari, discard the black ink (the black ink will discolor the rice, we don't want "dirty" paella). Add the garlic and the calamari to the pot. Stir for 3 - 4 minutes.

Step 3: Rinse off the black beans and add them to the pot. Pour the tomato sauce into the bean can and add water until the can is full. Add to the pot. Usually I would only use 1¾ cans of water for one pound of rice, but as the tomato sauce is a lot thicker than water, when using it to make rice we need to add a little more water. Now add a second bean can full of water to the pot. Basically we are adding 2 bean cans of liquid to the pot.

Step 4: Season the water, use the Sazon, oregano, garlic powder and salt to your liking.

Step 5: Bring to a boil on high heat, add the pound of rice and stir. When the water comes back to a boil, put the lid on the pot, reduce heat to low, and leave it alone for 20 minutes. Remove pot from the stove and let it sit covered so the rice continues to steam off the stove for another 10-15 minutes. When rice is tender and fluffy, it's done.

Now the rest of the paella:

Step 6: Clean the Jack Mack and break it into strips, half fillets are fine (A fillet would be half a fish, so our strips are quarter fishes, get it?)

Step 7: Dredge the Mack strips in the flour with the garlic powder and salt. Fry them on all sides until they are crispy. Set the fish aside and pour off the frying oil into a dry can and reserve it. Be sure to fry in hot oil, if your fish breading isn't crispy after 1½ minutes on each side, your oil is not hot enough. Turn the heat up. Fish sitting in cool oil will get chewy and absorb lots of grease.

Step 8: Using a little of the reserved frying oil sauté the diced onion. When the onion is lightly browned, set it aside, separate from the fish.

Step 9: Using a little more of the reserved oil, sauté the diced green peppers until just getting soft, but not mushy, and set aside by adding them to the onion.

Step 10: Using more of the oil, sauté the sausage and the pepperoni together until lightly browned, and add them to the pepper and onion mix.

Step 11: Remove the skin from the fried chicken and then take it off the bones. Rip it into small pieces and add them to the mixture.

Step 12: Assembly: When the rice is done, keeping the pot off the heat, gently fold in the diced pepperoni, onion, chicken, sausage and peppers. Decoratively place the fried Mack around the top of the paella and replace the lid. Let stand covered for at least twenty minutes so the flavors get a chance to come together and the fish will get reheated. Do all this off the heat.

Serve right out of the pot. Picture it, all the beans and octopus and other ingredients, especially if you use a red and/or green pepper, this pot full of paella will have quite a gourmet look to it.

My buddies mixed milk with orange juice and sugar to make a Spanish drink called "Morir Sonando". I would have preferred a Cuba Libre myself, but what can you do?

Viva Espagna!

TORTILLAS/QUESADILLAS

How is it that of the 60 guys in my dorm, only one other white guy and me knew what quesadillas were? I found that to be very strange, you don't have to be a Mexican to enjoy Mexican food. Well, in case you don't know, a quesadilla is like a closed-faced Mexican pizza made with tortillas. Here's a visual, a large round tortilla topped with your favorite ingredients (typically meats & cheeses) then another tortilla placed on top. Sort of a tortilla sandwich I guess. Traditionally, tacos, burritos, quesadillas and other wrapped foods made from various types of tortillas all begin with corn flour (maize). The various cultures that use maize mill their grains to different levels of fineness for texture differentiation among their tortilla products. Sometimes I feel that it's appropriate to quote an old marine credo: "Improvise, adapt, overcome." As I've said, prisoners are some of the most creative people in the world, we have to be, making what we want out of what we have is truly an art, whether it's making an FM receiver for a Walkman, or in this case making tortillas without maize. Regular all-purpose flour and a little pancake mix (my new favorite pantry staple) works just fine.

Before I go over how easy it is to make tortillas in prison without maize, I want to stress (as usual) that you should use your imagination. When it comes to filling them, don't be overly concerned with what will work because anything will work. I was in my boy J"oe Dirt's" cube when we came up with the idea of making quesadillas, so I checked his locker first. Dirt had a can of bean and beef chili, so I grabbed that, then I saw roast beef in gravy and more beans. Well, there's a base right? I sautéed some onion, green peppers and garlic and added them to the chili. I plucked the roast beef out of its gravy (I don't rinse off the roast beef when I use it in this recipe, a little gravy adds flavor and sauce) and threw that all in a pot. My neighbor had half a kosher beef sausage and some tomato paste, in it went. After cooking it for only about 20 minutes and adding some seasonings, I had a nice beef filling.

At this time four of us were sharing three large bags in the refrigerator, so after a quick inventory of our food pool, out came Jalapeno Jack cheese, Swiss cheese and some shredded Mozzarella. It was definitely "on". I drizzled about a tablespoon of oil in a pan and lightly cooked both sides of all my tortilla shells. After placing a healthy amount of my meat and bean mixture on half of the tortillas, I topped them with some diced, pickled Jalapenos and a little of each of the three cheeses. Last, I placed the other half of the tortilla on top, creating a sandwich effect -- or quesadilla. Thirty-five seconds in the microwave and they were hot, soft and packed with melted cheese. They were really great, the only things missing were some guacamole, sour cream and a little salsa.

Even if you only had a can of beans you could mash them up like refried beans, top them with cheese and fill your quesadillas. How about some chicken right out of the can, topped with some cheese from the mess hall? Cheese isn't necessary but they're a thousand times better with it, and when the cheese melts it helps the top tortilla stick to the bottom one. What a great way to utilize some leftovers. Pack whatever it is between two tortillas with cheese and you have a whole new meal.

TORTILLAS:

Ingredients for a dozen, six-inch tortillas:

2 Cups flour, plus more for dusting your work surface
2 Tablespoons pancake mix
1 Tablespoon sugar
1 Teaspoon salt
Cold water
6 Tablespoons oil.

Step 1: Place all your dry ingredients in a mixing bowl or large pot, and give them a quick stir to evenly incorporate them.

Step 2: Add a little cold water at a time. Literally, two or three tablespoons until a dough ball forms. Like all other doughs this one should be soft, supple and easily come away from the sides and bottom of your bowl or pot. Knead your dough gently for only about two minutes, don't overwork it or the flour will become glutinous and elastic. Make sure it's soft and dry to the touch, not sticky or tacky. This dough should not rest, use it right away.

Step 3: Dust your work surface with a little flour, and roll out your dough as thin as you can, dusting your work surface with a little flour as you go. These tortillas should not be any thicker than six sheets of paper stacked together.

Step 4: Using an inverted bowl that is about six inches around as a guide, press down and cut out your tortillas.

Step 5: When you have cut out all 12 tortillas, cook both sides of all of them using only a drizzle of oil for each side of each tortilla. Don't cook them until they get hard, they should be light brown and soft.

Step 6: When all of your tortilla shells are lightly browned on each side, sandwich them with whatever filling you have and some cheese.

Step 7: Nuke'em for 30 to 40 seconds, cut and serve with rice for a meal, or eat alone as a great snack.

CHILLIQUILLAS & FLAUTAS
(MEXICAN LASAGNA)

Here's another couple of great ideas for you. First the Chilliquillas, don't ask me how to pronounce it because I can't, I just eat it. There aren't any Mexicans here in E-dorm for me to ask, so I'm going to wing it -- chilli-KWEE-ya -- that might be close

I went to a pricey little Mexican restaurant in Manhattan on either 58th or 59th Street, called Rosa something or other, and had this lasagna-like dish. Mine came out much better. I think they overcooked theirs, which made their tortillas mushy. Maybe mine just don't get mushy because I don't use tortillas made with maize. Giving this dish a Mexican/Italian name I thought would assist in your generating a visual. Pasta-less lasagnas are exactly what these are anyway. We are just substituting the pasta with tortillas. You could use a traditional meat and tomato sauce for layering here, but I doubt you would ever see that done in Mexico. More commonly, chicken or seafood with sauces and cheeses are used.

This is going to be a kind of connect-the-dots recipe, so grab a pen and paper and you won't drive yourself crazy flipping back and forth and you won't get your book all messy.

CHILLIQUILLAS

Ingredients:

Tortilla dough
Cheese
Good filling

The difference between Chilliquillas and Flautas (FLAUW-tas) is basically that Chilliquillas are layered and Flautas are rolled. To make either Chilliquillas or Flautas you are going to need some tortillas, some cheese and a good filling. How many people you're feeding and the thickness of your layers will determine how many tortillas you need. With rice and beans on the side, one times the recipe for tortilla dough (see index) will be enough to make a Chilliquilla or Flauta that will feed four. So, make one times the tortilla recipe and pick a filling.

Now any saucy meat, poultry, fish or even vegetable mix will work. Use your own or try one of my recipes:

1. Beef & Cheese filling -- see Beef and Cheese Strombolis
2. The meat concept filling from the Quesadilla recipe
3. The roast beef filling -- see Roast Beef Dumpling
4. Even the Chicken and Turkey Pot Pie filling will work
5. Scrambled eggs, sausage & cheese filling -- see Breakfast Wraps
6. Gyro filling -- see Gyros
7. Beef patty filling -- see Jamaican Beef & Cheese Patties.
8. Any of the pasta sauces, just be careful not to add too much liquid. Use a slotted spoon when making your layers.

There are two ways to assemble your Chilliquillas. One way is in a microwaveable bowl. The other way is in a small heavy-bottomed pot with a lid. You should choose your bowl (any shape) or pot first so you can use it as a guide for shaping your tortillas. If I had an oven I would use a large rectangular baking dish. That would be the easiest route to go, I would just invert the baking dish onto my rolled-out tortilla dough and cut out perfectly fitting rectangles of dough. You are going to make your own tortillas and cut them the exact shape and size of the bowl or pot you are going to use.

Step 1: Choose your bowl or pot. Roll, cut out and sear off your tortillas until just lightly brown on both sides but still nice and soft.

Step 2: Choose and make a filling.

Step 3: Place enough of your filling and sauce into your bowl or pot, to just about ⅛ of an inch up the sides.

Step 4: Sprinkle some of your favorite shredded or grated cheese all over the top of your filling.

Step 5: The next layer is a tortilla, which will fit perfectly right? Continue layering in sequence until your bowl or pot is full or you run out of product. The last layer should be cheese.

Step 6 (a): If your Chilliquilla is in a bowl, microwave it for two minutes at a time without the lid, until it's very hot at the center and the cheese on top has melted. Place the lid on the bowl then let it stand (covered) for 5 - 10 minutes before you serve. If you can wait until the next day, you will be able to un-mold it and cut it into nice slices just like a regular lasagna.

Step 6 (b): If you opt to use a heavy-bottomed pot, use a small one. Follow the same building instructions as previously described in Step 6(a). To cook your chilliquillas in a pot I recommend putting a wide, hollowed-out can (like a 16 oz ham can) underneath your pot as a riser and cooking it with the lid on, using the lowest temperature for as long as it takes.

Step 7: To test for doneness, use anything you have that can be pressed into the center and gently pulled out without destroying it. For example, you can slide the handle of a plastic fork or spoon all the way through the center of the chilliquilla, pull it out, and using your finger feel it. If it's hot to the touch, it's ready.

FLAUTAS

Ingredients:

Same as Chilliquillas recipe, above.

Now Flautas, are another type of Mexican dish, using the same ingredients as the Chilliquillas, but they are rolled rather than layered and usually topped with a molé sauce. (Molé is a chocolate flavored sauce).

Step 1: You can roll out your tortillas and cut them exactly as you would the quesadilla, (see index).

Step 2: Place some filling on each of your tortillas and roll them up.

Step 3: Place some filling and its sauce on the bottom of your pot or bowl, then place a layer of rolled tortillas on top of that, then more filling and sauce, and finish with cheese. Cook according to Step 6(a) or Step 6(b) in the Chilliquillas recipe, and enjoy!

FAST & EASY BAKE BURRITOS
For 6-8 Medium Burritos

Ingredients:

3 Garlic cloves, chopped
½ Cup oil
3½ Cups flour
2/3 Cup pancake mix
2 Teaspoons oregano
1 Teaspoon garlic powder
1 Cup lukewarm water.
Filling, your favorite: beans, rice, vegetables, meat ...

To prepare the oil:

Step 1: Chop the garlic and place it in a small pot with the oil on a low heat. Let it simmer on a low heat until just lightly browned. Remove the pot from the stove and let it continue to cook off the heat. Do not burn the garlic, it will be bitter and unusable. If the garlic starts to get too brown, strain it out of the pot immediately because it will continue to cook.

To make the dough:

Step 2: In a Tupperware container, mix together the flour, pancake mix, herbs and spices, and half the warm water (4 oz). If the dough does not come together and is still dry after 2 - 3 minutes of mixing, add a little more water, about a tablespoon at a time. If dough is too wet and tacky, add a little more flour. When the dough is ready, sprinkle a little flour on your work surface, and knead by hand until the dough is smooth and supple, about 2-3 minutes.

Remember, to make a work surface, spread a garbage bag on your worktop and tape it down. If you don't have tape, you can lightly dampen the entire area where you plan to work with a little water and then place the bag on top. This works surprisingly well. Sprinkle a little bit of the extra flour onto your garbage-bag-covered work-surface so that you will have a clean work surface when you begin, and an easy to clean area when you are done.

Now you will need a pan, a spatula, a plastic bag to work on, a paper bag, and a rolling pin. I use full soda cans, they're better than other cans which have rough edges and will cut the dough while your trying to work. Most other things we could use or make will send us directly to jail without passing go, you know what I'm saying? The Box!

Step 3: Okay, this is so easy. Divide your dough into balls a little larger than your fist.

Step 4: Roll out one ball at a time into circles about 1/8th of an inch thick, not too thin or they will rip.

Step 5: Place your favorite filling in the center and roll it up, just as you would roll up a cigarette, roll the bottom flap over the ingredients, then fold over the left and right sides just enough to stop the filling from falling out. Continue rolling it up so it looks like a Chinese eggroll. Add a little water on the last little bit of edge, this will act like glue. Let them sit for 2 minutes flap-side down so they seal well.

This is a great way to use up leftovers. My favorite is ham and cheese with a little pizza sauce. I call them 'pizza burritos'.

Step 6: Put 1/4 inch cooking oil in a pan, and on medium heat. Fry your burritos on all sides until they are golden brown all over and the dough is cooked through.

Sometimes I even heat up more pizza sauce for dunking 'em. Viva Mexico!

SPICY JALAPENO RICE

It is still amazing to me how many different techniques I see here for making rice. When I first arrived at this correctional facility, I saw lots of Spanish guys judging whether they had the right amount of water in their pots by sticking a long spoon into the center of the rice. They told me if the spoon stands straight up without falling over, there's just enough water. Well, wouldn't the spoon stick up without any water at all? After actually standing there and watching the whole process, where they constantly have to stir and fold the rice, and at intervals have to add more water, I knew something was wrong. Some guys put paper towels on top of the rice, others tie plastic bags onto their lids. I even saw a guy put his hand into the water to judge the amount by how much water rose over his hand when it touched the rice.

To me, all these strange procedures seem ludicrous. It's not rocket science guys, it's just rice. On the back of every bag or box of rice are very simple instructions, basically two to one water to rice will always give you a nice fluffy rice. On occasion there are reasons for changing that ratio, for example, if you add two cans of octopus and a can of beans to your pot, those two cans of product have liquid, so this would lessen the amount of water you need.

Here's a simple equation: for each one pound of rice, I use 1¾ of a 16 oz bean can of water. That's 3 ½ cups of water. I always use a 16 oz bean can to measure my water because 16 oz is two cups. For one pound of rice I use 1¾ cans of water, easy, right? Now if you plan on adding any product to your rice that contains liquid, drain the liquid into the bean can first, then top it off with the water so you can keep your ratio correct.

Incidentally, to prevent having to go searching for cans, I keep a few empty, clean cans of various measurements in my cube. It's easier than transferring beans and mushrooms out of their cans at the last second just so you can use the empty can.

At first thought, keeping a bunch of cans in your cube or cell might seem like clutter, but I assure you every good cook everywhere has at least one measuring cup if not a set, so why shouldn't we? As we are allowed to have two boxes under our bed, most people seem to dedicate one box to stuff for cooking.

Anyway, here are a few simple steps, which, if followed, will turn two pounds (two bags) of rice into five large bowls of spicy, fluffy Jalapeno rice.

Ingredients:

2 lbs Rice
8 Pickled Jalapenos, minced
1 Package Sazon
1 Tablespoon salt
1 Teaspoon Adobo seasoning
3½ Bean cans of water (7 cups).

Step 1: Place water in heavy-bottomed pan.

Step 2: Bring water to a boil on high heat and add all the seasonings except the Jalapenos.

Step 3: Add the rice, leave on high heat, and bring rice and water back to a boil.

Step 4: Stir in the minced Jalapenos.

Step 5: Turn stove down to the lowest heat setting and put a tight fitting lid on your pot.

Step 6: Don't touch it for 30 minutes, leave it alone.

Step 7: After 30 minutes on low, remove the pot from the stove and let it sit on the side with the lid on for another 10-15 minutes so that the rice continues to steam off the stove. When rice is tender and fluffy, it's ready.

That's it. Now serve.

BEANS IN RED SAUCE
Serves 4

This recipe is sort of a play on a Spanish style of beans that we see frequently here. Many of the Spanish guys I have encountered in jail, no matter where they are actually from, seem to prepare their beans basically the same way. This style of beans in sauce is almost like a loose bean stew, and goes really well over rice, with fish or chicken. It's nice to have the wetness of the beans combined with the other meals they serve, like fried Mack or chicken with rice, which can be a little dry. You can serve these beans right on top of your rice or on the side, either way they're good.

The reason I say this version of Spanish beans is "a play" on what the Spanish guys here make, is because I took what they made and I played with it. It would seem that using a whole 8 oz can of tomato sauce for two 15 oz cans of beans is unheard of. Well, you're gonna hear it now. I asked one guy if he would put sugar or honey or a seasoning packet from a ramen soup in the mix, and he said "No, never". Well, these were my beans and I was gonna put whatever I wanted in 'em, right? Now, I wasn't looking for another thick type of baked bean recipe, I wanted them really flavorful and a little soupy. I ended up making two different types of beans on two separate occasions, both worthy of note. The only actual difference was that one time I used half a large green pepper and it added a whole new dimension in flavor to the sauce, so try both ways. If you have half a fresh bell pepper to use, slice it thin and sauté it with the onion and garlic, this makes a very nice change in flavor.

Okay, here is my played-with version of Spanish style beans in red sauce.

Ingredients:

2-5 oz Cans kidney beans
1-8 oz Can tomato sauce
3 Cloves garlic, minced
1 Packet Sazon seasoning
1 Packet beef seasoning from a ramen soup, any flavor will work, but
   beef is the best
3-4 Tablespoons honey
1 Teaspoon each of salt, garlic powder, oregano and Adobe
   seasoning
1 Medium onion, or two small onions, diced small
3 Tablespoons oil.

Step 1: Sauté onion and garlic in the oil on medium heat until tender, 3 - 4 minutes.

Step 2: Add all the dry ingredients -- the Sazon, garlic powder, oregano, salt, the Adobo seasoning and the packet of beef seasoning from a ramen noodle soup. Lower the heat and cook for another 3 - 4 minutes.

Step 3: Empty one can of beans into a bowl, and using the other unopened can crush half of the beans. (You can use whatever you have for the crushing process).

Step 4: Open the other can of beans, and add both cans of beans (one of them half crushed) and all the other ingredients to the pot.

Step 5: Let simmer on a low-to-medium heat for at least 20 minutes.

These beans are good to go right away However, I noticed that they taste even better the next day, so if you can plan ahead make them the night before.

Chapter 4

ASIAN CORNER

Sweet & Sour Crispy Mackerel
Orange Beef/General Tzo's Beef
Tempura Sardines with Spicy Tomato Sauce
Delicious Chinese-Style Fried Rice #1 With Pork
Delicious Chinese-Style Fried Rice #2 Without Pork
Fried Won-Tons with Diagram
Won-Ton Dipping Sauce

SWEET & SOUR CRISPY MACK
Makes 4 - 6 normal, human-sized portions, or 3 Viking bowls

This is a play on a Chinese sweet and sour dish. I wanted to create a Mack dish that would be crunchy and also bursting with flavor. Talk about extra crunchy, this came out amazing on the first try. Don't smother the fish in sauce cuz they might get soggy. I recommend you put some sauce on a plate, then put the fish on the sauce right as you're ready to eat so it doesn't sit for long. This 50-50 noodle cracker crust really did the trick. Just another example of slammin' jailhouse food, so go for it, and for goodness sake keep your fillets of Mackerel juicy, don't overcook them. See the introduction for Mac 11 Ways for detailed instructions on frying Mack.

Ingredients for The Mack:

3 Cans Mackerel fillets
6 oz Cold water
10 oz Maple syrup

4 Tablespoons sugar
12 Tablespoons lemon juice
2 Teaspoons salt
2 to 2½ Cups flour
2 Ramen soup mixes (Shrimp flavor, reserve seasoning for the rice)
2 Sleeves snack crackers
Oil for frying.

Ingredients Sweet & Sour Sauce/Syrup/Glaze:

Maple syrup
Sugar
Lemon juice
2 Tablespoons butter
Half a medium onion, diced. Optional.

Step 1: Open the cans of Mackerel and reserve one of the lids. Gently empty the fish out of the cans and discard all the liquid. Rinse the mackerel under slowly-running cool water, rubbing gently with your fingers to discard any discolored meat, the bloodline and the skin. Using the reserved lid gently split the Jack Mack into two whole fillets. One at a time, again put the fillets under the cool running water and gently remove the spinal bones. Yes, the key word here is 'gently'. If your fillets break up into tiny pieces you will end up making Mack patties.

Step 2: For the batter, in a bowl, mix the water, syrup, lemon juice and sugar, then slowly stir in the flour, adding a little at a time to avoid lumps. You want a smooth batter, the consistency should be almost as thick as pancake batter, so if you don't need all of the flour don't use it. Taste your batter, you can spit it out, it's not like it's got raw egg in it or anything. If you like it a little sweeter or more sour, adjust your seasonings.

Step 3: To make the breading, in a container large enough to work in, first crush the crackers. Next crush the noodles, but not into a fine dust, you want to see cool-looking little curly bits, then combine the two. I recommend transferring little amounts of the cracker-noodle mix to a small plate or bowl for actually battering the fish, that way any mix that is left over won't be soggy from the wet fish or the batter, and you can use it another time.

Here's a tip that Julia Child gave me after a few glasses of wine at her 75th birthday party (which I helped cater): "If you keep one hand wet and one hand dry, you won't bread yourself". Words to live by!

Step 4: With one hand place the fish fillet in the batter, shake off the excess batter, then place the fish in the container with the cracker-noodle breading. With your other (dry) hand dredge the fillet through the breading covering all sides with the crunchy coating. Repeat this process with all the fillets and set aside.

Step 5: Place enough oil in a frying pan to come up the side at least ¼ inch. Place the pan on medium heat (4) until you see light streams of smoke rising off the top.

Step 6: Fry all the fillets until golden brown (about a minute and a half on each side), then place on paper towels or a brown paper bag to absorb the excess grease.

This makes six portions depending on how hungry you are. If you're feeding Vikings, plan for three of them to be very happy.

FOR SWEET & SOUR SAUCE/SYRUP/GLAZE

Step 7: When you are ready to serve the Mackerel, place a small amount of maple syrup and lemon juice in a pan, use sugar and salt to season it. Make your glaze as sweet or sour as you like, then stir in the butter one tablespoon at a time. If you want to take this to the next level, soften half a diced onion in the butter then stir in the seasonings, that will make a nice glaze. You can drizzle it either over the fish, or on the plate, or both, and serve with your favorite rice.

ORANGE BEEF/GENERAL TZO'S BEEF
Serves 6 moderately hungry people, or fills 3 Viking bowls

This dish is amazingly authentic. If you like Orange Beef or General Tzo's Chicken, this dish is for you. I happened to have some bamboo shoots, one of the guys had a knob of ginger, and my buddy Sal came through with a can of sliced Mandarin orange segments. If you don't have bamboo shoots or ginger it will still be fine. Sal went around the dorm collecting oranges. Obviously this dish should be done when oranges are given out in the mess hall so everyone can bring them back. If you don't have a can of oranges, slice chunks out of the fresh oranges and add them in at the end. Try to get a little OJ from somewhere if you can. Even if you can't it will still be good, you'll see.

I went on a short trip to the Box for 30 days. A nice place to visit but I wouldn't want to live there. When I returned to my CF, I was moved to a new dorm. I knew some of the guys from the yard, and there was one guy I knew from Rikers Island when I first got arrested 2 years prior, but 50 out of the 60 guys in the dorm I had never seen before. This was the first dish I made in C-Dorm where I was now residing. After letting a bunch of guys taste my creation I instantly had many friends and gained some status in my dorm. I blew them away. Yeah, not to mention how nice it was to have a real meal, have you ever eaten at "Café Le Box"? Check please, I'm outta here!

Ingredients:

6 Oranges
¼ Cup thinly-sliced orange peel
2 Cans roast beef in gravy
1½ Cups granulated sugar
1 Medium onion, extra large dice (big chunks)
1 Can mushrooms, drained
1 Can orange segments in syrup
2 Cloves garlic or half teaspoon garlic powder
1 Can bamboo shoots, drained (optional - only if you have it)
1 Teaspoon fresh ginger, sliced thin (also optional, if you have it)
1 Cup flour
4-5 Teaspoons oil
2 Pickled Jalapeños, sliced, plus 5 tablespoons of their juice
1 Teaspoon lemon juice
Water to boil.

If you have someone sending you in a can of bamboo shoots, you might as well go the whole nine yards, ask them to check out the Asian section of their local supermarket and see if they can find cans of mixed Asian vegetables, baby corn, water chestnuts, etc.

Step 1: Using the lid of a can, slice the top and the bottom off all the oranges. Now the oranges will sit flat. Slice long, wide strips of peel, cutting from top to bottom. Place all the longest strips peel-side down on a counter, with the pith (the white part) facing up, and carefully slice sideways to remove all the pith, leaving only the orange skin. Now slice the orange peel into fine strips, the thinner the better (in French cooking they call this a 'Julienne').

Step 2: Place the Julienned orange peel in cold water in a pot and boil twice. Start with cold water both times. This will remove whatever bitterness may be left. Squeeze juice from the oranges and reserve.

If you don't have canned orange slices, section the six fresh oranges, that means make little orange wedges. After you extract the wedges, you can squeeze the remaining orange and skin for the juice, then reserve.

Step 3: Place sugar in a clean pan on medium heat. Let cook until it turns a sort of light amber- red color. Don't burn it.

Step 4: As the sugar starts to turn red, immediately add the canned orange or the fresh oranges or both. Reserve all of the orange slices for the end. Now you can add your orange peel and let simmer on a low heat.

Step 5: Remove the roast beef chunks from their gravy and toss them in flour until they're coated.

Step 6: Add the gravy from the roast beef to the sugar orange mixture and let cook slowly on low heat until all other steps are completed.

Step 7: Put half the oil in a pan on medium-to-high heat, and sear off the beef chunks until all sides of the chunks are evenly browned. Don't overcrowd the pan or the beef will end up boiling, do it in batches.

Step 8: When all the beef is seared remove it from the pan and wipe out the pan. Put the rest of the oil in the pan and on medium heat sauté the onion, garlic and ginger until the onion is just getting soft, 4 minutes max.

Step 9: Add the lemon juice to your orange sauce and taste. It should be great. If you like it sweeter add a little more sugar. If you want it a little more tart add more lemon juice. Remember, when you eat this dish you'll have added all the orange segments from the can which will add more orange flavor, so don't be discouraged if it's not overly orangey tasting yet, it's okay. If you find your sauce is not as thick as the General Tzo's we all know and love, take 2 tablespoons of the flour and mix it with enough cold water (about 1 tablespoon) to form a thick paste. The Chinese would use corn starch and make what they call a slurry, but in prison I don't think so, it's not in the Directive!

Step 10: To Assemble: Place all the beef in the pan with the onion mixture. Add the canned mushrooms without their water, the bamboo shoots, the Jalapeños, the canned orange segments, and any other vegetables you have, such as celery, carrots, green peppers or any of those Asian canned vegetables your people were able to send you. Pour enough sauce over the meat, vegetables and orange mixture just to cover. Gently fold in all the orange segments so as not to break them up. Let the whole pot come up to a light simmer, then serve it over white rice. Some guys like me to make fried rice to go with this dish, but I think it's more work than it's worth, once you ladle my slammin' sauce over the rice you won't be tasting anything but orange beef anyway.

Serve and take a bow!

TEMPURA SARDINES WITH SPICY TOMATO SAUCE

When I moved into C-Dorm it happened to work out that the other four main food contributors and myself all went to commissary around the same time each month. Life was good right after commissary and cooking was easy. Prior to everyone's buy-days, they would come to me, and I would fill out their commissary sheets for them after they had checked off whatever toiletries and personal items they wanted. So I basically knew what I had to work with and what combinations of stuff I could get from each contributor to create our meals.

This dish is one of those examples of what happens about a week and a half after the last buy. With 3 or 4 days left to go before commissary, everybody starts kicking in odds and ends from packages and what they have left over from the week before. At this point there is no such thing as menu planning, but winging it seemed to always work out fine. Some cooking schools give their students what's known as a "basket test". The students are given a basket of food without being informed of the contents of the basket prior to the test, and the students must create a meal using the mystery ingredients. They usually get duck breasts or squab, perhaps exotic greens and herbs, a lobe of foie gras, stuff like that. I got three large cans of sardines in tomato sauce, 4 boxes of macaroni and cheese, and a pepperoni. I laughed in the face of adventure. When others might have crumbled, I forged ahead.

I decided to make a tempura batter and fry the sardines. They were already in a tomato sauce, but it was very thin and very fishy. Macaroni and cheese in a box is also less than exciting, but since none of us had received a package for a while we were going to have to make do. After a little scavenging I came up with a stick of margarine, a can of evaporated milk and 6 slices of American cheese. Score! They all went into the Mac and cheese, along with the pepperoni diced up nice and small. After the noodles were cooked and drained I added the little cheese packets, the butter, the cheese slices, the milk and enough hot water until it was really runny and creamy. The pepperoni gave it a little zing and added some texture to it. It ended up going great with the tomato sauce and fish. Who woulda guessed? The sardines weren't fishy when I was done, don't be afraid of sardines, give them a chance, they're pretty good fried, all nice and crispy! This made a lot of food, so I'm going to cut the recipe down here.

Ingredients:

2-15 oz Cans sardines in tomato sauce
1 Cup flour
10 oz Cold water
½ 14 oz can crushed tomatoes
2 Pickled Jalapeños, diced
1 Medium onion, diced
1 Teaspoon Oregano
4 Tablespoons sugar
½ Teaspoon powdered garlic, or 2 cloves fresh if you have them
Oil for frying.

Step 1: Mix the water and the flour to make your tempura batter. Traditionally tempura has eggs, so do chickens – but I'm not a chicken and I didn't have any eggs. The batter should be a little looser than pancake batter. Stir well so there are no lumps, then refrigerate it until the fish is ready.

Step 2: Remove the sardines from their sauce and set aside in the refrigerator to keep them cold.

Step 3: Place onion in a small pot with 2 tablespoons of oil and sauté for about 3 minutes. If you're using fresh garlic add it to the pot at the same time. When the onions start to get a little soft add half the tomato sauce from the sardines, the crushed tomatoes, sugar, Jalapeños and oregano. Bring the sauce to a boil then lower the heat to the lowest setting on your range and let it reduce and get thick. By the time the fish is cooked, and whatever starch you make to go with it is ready, (rice, etc., in my case the creamy macaroni and cheese with pepperoni), it should be done. Check for seasoning, if you're a salt lover or you have basil, go for it.

Step 4: Carefully split the sardines in half leaving little fillets. Remove the center bones. Try to leave the fillets in as large pieces as possible.

Step 5: Heat about ¼ inch oil in a frying pan.

Step 6: Remove tempura batter from the fridge and give it a stir.

Step 7: Dip fish fillets in batter and place them directly into the pan with the hot oil. Don't overcrowd the pan or they will boil and spit. Only fry the fish for about 30 - 40 seconds on each side. Remember this fish is already cooked, you are just cooking the batter. If you overcook them they will get dry. When cooked properly, tempura batter stays almost white. It takes on a very light yellowish hue. If they start getting golden brown like fried Mac - they're getting over-cooked!

Step 8: Stir the tomato sauce well, it's ready.

Step 9: Place a large spoon of sauce on a plate. Top with tempura sardines, place your rice (or in my case macaroni and cheese with pepperoni) on the plate, and your good to go!

Yeah, I had to be a little fancy so I put a pile of macaroni on each of our plates, then stood the fillets up against the pile and made a nice design with the sauce on the plate at 6 o'clock (that's front and center). It looked as good as it tasted.

CHINESE-STYLE FRIED RICE, #1 WITH PORK

It is interesting how using the word Asian can mean different things in different places. Well, in NYC Asians generally prefer eating with chopsticks to using a knife and fork, and would rather drink their soup directly from the bowl than use those decorative porcelain spoons. Anyway, there weren't any Asian guys in this dorm to borrow cool products from, but after looking through what my mom had sent me, and scrounging around my dinner crew, I put together a nice little Chinese meal.

You can use leftover rice from the day before, or under-cook enough rice for as many people as you are cooking for. The rice is going to be cooked again so you want to stop it cooking while it is still a little hard, just under cook it slightly. Say two cups of cooked white rice per person. You can substitute any vegetable you have for the vegetable I use here. The only real necessity is soy sauce. I like dark, sweet soy sauce for my fried rice, but any soy sauce will work. Again, you may not be able to find all the ingredients I use here the first time, but you might be able to have someone send them to you for next time.

This technique is so easy and all you need is a rice pot and a large spoon. Ready? Here we go:

Ingredients:

2 Cups cooked white rice per person
2 Tablespoons hard cooked scrambled eggs (EggBeaters)
2 Tablespoons green onions, chopped
2 Tablespoons Red pepper, chopped
2 Tablespoons peas
2 Tablespoons cooked ham, diced
3 Tablespoons cooking oil
1 Teaspoon fresh ginger, chopped small*
1 Clove garlic, crushed and chopped fine*
Soy sauce to taste, add a little at a time, it might be strong stuff
  depending on the brand
Sugar, a tiny pinch, to counteract the soy sauce.
Cilantro, some chopped up at the end would be nice if you can get
  it, and of course a sprig on top for a garnish when you serve!

> **Note:** *One teaspoon of fresh ginger and one clove of garlic is sufficient no matter how many people you're cooking for.*

Step 1: Place oil in a large rice pot over a medium heat. When you see a little smoke start to come out of the pan add all of the vegetables, the ham, egg, garlic and the ginger. Everything except the soy sauce, rice, sugar and the cilantro.

Step 2: Stir until the green onion starts to get soft, about 2 minutes, add the rice and cook for another two minutes stirring all the time. Then, in intervals, add a little soy sauce and a tiny sprinkle of sugar, tasting as you go.

Step 3: When you are happy with the flavor, stir in the cilantro.

Step 4: Dish it out and top it with a reserved sprig of cilantro for a garnish.

Now don't get caught altering some item to make chop sticks, it ain't worth breaking up a chair over, just use a plastic fork. And for goodness sake have some couth and use a spoon when you have soup!

CHINESE-STYLE FRIED RICE #2, NO PORK

Lots of guys in my dorm didn't want to eat pork, mostly for religious reasons. Here are two easy adjustments for you to try if pork products aren't your thing.

Buy already-fried, frozen chicken from your commissary (my commissary always had it). Simply break or cut the chicken off the bone and substitute it for the diced ham in the pork fried rice recipe.

For seafood fried rice, open cans of your favorite seafood and drain them well. Dab the seafood dry before adding it, so your seafood fried rice doesn't get wet and mushy.

FRIED WON-TONS
Yields 30 - 35 Won-Ton Skins

I love all kinds of Asian foods, whether it's Chinese, Japanese, Thai, Korean, etc.

For some reason at this CF, they won't let us have most of the Asian ingredients I would need to concoct a true, say, Chinese meal. The female CO who works the package room here follows a set of directives inmates have never seen, and refuses to allow in many things I have sent to me. We are given the options to destroy, send home, or donate items that aren't allowed.

I'm still able to recreate many of my favorite Asian dishes, like Orange Beef, which comes out pretty close to authentic even without the ingredients you'd think there'd be no substitutes for.

Spring roll wrappers and won-ton skins were refused, so determined as I sometimes am, I decided to try to make my own won-tons.

Won-ton skins are used in Chinese cooking for lots of things, like won-ton soup and fried won-tons, and they are even stuffed with various fillings and boiled or deep fried, better known as dumplings.

I remember reading somewhere that won-ton wrapper dough is similar to Italian pasta dough. As pasta dough was easy I gave making won-tons a try and they came out awesome.

Now, every time I make something like my orange beef I make fried won-tons on the side. Your fillings can be anything you like. I can't get fresh ginger, a key ingredient in Asian cooking -- the package room CO says it's a spice and no spices are allowed, even though I explained that fresh ginger root is a root vegetable, not a spice, it only becomes a spice when it's dried and made into a powder. However, I was able to get some black bean sauce in a can which I turned into an Asian beef filling.

Use whatever you have, anything will work. Baby shrimps in a can either chopped up or whole with some sautéed vegetables works great, seasoned roast beef from a can, etc.

The one and only very important rule in making this won-ton dough, as in making pasta dough, is letting it rest. The dough needs to sit "un-refrigerated" for at least 30 minutes, preferably covered with a damp cloth or paper towel. This recipe will yield you between 30 and 35 three inch square won-ton skins. If you want less, just cut the recipe in half or make a quarter of the recipe.

Note: *If you refrigerate your dough for longer than an hour, like overnight, cover lightly with plastic wrap or tie tightly in two plastic bags.*

Ingredients:

3 Cups flour
4 Eggs, or one 8 oz container eggbeaters
4 Tablespoons cold water
2 Teaspoons salt
4 Tablespoons oil
Extra flour, for rolling out your dough
Filling of your choice.

Step 1: Place the flour and salt in a large bowl or pot.

Step 2: Using your hand or a spoon push all the flour mix up against the sides of the bowl creating a "well" (as it's called professionally) in the center.

Step 3: Pour all the liquid ingredients into the center of the bowl (the well).

Step 4: Using your fingers or a spoon stir the liquid egg-mix until all the flour mix is incorporated and the mixture has become a dough, and form it into a ball.

Step 5: If your dough seems to be overly wet and tacky use a little more flour. Gently work it with your fingertips until it freely comes away from the sides of your bowl or pot.

> *Do not knead the dough like bread dough. If you over-work this dough, glutens will form creating elasticity. It will be very hard to roll out later, the dough will bounce back instead of staying rolled out. It should be very soft to the touch.*

> *The flour well can be made right on a clean table if you like, the bowl or pot aren't really necessary, but I find making it in a bowl creates less mess to clean up later.*

Step 6: Cover the dough and let it rest for at least 30 minutes un-refrigerated.

Step 7: On a lightly floured flat surface, roll out small pieces of won-ton dough and cut them into approximately three-inch size squares. See diagram page 86. All sides should be about three inches long. If you are ambitious you can roll out a large piece of dough and just cut it into very thin squares, no thicker than 3 or 4 sheets of paper stacked together.

Step 8: Place a small teaspoon of filling in the center of each square.

Step 9: Now following the diagram, wet two adjacent edges of a square, and fold it into the official-looking won-ton shape you would find in a Chinese restaurant.

Step 10: Until you master this folding technique (it only took me ten minutes), you can cheat for speed. Theoretically you can make these won-tons any shape you want to, you can simply wet two adjacent edges lightly with water then press the square into a triangle (see diagram next page). Of course they will taste the same no matter what shape they are.

> **Note:** *Don't use too much water, and seal them well, otherwise they might pop open when you fry them.*

To deep fry won-tons:

Step 11: Deep fry your won-tons in oil at about 325-350 degrees, until they are golden brown and crispy.

 Drop a small piece of dough into the oil to test the temperature. If it darkens too quickly, lower the heat.

Step 12: Remove won-tons from the oil and strain. To drain off excess oil place them on something absorbent - paper towel or a paper bag. Lightly sprinkle them with salt while they're still hot so the salt sticks.

Step 13: Serve with Won-Ton dipping sauce (see next recipe) or sweet & sour sauce (see index), both are really good.

WON-TON DIAGRAM

1- Cut Dough into 3 inch Squars

2- Add filling

3- Lightly wet two adjacent sides with water

here→
hére

4- Fold Square into triangle Sealing it well

fold here→   into

5 - Wet one edge & fold Across so edges stick together

- this is what Your finished Shape should Look like →

wet here

WON-TON DIPPING SAUCE

In addition to eating your won tons in soups and broths, they are really delicious dipped in one of the many sauces I've described, or you can make an authentic-tasting Asian dipping sauce using the following ingredients, if you can get them sent in from outside. A little bit of sesame oil adds body and a nice binding finish. A little regular olive oil will work too, but it will not have the same intense flavor impact. If you don't have vinegar, lemon juice will work, or you can use the vinegar juice from canned pickled products, such as three-bean-salad. This recipe doesn't require exact measurements, as you make it to your own taste.

Ingredients:

Soy Sauce
White wine vinegar
Hot sauce
Ketchup
Fresh ginger grated, or pickled ginger is also good if you can get it
Green onion tops (scallion or spring onion)
Fresh ground pepper or any other pepper
A little bit of sesame oil or olive oil.

So, without actually measuring, start with some soy sauce and add a little of each of the other ingredients until you are happy with the flavor. It's best to let this sauce stand for at least one hour, but overnight is better.

Dip your Won-Tons and enjoy!

Chapter 5

LITTLE ITALY

Spaghetti Peché A La Crema
Summer Sausage & Tomato Sauce
Pizza Seafood Fra Diavolo
Chicago-Style Thin Crust Pizza
Traditional Italian Baked Ziti
Beef & Cheese Strombolis
Italian-Style Chicken & Broccoli Dinner
Garlic Knots
Garlic Oil
Fresh Pasta Dough

SPAGHETTI PECHÉ A LA CREMA
Spaghetti in Creamy Clam Sauce
Makes ten 8 oz servings

This is my version of a creamy clam sauce. We added a can of baby shrimp because one of the guys who chipped in for this meal happened to have one. He got it sent in from home, as did the guy who chipped in the garlic cloves. All the other ingredients were available at our commissary store.

If baby shrimps aren't available to you, add another can of minced or regular clams, and the number of portions will be the same. If you don't have garlic or onions, it will be just as good, just add a little more garlic powder, and if you have it, onion powder to taste.

This recipe will yield ten servings, about 8 oz each. However, four of us chipped in for this meal and five of us ended up eating. We all went back for seconds and polished off two boxes of spaghetti. Try the recipe for garlic knots with this dish, they go great together

Ingredients:

1-10.5 oz Can white clam sauce
1-4 oz Can tiny shrimp
2-10.5 oz Cans cream of mushroom soup
1-5 oz Can evaporated milk
2-10 oz Cans whole clams
1-6.5 oz Can minced clams
3 Small onions, diced
3 Cloves garlic, minced
1 Teaspoon Adobo seasoning
1 Teaspoon garlic powder
2 Packets shrimp seasoning from shrimp ramen noodles
1 Teaspoon Oregano
3 Teaspoons Oil
Parmesan cheese to taste (optional).

Step 1: Place oil and onions in pot over low heat and sweat the onions with the lid on for about five minutes or until tender.

Step 2: Add Garlic and cook for two more minutes without the lid, stirring constantly.

Step 3: Raise your cooking temperature to medium and add all the other ingredients.

Step 4: Simmer for ten minutes, then serve over pasta. If you have it, top with some grated parmesan cheese when you are ready to eat.

If they had linguini for sale at our commissary I would have used it. Of course, if you're ambitious like me, you can make your own fresh linguini, see index for recipe.

SUMMER SAUSAGE &TOMATO SAUCE
Makes 15, 8 oz servings

At our commissary store they sell Sparrer Summer Beef Sausage. There are a lot of things you can do with sausage. This particular variety does not need to be refrigerated before opening, it's kind of like a soft salami. Unfortunately, there were no fresh bell peppers available or I would have cut up a few and cooked them with the onion.

For this dish we thought rigatoni would be good because each individual rigatoni tube can hold so much sauce. Choose your favorite pasta or whatever you have at your disposal, and top it with grated Parmesan or mozzarella cheese. It's a little spicy but that's easy to adjust, just add less Jalapeños, or omit them entirely.

Ingredients:

2 Summer beef sausages, cubed
3 Small onions, diced
3 Garlic cloves, sliced
2-8 oz Cans tomato sauce
1-28 oz Can crushed tomatoes
1-28 oz Can Italian-style spaghetti sauce
1-4 oz Can sliced mushrooms
2 Tablespoons tomato paste
3 Tablespoons sugar
2 Teaspoons oregano
2 Teaspoons Adobo seasoning
1 Teaspoon garlic powder
Several handfuls grated cheese, preferably Mozzarella
2 Teaspoons oil.

Step 1: First you must remove any skin or casing from the beef sausages. Then slice them length-wise four times to give you four even logs. Then slice them in the other direction into about quarter inch chunks.

Step 2: Put the two tablespoons of oil in a pot on a medium heat, add the chunks of sausage and cook until evenly browned, about five minutes. Add the diced onions and sliced garlic and cook while stirring for about another 3 - 5 minutes, or until the onions are tender. Add all the other ingredients including the mushroom liquid, and bring to a boil.

Step 3: Reduce the heat to low and let simmer with the lid on for 20 - 30 minutes, stirring occasionally. If you have enough stove time, cook the sauce for an hour, if you don't, 20 - 30 minutes will still be good.

Serve over your favorite pasta, and don't forget the cheese, shredded/grated mozzarella on top works out great for this sauce. Give each plate or bowl of pasta a good sprinkling of shredded mozzarella, then microwave it for a minute or just until the cheese is melted. It gets all melt-y and stringy -- Happy, Happy!

PIZZA-SEAFOOD FRA DIAVOLO
Makes three, 9 inch pies

I can't believe I made pizzas in jail, and without yeast, baking soda or baking powder. Look how I did it.

For lunch one day we had sheet pan pizza in the mess hall, and it was pretty bad, to say the least. For the next few days I had pizza on the brain. No one in my dorm had any pepperoni, mozzarella cheese, sausage or even mushrooms. I had already received my 35 pounds monthly food allowance sent in from home, and commissary was over a week away. I couldn't wait, I had to have some kind of pizza.

After evaluating what we had available, I decided to make a rendition of a seafood pizza I had made back in NYC. In one of the fancy restaurants I worked in, we made an awesome seafood pizza in a proper pizza oven, with scallops and baby shrimps. Patrick, the Executive Chef, used to run it on weekends as a special. At first a few of the guys in my dorm weren't too keen on the idea, but after trying it, it became a regular request. It's not fishy-tasting at all, it's delicious. Three thumbs up. Of course if you aren't into "spicy food", omit the Jalapeños, and if you have mozzarella cheese and pepperoni, you're set. Just follow the pizza dough recipe, top it with the pizza sauce recipe, and use cheese or whatever toppings you like. Get creative. This recipe was inspired by and dedicated to Patrick V. Thanks Pat.

Ingredients for the Garlic Oil:

½ Cup oil
3 Garlic cloves, chopped.

Ingredients for the Dough:

3½ Cups flour
⅔ Cup pancake mix
2 Teaspoons oregano
1 Teaspoon garlic powder
1 Cup lukewarm water.

Ingredients for the Sauce:

14 oz (half large can) Crushed tomatoes
14 oz (half large can) Italian spaghetti sauce
2 Pickled Jalapeños
1 Teaspoon garlic powder
2 Small onions, diced
2 Tablespoons garlic oil (see Step 1)
1 Tablespoon oregano
2 Tablespoons sugar.

Ingredients for the Seafood Topping:

1 Can smoked clams
1 Can scallops
1 Can Octopus, diced small
1 Can smoked kipper snacks, or any seafood you have (shrimp, etc.) broken into small pieces.

To make Garlic Oil:

You need to make the garlic oil first, so it will be ready to use in your authentic pizza sauce in Step 5, and in Steps 6 and 7.

Step 1: Chop the garlic and place it in a small pot with the oil. Let it simmer on a low heat until just lightly browned. Take the pot off the stove and let it continue to cook off the heat. Do not burn the garlic, it will be bitter and unusable. If the garlic starts to get too brown, strain it out of the pot because it will continue to cook.

To make the Dough:

Step 2: Mix the flour, pancake mix, oregano, garlic powder and half the warm water (4 oz) in a Tupperware container. If the dough does not come together and is dry after 2 - 3 minutes of mixing, add a little more water, about a tablespoon at a time. If dough is too wet and tacky, add a little more flour. Knead by hand on the table until the dough is smooth and supple, 2-3 minutes.

To make a work surface, spread a garbage bag on a tabletop and tape it down. If you don't have tape, you can lightly dampen the table with just a little water on the entire area where you're going to place the bag, then place the bag on top. This works surprisingly well. Sprinkle a little bit of the extra flour onto your garbage-bag work-surface.

Step 3: Divide your dough into 3 even balls. Using a full can of soda (or whatever you have) for a rolling pin, roll the dough out into about a 10 inch circle. Press a large lid from a frying pan or pot onto the dough and cut around it. This will give you a perfect circle of dough for your pizza shell, and it will fit into the pan that goes with the lid.

Step 4: Using a plastic fork or the back edge of a spoon, press about a half-inch of the dough all the way into and around the pan. Cover your pizza shells and let them rest while you make the pizza sauce.

To make the sauce:

Step 5: Place garlic oil (which you made in Step 1) in a pot with the diced onions. Place on medium heat until onions are a little tender. Add all the other ingredients except the seafood, and bring to a boil. Remove from the heat and let stand for 5 minutes before using it. The idea is to end up with little pieces of tomato from the crushed tomatoes, not to cook it down into a liquid. Chunky is a good thing.

Of course, in a pinch, you can use any type of tomato product: pre-made sauce, leftover sauce, anything will work.

Step 6: When the sauce is ready, take one tablespoon of the garlic oil (with the garlic) and spread it evenly on one of the pizza shells. Place the shell, oiled side down, into a non-stick frying pan on medium heat (4 - 5). Keep the shell moving in the pan, spin it with your fingers checking the underside frequently making sure it doesn't burn. When it is lightly browned remove it from the pan and repeat this process with the other two shells. Make sure not to put the shells hot side down onto the plastic garbage bag, melted plastic is not part of this recipe! These shells can be refrigerated, or frozen and used at a later date if you wish. We were hungry so there wasn't going to be any refrigerating for later.

Step 7: Spread another tablespoon of garlic and oil onto the un-cooked side of one of the pizza shells, and place it -- uncooked side down -- back into your pan. Adjust the heat to medium-to -low (2 - 3). Spread a thin layer of sauce around the shell, leaving about an inch for a crust. Top sauce evenly with the seafood, sprinkle a good amount of Parmesan on top of that, and then balance the lid on the pan leaving a tiny space for steam to escape so the dough won't get soggy.

Step 8: In only another 3-5 minutes, or when the seafood is warm enough to the touch and the cheese has melted, cut and serve.

I've seen some guys put their rolled-out dough in a pan with sauce and toppings and cook it slowly. That works fine, but it takes like 30-40 minutes on a low heat, and it never really gets as crispy as my double-cooking method. Cooking the pizza crusts twice will truly yield a better product, you'll see.

CHICAGO-STYLE THIN CRUST PIZZA

The pizzas I had originally made here were really good but kinda labor intensive, with lots of steps. Truth be told, the concept came from my buddy Yum Yum. I knew however, if I put my mind to it I could come up with something both simpler and just as good, if not better. Once I started making pizzas in the kitchen, people started coming out of the woodwork asking what they could contribute to "get down", and as usual asking me how many stamps for a pie. I decided not to charge anyone, I told them all to just give me product and I would make it happen.

The next thing I knew, my partner Joe Dirt and I had two frying pans going simultaneously and we jammed out 32 pies. Most of the process I perfected was similar to Yum Yum's except for a few steps. Any toppings will work here, but unlike a real pizza oven, which is often around 600 degrees, we are using pans. Because we don't have such intense heat to cook our toppings on the pies, the toppings must be cooked first. If you're using vegetables like onions or green peppers, they need to be sautéed in a little oil first, until they are just turning soft. Any meats, like sliced sausage or pepperoni, should also be sautéed in a little oil until lightly browned on both sides.

Here's a little overview before we get into the method steps.

Make your dough first because it needs to rest for at least 15 minutes, preferably covered with a damp cloth or paper towel, and while it's resting you can pre-cook your toppings. Then roll out the dough into thin circles, drizzle them with a little oil, and pan fry them on both sides until they are a light brown. Place the pan on top of a riser (a ham can, or a large sardine can, with the top and bottom removed) and lower the heat to 3 or 4.

Top your pizzas with sauce, your favorite cheese, then your toppings, and put a lid on the frying pan. After about 5 minutes your pie bottom should be crispy, the cheese melted, and your toppings hot.

ABOUT PIZZA SAUCE

I made a nice pizza sauce using onions, garlic, crushed tomatoes, oregano and sugar. However, after about 15 pies my sauce was gone and people started bringing me every kind of tomato product they had. Well, cans of tomato sauce, pre-made spaghetti sauce, and even tomato paste all worked well. It's okay to be lazy here, especially if you end up making pies into the double digits.

Ingredients for a Quick & Simple Pizza Sauce:

1 Teaspoon oil
1/2 onion, minced
1/2 clove garlic, minced
1 large can (28 oz) spaghetti sauce, or 2 small cans
1/2 Teaspoon oregano, optional
Salt to taste
Pepper to taste
Sugar to taste

Step 1: Saute the minced garlic and minced onion in the oil.

Step 2: Add the spaghetti sauce and seasonings.

Step 3: Simmer for about five minutes.

Nice and easy, but taste it. You're only going to use a very thin layer of sauce, so don't be overly concerned with it being an awesome sauce, it's really not that important here.

ABOUT PIZZA DOUGH

Like I said, every time I make pies people bring me flour, pancake mix, cheese toppings, and other ingredients, making it difficult to get an accurate count on how many pies I get per recipe because I keep adding to it. So, I'm going to give you the proportions, but not to worry because (a) you can always make more dough, and (b) leftover dough -- if you have any -- will keep refrigerated or frozen.

You will need your pans, a riser, a spatula, a plastic bag to work on, a rolling pin (I use full soda cans, they're better than other cans which have edges and cut the dough, and most other things will send us right to jail without collecting Jack, you know what I'm saying? The Box), a paper bag or cardboard pieces to put the finished pies on, and a lid from a pot that fits over your frying pan.

Ingredients for Pizza Dough:

3 measures (3 cans-full are fine) flour
1 measure (1 same-size can you used for the flour) pancake mix
Savory seasonings for a savory pizza, or

Sweet seasonings for a sweet-topped pizza
Warm water.

For Chicago-Style thin-crust pizza dough I use a ratio of 3 to 1 flour to pancake mix. For a lot of dough, use a large can as a measuring cup, fill it three times with flour, then once with pancake mix, and you'll have achieved a three to one ratio. For less dough use a smaller can. As you are working with pancake mix, which is sweet, you need to add salt when making savory dishes. You can add whatever seasonings you like, such as garlic powder or Adobo, but they are not necessary. Taste your dough when it's done (you can spit it out). If it needs more salt just sprinkle a little onto each pie after you roll it out. Cover and let the dough rest for 15 minutes.

Note: *If you refrigerate your dough for longer than an hour, like overnight, cover lightly with plastic wrap or tie tightly in two plastic bags.*

Step 1: Mix the flour, pancake mix and your seasonings in a large pot or bowl. Add warm water, a little at a time while mixing it gently with your fingertips, until it comes together into a ball. Your dough should be soft to the touch but not tacky or sticky. When there is no flour mix left on the bottom and the dough easily pulls away from the sides, it's done. Cover and let rest in a warm spot for 15 minutes.

Step 2: While your dough is resting, chop, slice and half-cook your favorite toppings, (the toppings are going to continue to cook later). If you're going to doctor a can of pre-made sauce, now is the time. If not, just open a can or utilize some leftover sauce.

Step 3: Choose your cheese, shred if necessary, or if you're using slices, just chop them into tiny pieces.

Step 4: Take a piece of dough just larger than a handball and roll it out very thin, to a thickness of no more than ⅛ of an inch. Place the lid which fits your frying pan on the rolled-out dough, and cut around the lid to form a large circle.

Step 5: Place your frying pan (non-stick works best but any pan will do) on a medium to high heat (4-5). Drizzle about a tablespoon of oil into the pan and place your dough circle in the pan to cook the first side. Using your hand or a spatula, spin the dough around ensuring an even distribution of heat.

Step 6: When the bottom of your pie starts to get a nice light brown color (4 or 5 minutes should do it) drizzle the top with another tablespoon of oil then flip it over.

Step 7: Place your riser (see explanation under "Equipment" in the index) under the pan and reduce the heat to around low-to-medium (about 3-4).

Step 8: Spread a little sauce on your pie shell, leaving about half an inch uncovered all the way around for a crust. Sprinkle the cheese liberally over the sauce, avoiding the edges. Now top with your favorite pre-cooked toppings. Try arranging them nicely. Long strips of peppers with pepperoni slices in between, then olive halves, whatever. Make it look appealing.

Step 9: Lastly, place the lid on the pan and let cook for around five minutes more or until the bottom is crisp and the cheese has fully melted.

Step 10: Slide pie onto a paper bag or a piece of cardboard and let it cool for a minute, then cut and serve.

Step 11: Repeat steps 1 - 10 and enjoy, and enjoy, and enjoy ...

TRADITIONAL ITALIAN BAKED ZITI

Now that I live with, and cook for four Italian guys, red sauces and anything Parmesan are frequent requests. Even though I do the cooking, as their combined equal contributions outweigh mine 4 to 1, I tend to have to give in. When four Italian guys give me tomato sauce, crushed tomatoes, mozzarella cheese and a couple of boxes of ziti shells, do you think they're trying to tell me something?

OK, so I'll make the ziti. They were always good about giving me what I needed to cook with, and now I'm filling in all their commissary sheets so I know who's got what. Why nobody thought to plant green bell peppers or red peppers in the little garden patch outside the dorm, I'll never understand. I pray I won't be here next season, but if I am I will make sure I have a hand in what's planted around the facility.

Even though I'm not Italian, I would surely give up what little kingdom I have left for a basil plant. Anyway, this baked ziti is really easy to make and it became a favorite among the guys in my dorm.

Ingredients:

2 Medium onions, diced
3 Garlic cloves sliced, or 1 teaspoon powdered garlic
1-12 oz Can corned beef
2 Tablespoons oregano
4 Tablespoons oil
1-28 oz Can crushed tomatoes
1-8 oz Can tomato sauce
2-4 oz Cans mushrooms (stems & pieces are okay). Do NOT drain off the water
1-11 oz Beef sausage, diced very small
6 Tablespoons sugar
2 Cups water
1 Large bag shredded mozzarella
2–1 Pound boxes ziti shells
1 Tablespoon Adobo seasoning
Salt to taste.

Step 1: In a large sauce pot cook the ziti noodles in well-salted water. Taste it. What your water tastes like, is what your noodles will taste like. When they are al dente (cooked but a little chewy), rinse them off with cold water. You don't want your noodles to be cooked all the way because they're going to get baked in the sauce later. Set noodles aside.

I put the noodles in a garbage bag and use the same pot over again for the sauce. This way I only need one burner for my dish, and I only have to wash one pot when I'm done. OK, I never washed the pots, I did the cooking, that was part of my contract, no pot washing.

Step 2: While you are waiting for the water to boil, or while the noodles are cooking, open all your cans. Dice the onion and the beef sausage and slice the garlic.

Step 3: Place the onions, garlic and oil in either the same pot when it's free, or in another pot, and place it on a low-to-medium setting. Cook for 3 to 4 minutes or until the onion starts to get a little soft.

Step 4: Add the corned beef, the Adobo and the oregano and cook for 10 minutes more.

Step 5: Add all other ingredients to the pot except the mozzarella, the salt and the noodles.

Step 6: A small tomato-sauce can equals one cup, so add two small tomato-sauce cans of water to the pot, pour in the mushrooms and their liquid, and the beef sausage, diced very small.

Step 7: For best results, let sauce simmer on the lowest setting possible for at least 45 minutes. Cook with the lid on for the first 30 minutes, stirring frequently.

Step 8: The assembly: this recipe fed four of us. We all used large Tupperware bowls and we had leftovers. Ladle enough sauce into each container to just cover the bottom. Top with a layer of ziti noodles, then more sauce to cover, then mozzarella cheese. Keep alternating layers of sauce, cheese, noodles, sauce, then cheese until all of your bowls are full. The last two layers should be sauce then cheese.

Step 9: Nuke your bowls with their lids slightly off, so steam can escape, for 2 - 2 ½ minutes on high, or until the sauce is bubbling and the top layer of cheese has melted. That's it, Baked Ziti!

I called this Traditional Italian Ziti because it actually tasted authentic. It was as traditional as I could get without ground veal, pork, beef, peppers, etc., capeesh?

Buono Appetito!

BEEF & CHEESE STROMBOLIS
Makes 10 nice Strombolis

I used to work in a restaurant where the chef took some of the bread dough from the baker every morning. He would stuff it with peppers, beef, cheese and basically whatever we had lying around, then bake it off. He used to call them "braciole" because they were rolled.

The Italians here in my dorm said the proper name for what I made is 'Strombolis', named after Stromboli, a small island off the north coast of Sicily, so that's what I called them. Whatever the name, these came out so good that word got out into the yard and people started offering me stamps to make them. One guy took a stromboli out into the yard in his pocket somehow. It must have been sticking out like a weapon because they came out the size of small sub sandwiches. The bidding went up to 12 stamps, but (a) I didn't want to start smuggling strombolis into the yard or open up a stromboli stand, and (b) they were too good to sell.

This is definitely a winner and this dough recipe is good for almost anything savory. I have definitely perfected my dough making at this point. It's like a Catch 22. More than one of my bosses has said either to me or someone else, 'never think you're the best'. However, on the other hand after cooking professionally for 15 years in NYC, if anyone in jail can bake better than me I would feel like a jerk. I think at this juncture in my career it's safe to say "I am the best stromboli maker at this correctional facility". I may be the only one, but that still makes me the best!

Some of the guys who have been in prison for years said this was the best dough they've had inside. There is one secret, and that is the technique for kneading the dough. Pay attention here.

After mixing all your dry ingredients well, you need to add just enough cold water (a little at a time) until your dough forms a ball.

For clarification, the trick is after you have a ball, sprinkle a little flour on top and under it, and then press it down into a flat disk. Press lightly with your fingertips, don't use your fists or your palms, be gentle with her. Now fold it in half twice, forming a triangle shape, then with your fingertips, gently press it down again into a flat disk. I found the easiest way to do this is in a large pot. Mix and knead right in the same pot. You have to sprinkle flour and repeat the kneading process about 8 - 10 times until the dough is soft and smooth. This dough is extremely versatile, it will make dumplings, patties, strombolis and pizzas, it's all in the kneading process. It doesn't have to rest, you can roll it and use it right away. It can also sit or be frozen.

> **Note:** *Remember if you refrigerate or freeze your dough, let it come back to room temperature when you want to use it. If you refrigerate your dough for longer than an hour, like overnight, cover lightly with plastic wrap or tie tightly in two plastic bags.*

Here is my perfected dough recipe and my stromboli filling. Of course you can roll this dough out and fill it with whatever you want, but this recipe is a winner. To make measuring easy, instead of using a cup measure I used an empty bean can. The ratio of flour to pancake mix is always going to be 2 of flour to 1 of pancake mix, whatever you use to measure with. The bean can I used was a 15 oz can which is about two cups. So basically this recipe calls for two cups pancake mix and four cups all purpose flour and yields ten large strombolis.

Ingredients for the stromboli dough:

2 Bean cans (4 cups) of flour, plus extra for rolling the dough
1 Bean can (2 cups) of pancake mix
3 Teaspoons salt
2 Teaspoons garlic powder
1 Teaspoon Adobo seasoning
2 Teaspoons dried oregano
About ¾ bean can filled with cold water.

Step 1: In a large pot mix the flour, salt, pancake mix, oregano, Adobe and the garlic powder. Mix well.

Step 2: Add half the water and gently knead with your fingertips, wear a rubber glove if you can get one. Keep adding the rest of the water a little at a time, gently kneading until a dough ball forms and it comes easily away from the sides of your pot. If you don't need all the water, don't use it. When you can pick up the dough ball in one large piece and there is no flour mix left on the sides of the pot, you have added enough water, and you are ready for my new and improved kneading technique.

Step 3: Lift the dough out of the pot, sprinkle just a little of the extra flour on the bottom of the pot. Replace the dough on top of the flour, and lightly dust the top of the dough with more flour. Press the dough down until it is spread out evenly touching all sides of the pot (it's now a large disk). Fold the dough in half, then in half again, forming sort of a triangle. Press dough down into a large disk again, and then lift it out and dust the bottom of the pot with more flour, sprinkle more on top, and fold again. Repeat this process about eight times or until you have a smooth, soft dough and it isn't at all tacky. Set the dough aside. Remember be gentle, only kneading (pressing down) with your fingertips.

Ingredients for beef & cheese filling:

2 Cans roast beef in gravy
1-8 oz Bag shredded mozzarella
1-5 oz Pepperoni stick
2 Medium onions, sliced
3 Pickled Jalapeños
1-5 oz Can mushrooms, drained
3 Tablespoons oil, plus more for frying.

Step 4: Open all the cans and set them aside. Take one of the lids from a can of roast beef, rinse it off and bend down one corner to make your cutter, if your COs let you. Most of mine did as long as we threw them away when we were done. Otherwise, use whatever you have to get the job done, like the US Marine Credo: "Improvise, Adapt, Overcome..."

Step 5: Peel and slice your onions as thin as you can get them. Sauté the onions in the oil on medium to low heat until soft. 4 - 5 minutes.

Step 6: While the onions are cooking, remove the roast beef from its gravy. If you press the can lid down on the beef in the can and pour out all the gravy, you must add back 3 teaspoons of gravy to the meat so it isn't dry. If you just pick the meat out of the can, enough gravy will stick to the chunks. Save the rest of the gravy for another day, it freezes well.

Step 7: Mash up the Jalapeños and cut the pepperoni into small pieces.

Step 8: Spread out a plastic bag on your work surface; putting a tiny amount of water underneath the bag will prevent it from sliding around. Put all your ingredients in small containers near your workstation for easy access. Don't forget to drain the water out of the mushrooms. You can put the mushrooms, onions and Jalapenos in one bowl, but keep the rest of the ingredients separate.

Step 9: Pull small balls from your dough and one at a time, using an unopened full soda can, or a stick, or a rolling pin if you happen to have one, roll them as thin as you can into large rectangles. The length of your stromboli should be the same as the width of the pan you're going to fry them in. If you roll them out too big, use your cutter to cut the rectangles down to the width of your pan. My rectangles were about 7 inches wide by 5 inches long.

Step 10: This is going to be sort of like rolling a cigarette. Place a small schmeer of the Jalapeño, onion and mushroom mix along one of the long ends, top with meat and then cheese.

Step 11: Roll your dough up half way. Now fold the short ends over, (to seal in the filling), dab a little water on the flap like the glue strip on a rolling paper, then finish rolling upward. It should look like a large egg roll.

Step 12: Place about a ¼ inch of oil in your pan and on a medium setting (4 or 5) brown off your strombolis. Don't forget to brown the ends if they are not submerged in the oil. Go vertical if you have to (hold the ends in the oil), but be careful, hold them with a towel and don't let go

Diagram
Filling and Rolling The Stromboli

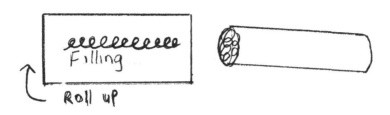

For best results eat right away, although they're good cold later too. But I don't personally recommend putting them in the microwave. Microwaves tend to make bread chewy, but other people told me 30 - 40 seconds in the microwave worked for them. They said the insides got warm and melted the cheese. I would rather eat them cold than risk making the dough tough and chewy. It's up to you. If they come out as good as ours did, you shouldn't have to worry about leftovers.

ITALIAN STYLE
CHICKEN & BROCCOLI DINNER
For 3 Viking portions

My neighbor Yum Yum, who was also relocated from F-Dorm to C Dorm, insisted I try this recipe. At first I thought putting Italian dressing on pasta sounded more like a pasta salad. As this recipe was going to be served hot, I was a little skeptical. With my input, the store-bought salad dressing and some chicken stock became a sauce. If you don't have any chicken stock use the chicken powder seasoning from a ramen noodle soup, add just a little water so it will have a very strong chicken flavor and add this to the water from the canned chicken for your sauce base. Yum Yum received a half head of broccoli from his brother in a package, and I had a couple of cans of chicken in water. My buddy Jacques who went out on a court call-out asked me to hold his stuff for him. Jacques said I could use whatever foodstuff I needed and lo and behold, he had Italian salad dressing, chicken stock, mushrooms and more. Perfect. I put three tablespoons of Parmesan cheese in the sauce, if you do that, sprinkle it with a healthy portion of cheese when you serve.

The only one real problem I have with this meal is how we have to eat it. If you are now, or have ever been incarcerated, you know, but if you haven't, then let me enlighten you. We eat like Vikings. That's right, like Vikings, we even slurp pasta out of huge Tupperware bowls with only spoons for utensils, sauce dripping down our faces as we slurp. It's quite a sight, I assure you.

The problem, you see, directly relates to this dish, and any loose sauces served for example on spaghetti. If I were serving this pasta dish on the street, I would fork the pasta onto the plate or into a flattish bowl, then ladle just enough sauce over the pasta to cover it. Eating this dish like a Viking makes it hard to enjoy. In a two-quart bowl all the sauce sinks to the bottom of the bowl. The pasta on the top of the bowl has all the chunky chicken and vegetables, but isn't as good as it would be with a mouthful of sauce. Eat this however you want to, but I recommend eating it like a more modern human being. Take a good scoop of pasta, top it with sauce and cheese and enjoy. Go back for seconds or thirds rather than over-filling a pot-sized bowl and chomping like a Viking. "Take human bites!"

Ingredients for three Viking size portions:

1-14 oz to 16 oz Can chicken broth (or make your own using a chicken ramen packet as I described)

1-4 oz Can mushrooms, drained

2-10 oz Cans diced chicken breast in water

1 Teaspoon each oregano, garlic powder and Adobo seasoning

2 Small onions, diced large

9 Tablespoons cooking oil

½ Teaspoon salt

3 Tablespoons butter

4 Cups small pieces of broccoli (florets)

4 oz Italian dressing

2 Tablespoons Parmesan cheese, plus more for shaking

½ Cup flour.

Step 1: Empty the can of chicken broth, and the liquid from the canned chicken into a small sauce pot. Place on high heat and let it reduce by half.

Step 2: While broth is reducing, dredge the chicken chunks in the flour then gently shake off any excess flour.

Step 3: Place 3 tablespoons of the oil in a frying pan on medium heat (4 - 5). Sear half the chicken until golden brown on all sides. Don't overcrowd the pan because the chicken will end up boiling in it's own juices instead of searing.

Step 4: Remove the first half of the chicken from the pan, and repeat this process with the other half. Set aside in a large pot.

Step 5: Place the onions and the rest of the oil in the same frying pan you cooked the chicken in, and sauté for 3 - 4 minutes, or until the onions just start to brown. Add the onions to the large pot with the chicken.

Step 6: Add the drained mushrooms to the pot with the onions and the chicken.

Step 7: Put the reduced chicken broth in the same frying pan you've been using. Bring to a boil then add the butter, cheese and seasonings. When this broth tastes good to you, and looks like a pan sauce rather than just stock, add the broccoli florets and boil about two minutes. Don't overcook the broccoli, you want it to stay a little crunchy (al dente).

Step 8: Pour the sauce over the chicken mixture.

Step 9: Add the Italian dressing to the chicken and sauce and stir gently. Heat the pot with all your ingredients, just for a minute or two, to get it hot.

Step 10: Serve sauce over a pound and a half of cooked pasta divided into three Viking sized bowls, and sprinkle with more Parmesan cheese.

It's so good!

GARLIC KNOTS

There are three ways to make garlic knots. The First: if you have fresh garlic, simply follow the recipe for dough in the *Pizza Fra Diavolo.* recipe. The Second way is if you don't have fresh garlic, in which case follow my universal dough recipe, which is two to one, flour to pancake mix. For every cup of flour (8 oz) add half a teaspoon of garlic powder and salt. The Third way is to use fresh garlic and garlic powder.

For a little extra zing shake extra garlic powder on your knots just as they come out of the cooking oil, because while they're still hot and a little wet is when the powder will stick. This holds true for any fried item. Take French fries for instance, if you salt fries just as they come out of the fryer the salt will stick, when they cool even slightly and the oil dries, salting becomes useless because the grains will just bounce right off. I suggest dusting your garlic knots with garlic powder, salt and grated Parmesan cheese no matter which version you choose.

My point in giving the pizza dough as a reference, is because if you have leftover dough sometime, you can either make some knots or save it for later knotting. As I said before, the stromboli dough, pizza dough and patty dough are all the same ratio of flour to pancake mix, so follow the directions for any of these to make your dough. (If you follow the directions for the patties as a reference, omit the Sazon from the recipe, yellow garlic knots might look a little atomic!)

Step 1: Make some garlic-y dough, using 2 to 1 flour to pancake mix, add half a teaspoon of garlic powder per cup of flour. If you have fresh garlic and are also going to use powdered garlic, add only one clove of toasted, minced garlic per two cups of flour.

Here's an example: One 16 oz bean can full of flour (16 oz = 2 cups), half a bean can (8 oz = 1 cup) of pancake mix, therefore a ratio of two to one, right? One teaspoon garlic powder (half teaspoon per cup), one clove minced and toasted garlic (one clove per two cups flour), two to one again. Sautee garlic until light brown (toasting) then add to the flour mix without the oil. Using water and any of the dough-making instructions from the aforementioned recipes, make a dough.

Step 2: Roll out dough into thin logs and tie them into little knots.

Step 3: Deep fry your knots following the same directions as for chocolate frosted doughnuts, (see index), the cooking process is exactly the same.

Step 4: When your knots are nice and golden brown and they're out of the pan draining on either paper towels or a paper bag, dust them right away with a little more salt and garlic powder, and if you have some grated Parmesan use it, it will make a big difference. If you're planning ahead to make garlic knots, get some Parmesan or any other shake-able grated cheese.

These make a great snack but what better than garlic bread (knots) to have with any pasta dish? Oh yeah, well I don't happen to have a thick steak, but even if I did I would still make knots!!!

FRESH PASTA DOUGH
Feeds 4 hungry people
(With sauce or ravioli filling, of course!)

Yeah, I know pasta is cheap to buy and there is probably a pretty good variety available at your commissary. Well, at our commissary it's spaghetti or rigatoni, that's it. Others here seem to be content without elaborate types of noodles to choose from. However, I am not one to sit around until dinner time and just open a box of rigatoni, sorry. Since I only have a morning program, my afternoons and evenings are free. So why not make a nice lasagna, right? How about tortellini filled with cheeses, fresh linguini for your clam sauce, or my favorite, raviolis? Here's a recipe and directions for an all-purpose pasta dough that should suit all your noodle needs.

Being as creative as we are here, a buddy and I designed and built a pasta machine out of commissary items that actually works. I believe the total cost was $1.90. But that's another story, isn't it?

Ingredients for Fresh Pasta Dough:

3 Cups flour (24 oz)
1 Container EggBeaters (8 oz) or 4 fresh eggs, lightly beaten.

Step 1: The easiest way to make your dough is to place all three cups of flour in a large bowl or pot.

Step 2: Using your hand inserted into the center of the flour and spinning your bowl or pot around, press the flour out to the sides. This is called "making a well". There should be enough room in the center of the flour to pour in all the eggs or EggBeaters without them running all over the place. This can be done right on a table without using a pot or bowl, but I find this creates more of a mess to clean up later.

Step 3: If you can get your hands on fresh eggs, beat them for a minute or two with a fork before pouring them into the well.

Step 4: Using your fingers gently stir the eggs around in circles, slowly incorporating the flour until a dough ball forms. I know this is going to sound crazy, but depending on the humidity (the amount of moisture in the air) you may not have to mix in all of the flour.

> *Believe it or not, if it's raining or someone is boiling water in the kitchen, it can affect the dough. I often make my dough right on my locker in my large sauce pot before I go anywhere near the kitchen, because someone is always in there doing something. A cool dry place is preferable.*

Step 5: Remove your pasta dough ball from the pot. It should still be a little tacky, unlike all the other dough recipes in this book.

Step 6: If you have any leftover flour in your "well" and it has lots of lumps of dough in it, don't use it for the next step. Pick the pieces out of the flour and use them for something else later, like making fish cakes or patties.

Step 7: Cover your work surface with a garbage bag. I find if I want to make my garbage bag stick really well, (so it doesn't slip around), I put two or three tablespoons of water on my locker or on a table, then wipe it off with a towel without drying it completely. Then I lay the garbage bag on the damp surface, and it sticks on it really well.

Step 8: Lightly dust your work surface with some flour and knead your dough, dusting with flour as required for at least ten minutes. Time yourself, you need to work the dough gently for the full ten minutes for glutens to form and to create an elastic dough. Use the heel of your palm to press the dough, then fold it in half and give it a half turn. Keep doing this for ten minutes, I'm serious. You want your dough to still be a little tacky when you're done (not wet, but not dry).

Step 9: Put your dough in another garbage bag, press all of the air out and tie the bag into a knot.

Step 10: The dough must rest, covered, at room temperature (70 degrees) for at least two hours. If the kitchen is hot leave it in your cube, more than two hours is okay, but less is 'no buono'.

That was simple, right? As they say "the waiting is the hardest part". I'm so funny, at least once a week when people pass my cube they see sheets of pasta and strands of fresh linguini hanging from strings all over the place. Drying your pasta is not necessary if you're going to cook it right away, or if you freeze your raviolis and other stuffed pastas. I like to make big batches and play, it just adds to my rec., gotta pass the time right?

Rolling out pasta is really easy too. Sometimes we have a cardboard tube from a plastic wrap with a little plastic still on it smuggled in from the mess hall to use as a rolling pin. Sometimes we loose 'em on cube searches and then I use a full soda can. I find all other cans at my disposal have at least one edge if not two and they cut the pasta, so a full soda can is the way to go for smooth rolling.

Now that you have sheets of pasta, check out the many different pasta dishes in this section.

Step 11: Dust your work surface with flour. Now, using your soda can or your improvised rolling pin, roll out small pieces of dough as thin as you can get them. Your pasta needs to be no thicker than two or three sheets of paper.

Once you have mastered making pasta dough (don't forget it needs to rest), you need to become proficient at rolling it out. There are so many different types, shapes and sizes of pasta it's hard to decide where to begin and where to end. Rolling it out is the fun part. Choose a noodle shape. Here are a few examples, but make any kind you can think of. Remember to let your dough rest, covered, at room temperature (70 degrees) for at least two hours before you roll it out.

Note: *Again, remember if you refrigerate your dough for longer than an hour, like overnight, cover lightly with plastic wrap or tie tightly in two plastic bags.*

For LASAGNA:

First use your hands to roll out long, thin logs. On a well-floured surface, using both hands, roll dough into logs about the thickness of a magic marker. Don't over-work your dough. Your sheets should be about 2 ½ inches wide.

Cut the sheets of pasta into strips the length of the dish or bowl in which you're going to cook your lasagna. This dough does not need to be cooked for very long, about a minute should do it, in salted, boiling water.

When cooked, transfer the lasagna noodles to cold water then proceed as you would normally to assemble your favorite lasagna.

That would be placing some sauce in the bottom of your dish or bowl (a good meat sauce), placing noodles on top of the layer of sauce, overlapping them, then adding more sauce, then sprinkling cheese, then more noodles, etc. Your last layer should be cheese. Now microwave for as long as it takes for your lasagna to come to a boil. When it's bubbling, take it out and let it rest for at least an hour. Serve at room temperature or cut and reheat individual squares.

For RAVIOLI:

Roll out your dough just as instructed in the lasagna recipe above. Long sheets 2½ inches wide are the fastest way to go. Imagine a long length of pasta dough. Now imagine cutting it into squares. Place a little filling in the center of each square. Wet the edges with beaten egg or water and fold your squares into rectangles, that's it.

Use your rolling pin (a full soda can) to roll the dough as thin as possible. Now you can make your raviolis any shape you want. Use an empty can to punch out nice round disks. Place the filling in the center of one pasta disk, wet the edges with egg or water, and place a pasta disk on top. Crimp the edges with a fork to seal it. Alternatively, you could place a small amount of filling on all of your pasta disks, wet only half the edges and fold them over into half moons. In Italian these are known as "agnolotti" or "mezza lunas".

You can use anything to stuff your ravioli. Most fillings have something that will act as a 'binder' or a thickener like cheese. I personally don't mind my filling not being 'bound' with cheese, especially if the whole ravioli fits in my mouth. Here is yet another example where you get to be creative, and a great way to utilize leftovers. You can even fill raviolis with just a meat sauce, it will work. My favorite so far here at this CF is my sausage and pepper raviolis with tomato sauce. Stuff 'em with anything, really. Drop in boiling salted water, cook until tender.

For LINGUINI:

Lastly, an easy way to make fresh linguini for that linguini in clam sauce or your favorite Alfredo recipe.

After your dough has rested, using a full soda can, roll it out as thin as you can get it (not thicker than two or three stacked pieces of paper). Flour your rolled out dough really well. Cut the dough into widths that are the same as whatever you are using for a rolling pin, presumably a soda can. Remember of all the different cans we have at our disposal, a soda can works best as a rolling pin because it doesn't have edges that will cut the dough while rolling. If you have something better like a rolling pin, great, use it. Place your rolling pin device at one edge of your dough then gently roll up the dough over itself, this will give you many layers wrapped over your rolling pin.

Now using a can lid gently cut the dough into strands the width of linguini (just smaller than the width of the lines on a sheet of lined writing paper.) Drop them in boiling salted water, cook until tender.

For PARPARDELLA:

After rolling the dough out very thin, you can just cut out all different shapes, and roll into other shapes, this is what's known as parpardella. Drop then in boiling salted water, cook until tender, and serve with your favorite sauce.

You're on your own now, but with a little practice you should be bangin' out shells (use a clean comb for the lines) and even tortellini (squares folded into triangles with the ends twisted together) in no time at all. You've got time right?

Cooking times will vary depending on how thick you roll your dough or how large your pasta is. There are many factors which will adjust the cooking time, like how much pasta you put in your water, or if you have let your pasta dry. Fresh pasta should be ready in 4 to 6 minutes. Just keep tasting pieces until it reaches the doneness you prefer.

Chapter 6

SOME SAUCES & A FEW EXTRAS

Sauces
Chocolate Sauce
Demon Cave Hot Sauce
Honey Mustard Glaze With A Kick
International Dipping Sauce
Salsa and Fresh Baked Chips
'Secret' Gyro White Sauce
Sweet & Sour Sauce, *(see recipe Sweet & Sour Crispy Mackerel)*
Tangy BBQ Sauce

Extras
Dirty Vermicelli, Jailhouse Approved
Indian Onion Bread - Naan/nan
Sweet Prison Biscuits
Microwave Jambalaya
Quick & Easy Almost Baked Beans
Roast Beef Dumplings
Savory Fried Hush Puppies
Wings and Things
Wing Sauce Recipe #1 - Sweet Soy Orange Glaze
Wing Sauce Recipe #2 - Onion BBQ Picanté Glaze

CHOCOLATE SAUCE

This chocolate sauce recipe is quick and easy to make, and you can use it on literally anything, from pancakes to breakfast wraps.

Ingredients:

Any kind of chocolate
Any kind of milk, coconut, evaporated or fresh
A little sugar.

Step 1: Place the chocolate in a small pot or a microwaveable bowl.

Step 2: Heat it slowly adding a little milk and a little sugar. Then, as it starts to melt, a little at a time add the rest of the milk, stirring until you have a sauce consistency. The more chocolate you use the more milk it will absorb.

DEMON CAVE HOT SAUCE

I have only one word to describe the hot sauce they sell at my particular commissary - Nasty! I love hot sauces and I have literally tried hundreds of different brands. On one trip I made down to New Orleans I sort of became a connoisseur, trying every one I could find. My favorites however, ended up being those I found in Manhattan's Chinatown. The Chinese chili pastes are awesome, some of them have roasted garlic or onions and are sweet with hints of honey. I always doctored them with more sugar and vinegar to get them just the way I like them, but they were also good just as they were. Undoubtedly, the hot sauce here is their sauce of choice because of the price, well you get what you pay for. So for 37 cents, with no other choice, everyone buys this red spicy salt water. I won't mention the name of the brand, but suffice to say it's not a "name brand".

One day when I needed some hot sauce I said to myself "You know what? Even though I don't have all the ingredients to make the kind of hot sauce I'd like right now, I'm gonna make some! anyway". I took out a request slip and started to write a list of suitable ingredients, and across the top I wrote catchy names for the sauce.

After several tries, the perfect name came to me. The address here at my correctional facility is Demon Cave Road. How perfect is that for a name? "Demon Cave Hot sauce".

This recipe makes a lot, but if you like hot sauce, so what? Keep it in the refrigerator or in your locker. It will probably have a shelf life much longer than I'll be here, but no doubt I'll go through it and have to make more.

When I made my hot sauce I decided not to strain out the Jalapenos, I tore them into large pieces and left them in. Originally, I was going to strain the sauce then funnel it into an empty hot sauce bottle for easy shaking. Way too much trouble. There is a cooking term known as "steeping". This is where liquids are usually brought to a boil, taken off the stove, poured over whatever you want to "steep", covered, and allowed to cool at room temperature to infuse all of the flavor from whatever is being steeped, with minimal flavor loss. After adding all the juice from one can of pickled Jalapenos, I needed more heat, so I tore three large Jalapenos into large pieces, threw them in my sauce, brought it back to a boil, and took it off the stove. I placed a plate on top of my sauce pot and let the peppers steep until the sauce cooled, (about an hour). Not only was my sauce hot but it tasted pretty good too. This recipe makes about 3 cups or 24 oz. If that's too much for you (which can't possibly be true) cut the recipe in half. This isn't the best hot sauce I've had, but it's definitely better than what they sell at my facility. Give it a try, you won't regret it.

Ingredients for one large, kick-ass pot of Hot Sauce:

1-6 oz Can tomato paste
4 oz Jalapeno juice
3 Tablespoons sugar
2 Tablespoons honey
2½ Tablespoons lemon juice
4 Shakes garlic powder
¼ Teaspoon salt
2 Tablespoons yellow mustard
3 Large jalapenos, torn into large pieces
10 oz Water
½ Teaspoon Adobo seasoning.

Step 1: Place all ingredients except the jalapenos into a small pot.

Step 2: Bring mixture to a boil, then lower the heat and let simmer for 15 minutes.

Step 3: Add the Jalapenos and let simmer for only another 5 minutes.

Step 4: Cover pot and let steep until cooled to room temperature.

This hot sauce is even better the next day, after the flavors have had a chance to marry (come together) overnight, and it should keep you sweating it off, wear a headband and enjoy!

HONEY MUSTARD GLAZE WITH A KICK!

Lots of people make honey mustard Jack Mack and honey mustard sauces for chicken and other dishes. When reduced until thick, this sauce recipe resembles what I consider a glaze. I like to cook with sugar and I have gotten good at it. Mixing equal parts of honey and mustard works just fine, but if you want something more flavorful and complex give this a try.

This recipe came about because one of my friends wanted honey mustard and we were all low on honey. There were five of us eating and combined we had exactly a quarter bottle of honey (3 oz). Instead of just scrapping the idea and moving, on I decided to try using sugar to supplement the honey we didn't have. This recipe has now become one of our staples here in G-dorm, it's much less expensive than using all honey, and actually much better.

Just like we did in other recipes, we're going to put some sugar in a clean, dry pot, put it on a slow heat and let it caramelize. When the sugar starts to melt and turn an amber color, you must stir it or swirl the pot around to ensure even meltage. Don't worry if some of the sugar gets lumpy, just stir it in. Don't let it burn, if it does, start again or your sauce/glaze will be bitter and nasty. When your sugar is a nice red color you're going to add a little water. This will stop the cooking process and lighten the sugar, but we are going to simmer it and the water will evaporate. The water is going to seize up the sugar and it's going to look funny and all crackly, don't let that discourage you, it's normal. Just leave the pot on a low heat and the sugar will melt again with the water and become more stable. The reason we don't just melt sugar in water and add the other ingredients is because the sauce would be too sweet, it would be more like sugar-water syrup. We want to start our glaze with a caramel base, which is why we are caramelizing our sugar first.

I like spicy food so I added Jalapenos and Jalapeno juice to this recipe. If you're not into spicy stuff, omit all of the Jalapeno product and substitute water for the required amount of Jalapeno juice. You may also have to adjust the seasoning, a little more lemon juice and salt will probably do it. After all of your ingredients are in your sauce pot, reduce it very slowly for about ten minutes, it should be very thick. This glaze is great on fried chicken or Mack. Try dunking onion rings in it, mmm.

Ingredients to glaze 12 pieces of fried chicken or 4 cans of Jack Mack:

4 oz Sugar
2 oz Warm water
3 oz Honey
2 oz Mustard
6 Tablespoons butter
1 Tablespoon lemon juice
½ Teaspoon salt
1 Small onion, diced small
2 Pickled Jalapeños, diced small
2 oz Jalapeno juice.

Step 1: Caramelize your sugar (in a dry, clean pot). Place pot on a low-to-medium heat and when sugar starts to turn red, swirl the pot for even caramelization. It turns a deep red (not brown).

Step 2: When your sugar is a nice amber reddish hue add the water and the Jalapeno juice and bring it back to a simmer.

Step 3: When smooth and incorporated, add everything else except the butter and the onion.

Step 4: In a separate pot or pan place the diced onion and two table-spoons of the butter. Sauté until tender, 4 - 5 minutes. When transparent add them to the pot with the sugar.

Step 5: One at a time add the remaining 4 tablespoons of butter, keep the heat at medium, and keep stirring to incorporate them.

Step 6: Let the sauce simmer on the lowest heat possible for almost 10 minutes. If you want to adjust this to your own liking now is the time. More mustard, lemon juice, and salt, as they say "Do You?"

Step 7: You're ready to go. Glaze away! Glaze your meat or fish, or dunk your onion rings and other dunkin' foods.

INTERNATIONAL DIPPING SAUCE

This is a very easy and simple sauce to make. It's sort of a cross between a Russian dressing and a French dressing. If you have some pickled relish, scoop some of it into this recipe and turn this tasty dipping sauce into A Million Island Dressing! You can use it with just about everything.

Ingredients:

Equal parts Ketchup and mayonnaise
Honey to make it sweet, add to suit your taste
Pickled relish, again add to suit your taste.

Step 1: Mix all ingredients in a bowl until they are well blended.

Step 2: Dip!

SALSA & FRESH BAKED CHIPS

Okay, at this point I am realizing there is nothing I can't make in prison (food-wise). After spending only four months in a facility where I am allowed to cook and have access to a kitchen, I have found no challenge too great.

Once I mastered three-layer cakes and gyros that tasted better than they do on the street, there was no stopping me. Cooking became my rec. I wanted people to give me ideas. I thought it was fun to make stuff out of what I had available at any given time. Well, let me tell you, being a chef and having people request things they missed from home that I hadn't thought to make, was even more fun. For example one night a young guy named Black came into my cube and said "You know what I miss? Gyros". "Hmm" I said, slipping deep into thought for only a minute or so, then smiling. What a great idea. The next day we had fresh gyros with the secret sauce and everything. See Index for Gyros and for secret sauce.

Mid-September and football season, we didn't have any cold beer, but when my boy Sal said he wished he had some chips and salsa, that's all I needed to hear. This dish actually has a bit of history to it.

One of my buddies wanted me to make, among other things, lasagna for his birthday. Another challenge that of course I was up for. No ricotta, lasagna noodles, chopped meat, etc., etc., etc. Of course I made lasagna for him, making a mock ricotta out of cream cheese, and I rolled out fresh pasta dough. It took me three tries to get the pasta dough just right. Not having the right kinds of flour - semolina durum - kinda threw me. The first two attempts came out more like dumpling doughs and when I made raviolis the edges were tough. Well I never throw anything away, especially as food product is so hard to come by, I figured I could make little tiny raviolis and fry them in oil. Kind of an appetizer with some kind of dipping sauce.

A week earlier we got some new recruits in my dorm and one of them named Van had been watching me in the kitchen every day since his arrival. He admitted being astonished. He told me in all his years he had never seen any cooking in prison like I was doing. To myself I said "I should hope not", and accepted the compliment politely. Van said to me on the day of my first pasta failure: "Why don't you try micro-waving it?" He was referring to the dough. "Well, because I don't want micro-waved dough" I said. He asked if he could try it, so I let him and holy cow wouldn't you know it, when this simple dough is rolled out thin and micro-waved for 15 seconds on each side, it tastes just like a tortilla chip. Now, just to show you how into this I was getting, with the help of a friend I created a pasta machine to roll out our dough. Another story ...

But you can roll out your dough using a rolling pin, or a full soda can which will work just fine. I'm not going to give you exact proportions for either the chip recipe or the fresh tomato salsa. I am however going to educate you on the basic theory and techniques of both, then let you get creative on your own, okay? Here we go. We'll make the Salsa first, as it has to sit awhile.

ABOUT MAKING SALSA

When making fruit salsas like mango salsa or green apple salsa, I always start off with a puree of the fruit, then fold in a small dice of everything else I want to use. These fruity salsas are the only ones that I don't start off by using a crushed or pureed tomato product. I start all my other salsas like this: I chop tomato, onion, peppers, and Jalapenos, and fold them into crushed or pureed tomatoes, then season. This recipe is going to be a base for you to build upon, another technique which you can run with. It's fine as it is for chip dipping, but I recommend that you expand your culinary creativity. Try adding canned corn, parsley, cilantro, vinegars, how about a can of crab meat for a crab meat salsa? Mmm. Doesn't that sound good? Chunky fresh salsas I grew up with were called "Pico de Gallo", and thick chunky salsas were great, but after I made a toasted corn and crab salsa there was no turning back. Here's my simple base, run with it, get creative.

Ingredients for a large bowl of Salsa:

5 Tomatoes, chopped small
1 Small onion chopped small
⅓ Green pepper chopped small
About ⅓ of a 28 oz can of crushed tomatoes (10 oz)
3 Tablespoons lemon juice
2 Jalapenos chopped fine and 3 tablespoons of its juice
Salt, garlic powder, and Adobo seasoning to taste
4 Shakes Tabasco sauce.

Step 1: Mix all ingredients, then adjust seasoning. If you don't like it too spicy cut back on the spicy stuff. If you like it more acidic, use more lemon juice.

Step 2: Let sit a while. This mix is better after it sits for a while and the flavors have time to marry (come together). Give it at least an hour, even overnight if you can wait. Now add your favorite ingredients, how about a couple of cans of baby shrimp? Shrimp and tomato salsa, wow! Go for it.

NOW ABOUT MAKING CHIPS

This chip dough is so easy it's really a no-brainer. I like my chips to be very bland and almost flavorless, so I can get the full flavor from my dipping sauces and salsas. You can of course season your chips anyway you like. My chip recipe is just EggBeaters and flour with a pinch of salt. That's it. Now here's where you have to get creative on your own. I'm going to give you a few ideas, then you see what you can come up with. Cheese tortilla chips? Add a packet of cheese mix from a macaroni and cheese box to the EggBeaters. Spicy tomato chips? Add a little juice from a can of Jalapenos and a little tomato paste to the EggBeaters and BAM! -- spicy tomato chips. Now you try it. Here's how it's done.

Ingredients for the Chips:

Flour, start with 3 cups
Chilled EggBeaters, less than half an 8 oz container
Salt, pinch.

Step 1: Place 3 cups of flour in a large pot or bowl. This can even be done right on a counter covered with a plastic bag. We are going to make what's called a well. Press your fingers into the center of the flour and pressing outward make what looks like a volcano. Pour the EggBeaters and the pinch of salt into the center of the well. Now, using a spoon vigorously stir the EggBeaters. As you stir, flour from all sides will start to incorporate into the EggBeaters. When a nice tight ball of dough has been accomplished, you've got your tortilla chip dough. If you need more flour, add it. Now knead the dough on a well-floured surface for 3 - 5 minutes. Keep dusting it with flour until it's nice and smooth and not at all tacky to the touch.

Step 2: Cover dough and let it rest for 30 minutes minimum, refrigerated. This dough will freeze well and stay fresh refrigerated for up to about a week. If you see little black specks in the dough after a few days of being refrigerated, throw it out, that's mold.

> **Note:** *Don't forget, if you refrigerate your dough for longer than an hour, like overnight, cover lightly with plastic wrap or tie tightly in two plastic bags.*

Step 3: As a rolling pin we're going to use your full soda can which works well. I tried different types of cans and they all have edges that end up cutting the dough. I found a soda can to be my first choice for a rolling pin. Dust your work surface and soda can well with flour. Roll out your dough as thin as you can, turning it over and continuously dusting it with flour so it doesn't stick to anything.

Step 4: Place the large flat strips of thin dough in the microwave for 15 seconds. Turn them over, then nuke for another 15 seconds. Let cool, and they're done.

SECRET GYRO WHITE SAUCE
Enough for a dozen gyros

When Gyros are served in New York the server will always ask you what kind of sauce you want. Typically they all carry hot sauce, BBQ sauce and that secret white sauce. When I was growing up it was pretty clear that at these gyro stands the white sauce was for the gyros, the BBQ sauce was for their street side versions of a Philly cheese steak, and the hot sauce was for the shish kabob. I always had them drench my gyros with hot sauce and that secret white sauce. Well that white sauce is no secret to me now, it's a yogurt sauce and of course at my facility I'm not allowed to have yogurt, "heaven forbid"! Yeah, it would be much easier to escape on the yogurt truck than in the cab of the Frito Lay guy's 18 wheeler!

Anyway, I made gyros therefore I made white sauce. I used cream cheese and it came out just as good as the yogurt version.

Ingredients for Secret White Sauce for a dozen Gyros:

4 oz Cream cheese
1½ Teaspoons lemon juice
1 Teaspoon honey
½ Teaspoon yellow mustard
6 Teaspoons water
4 Teaspoons juice from pickled Jalapenos
1 Teaspoon salt
½ Teaspoon garlic powder
1½ Teaspoons Adobo seasoning.

Step 1: Microwave the cream cheese until its very soft, 20 seconds or so.

Step 2: Mix all other ingredients into the softened cram cheese really well, and let stand at room temperature for ten minutes.

Step 3: Stir well again and it's ready to serve.

If you find your sauce to be too thick and un-pourable, use a little more water and check your seasoning.

TANGY BBQ SAUCE

Who doesn't like BBQ sauce? Not you, right? I hope not. I haven't met anyone in my facility who doesn't like BBQ sauce, so when I make it I have two basic rules: (1) I make it strong, I mean really flavorful, and (2) I make a lot of it. Although it isn't necessary, it is my habit to add a little butter to my BBQ sauce when I heat it up, before I coat my chicken or whatever I'm turning into BBQ. Making the BBQ sauce strong is okay because when the butter melts into it, the sauce not only becomes nice and creamy, the butter mellows it out a little.

This sauce doesn't need any heating or chopping, and will refrigerate for a long time. Like my other sauces, it's hard for me to gauge how long it will last because every last drop gets eaten. I must say that this BBQ sauce gets better and better the longer it sits. If you want to have BBQ Mack or chicken or tuna cakes or whatever, make the sauce the night before. It's still good on day one, and it doesn't have to be made up in abundance, but you'll see it tastes better the next day.

Now like I said, I make a lot, so if this recipe sounds like too much for you, simply make half or a quarter. At my facility they sell Ketchup in 24 oz bottles. Although I do like ketchup on scrambled EggBeaters, I haven't found anything else I would really put it on. I buy the 24 oz bottles of ketchup specifically with BBQ Sauce in mind. Instead of messing around with one cup of this or two cups of that, to make life easy I just started by emptying the whole 24 oz bottle of ketchup into a bowl. I figured when I was done I could just funnel the BBQ sauce back into the plastic ketchup bottle and squeeze away when I wanted some BBQ sauce. Of course when I was done I had enough sauce to fill one and a half bottles, so I had to get another bottle from one of my buddies for the excess. No problem there, like I said, it lasts and by making a lot you won't have to make it too often. They don't sell BBQ sauce at my commissary so it's nice to have a bottle on hand in my pantry (i.e., my foot locker).

OK, ready? BBQ sauce lesson one: The secret ingredient to most BBQ sauces is some type of beef base. The ramen noodles only cost 11 cents a piece and they come in chicken, shrimp and beef flavors. I buy four or five of all 3 flavors almost every commissary buy (every two weeks). They never sit in my locker for very long as I use the flavor packets for my seasoning bases, and the noodles to bread stuff, so it doesn't matter which I use first, because neither the seasoning packets nor the noodles ever go to waste. In this recipe we're going to use two packets of ramen beef seasoning. I empty the packets into whatever large container (bowl or pot) I'm going to mix my sauce in. I add just enough water to liquefy the powder, but in this recipe we're going to use 6 oz. This not only acts as my secret ingredient for authentic BBQ flavor, but it gives the sauce a nice dark color.

Ingredients for 40 oz of Tangy BBQ Sauce:

24 oz Ketchup
6 oz Honey
8 Tablespoons yellow mustard
1 Level teaspoon garlic powder

½ Teaspoon salt
4 Tablespoons sugar
1 Level teaspoon Adobo seasoning
2 Tablespoons lemon juice
4 oz Demon Cave hot sauce, see Index, or any hot sauce
2 Packets beef seasoning from ramen noodles
6 oz Cold water.

Step 1: Place the water and the beef seasoning in a large container and stir well until it's all dissolved.

Step 2: Add all the other ingredients, mix well and you're done!

This BBQ sauce becomes a great base in itself. Now get creative. Add some soy sauce, or plum sauce, or some sesame oil, or a little of each, and it becomes an Asian BBQ sauce. Any exotic products you may have will work. Trust me.

The next step is optional, you decide: When I make my extra crispy Jack Mack, or I want to turn our commissary fried chicken into a BBQ feast, I place about ⅛ of a cup of sauce to one tablespoon of butter in a pan, when the butter has melted and the sauce is hot, I roll my chicken or fish around in the pan until it's coated and hot and Voila!

DIRTY VERMICELLI,
JAILHOUSE APPROVED!
Serves 6

I know what you're thinking, dirty vermicelli, nice name to give a rice dish, right? Well, this one is an old, traditional Spanish rice dish, the difference here is we are going to add broken spaghetti to it, converting it into a vermicelli. Lots of people use the black squid ink that comes with both packaged and fresh squid (calamari) to flavor and color their rice. In Italy, adding squid ink to pasta dough is very popular for seafood pasta dishes, and in Spain dirty paella is very popular. Believe it or not, black squid ink pasta definitely complements various seafood pasta sauces, and it looks really cool too. Don't be afraid to use the ink, its not overpowering or fishy when its mixed with other foods. I wouldn't take a shot of the stuff, gag, but cooking with it is fine.

The only advice I need to pass on to first-timers is that when using canned squid you need to pick through the squid and its ink before you use it. There tend to be little twigs of I-don't-know-what -- I hope they're herb stems -- in the cans which need to be removed. I suggest emptying the cans of squid onto a plate so that you can see any of those little branches that might be hiding in there. Nobody likes little chewy bits of wood in their rice, and who needs a frivolous lawsuit from a choking victim, right?

So, with all that said, here is a jailhouse version of dirty vermicelli. Obviously you can serve this with whatever you want, but I served it with my now-famous sweet and sour Mack, and they went great together. I know Spanish rice and Italian style vermicelli served with a Chinese-style fish may sound strange, but I will chalk it up as jailhouse fusion and file it under artistic licence.

Ingredients:

2 Tablespoons butter or margarine
2 Medium onions, sliced
4 Tablespoons oil
4 Pickled Jalapeños, chopped up
3 Cans calamari with the black ink (picked through)
2-One pound bag of rice
5 Cups water (almost 3 Mackerel cans filled)
3 Cans mushrooms, drained
2 Tablespoon each garlic powder, oregano, and Adobo seasoning
2 Shrimp seasoning packets from ramen noodle soups
2 Tablespoons salt
¼ Pound (¼ package) of spaghetti, broken up into very small pieces, about half-inch lengths.

Step 1: Heat oil, butter and the sliced onions in a pan until just lightly wilted. About 3 minutes.

Step 2: Add the rice and the pasta lengths and cook until the pasta turns golden brown. Then add all of the other dry ingredients: the shrimp seasoning packets (from the ramen soups), the garlic powder, oregano, salt and Adobo seasoning and cook another 2 – 3 minutes, stirring continuously.

Step 3: Add the mushrooms and the peppers and the water and bring to a boil.

Step 4: Last, add the calamari with the ink. Stir well, then lower heat to the lowest setting and cover with lid. Let cook slowly for 15 minutes then check it. If the rice is still a little firm just pull the whole pot off the stove and let it sit covered for another 5 – 10 minutes. The carryover heat will finish it off.

Step 5: Serve topped with sweet & sour mackerel or other fish of your choice, then if you like, baste fish with glaze and enjoy! (See index for glaze).

INDIAN ONION BREAD/ONION NAAN

This is my version of an Indian bread called Naan. I take these cans of curry sauces and cut them with coconut milk, and add all kinds of meats and vegetables to make West Indian stews and East Indian curries. In every Indian restaurant I've ever been to there were always two breads offered, and this one actually comes out better than any I ever had in a restaurant. The best way I can think of to describe this bread is it comes out like a soft, fluffy pita bread with onions. In Indian cooking a lot of sautéing is done in burnt butter, they call it ghee. The French clarify their butter by heating it until it froths then removing the froth, which is actually a milk solid. When this solid is removed it raises the "burning point" of the butter so it can be used at higher temperatures. In Indian cooking they do the opposite. They heat their butter until the milk solids turn brown (burnt butter), which adds a nutty flavor, then they cook with it.

In keeping with the Indian theme, I burned some butter then added some small diced onion to it. When the onion was very soft and translucent I added some cold water to cool it down.

I added the onion-ghee-water mix, a little at a time, in place of the plain water to the flour and pancake mix. I still had to add more water after my flour and pancake mix had absorbed my onion water, but the outcome was this soft, nutty, buttery, onion-y pita-like bread.

Here's a recipe for you, but for a more in-depth description see the recipe and directions for Gyros (see index). However, for every bean-can's worth of flour (2 cups =16 oz) add half a small onion diced very small which you've already cooked in 3 tablespoons of burnt butter. The rest of the procedure -- the rolling and cooking -- will be the same as the Gyro recipe.

Ingredients for 16, 9-inch Onion Naans (onion breads):

2 Cups flour, plus extra for dusting your work surface
1 Cup pancake mix
½ Small onion, diced
3 Tablespoons burnt butter
2 Teaspoons salt
1 Teaspoon Adobo seasoning
1 Teaspoon garlic powder
Cold water
Oil for cooking.

Step 1: Put the three tablespoons of butter in a small pot and cook on a medium heat (3), until it starts to turn light brown and gives of a nice nutty smell (as I mentioned before, what the Indians call ghee).

Step 2: Add the diced onion to the pot, reduce the heat to low and cover with a lid or a plate. This type of cooking with low heat and very little fat (the butter) and a lid is called "sweating". So, sweat the onions for 3 or 4 minutes or just until they are turning transparent.

Step 3: Add one cup of cold water to the onions to stop them cooking and to cool down the butter. If it's still hot set it aside until it's cool. Don't add hot butter or a warm mix to the flour because it will start to rise prematurely.

Step 4: Mix all of your dry ingredients in a large bowl.

Step 5: Slowly add your onion, butter and water while mixing with your hand or a spoon. Add more cold water as needed until the dough forms a nice soft ball.

Step 6: Knead the dough ball for only about three minutes right in the bowl, lightly dusting with extra flour until the dough is soft and supple, not at all tacky to the touch, and comes away easily from the sides of the bowl.

Step 7: Cover, and let dough rest in a warm spot for 20 minutes.

Step 8: Roll out and cook just as you would for the Gyros, (see index).

Serve while still warm and soft. They go great with stews, and like I said are great with curries for mopping up your extra sauce.

SWEET PRISON BISCUITS
This makes two-dozen small sweet biscuits

You know what? Considering we don't have any baking powder or baking soda we're doing alright. You must agree, so far no setbacks, there isn't anything I've wanted to make that I couldn't figure out.

These sweet biscuits are great anytime of day, they are lighter and fluffier than my other biscuit recipe, and may take a little practice to make perfectly. Biscuits aren't just for breakfast any more. Even though they're sweet, you should still be creative with them after mastering my version. Try a little cayenne pepper or diced green bell peppers, or both. How about grating a little of your favorite cheese and dicing up a fresh Jalapeno pepper? Add them to your dough, yeah baby, sweet and spicy Jalapeno cheese biscuits, woooo-woooo, now we're cookin'. Split 'em in half and use 'em like bread for sandwiches, eat 'em with stews, smother 'em with gravy, whatever you do with 'em I guarantee you'll enjoy them.

The number of biscuits this recipe yields will be determined by the size of the cutter you use to punch them out. When I want small biscuits I use a 4 oz mushroom can as a puncher and I get around two dozen. Cut the recipe in half if you like, or just freeze the dough circles you don't need for next time. This dough freezes really well.

So, for two-dozen small biscuits you will need:

Ingredients:

3 Cups of All Purpose flour, plus a little extra for dusting
¾ Cup sugar
1 Teaspoon salt
⅓ Cup butter or margarine, chilled
1-5 oz Can evaporated milk.

Step 1: Mix dry ingredients together.

Step 2: Work in the butter or margarine as if you were going to make a pie dough, crumble the cold butter or margarine into small pieces, then using a fork mash it into the flour. When no pieces of butter or margarine are visible and the flour looks like wet sand, it's ready for the next step.

Step 3: Slowly add the milk and keep working the mixture until you have formed a nice, tight dough. It should be almost hard to the touch, not supple like pie dough. If the dough absorbs all the milk and is still dry, add a little more. If you don't want to open another can of milk, use a little water.

Step 4: This dough doesn't need to rest, so dust your work surface and your rolling pin (use a soda can) with flour, and go ahead and roll it out to about a quarter to half an inch thick, don't roll it out too thin. Then, using an empty can (your choice of can size) with the edge dusted with flour so it doesn't stick to the dough, punch out your disks. Only punch one at a time, re-dusting the edge of the can between each punch.

Step 5: Place a riser (an empty ham can or other large can) on the stove. Grease the bottom of a heavy-bottomed rice pot really well. A non-stick pan and a lid that fits nice and snug will also work. Dust the inside of the pot with flour then literally bang out the excess.. Place the pot on top of the riser, and heat the stove to only medium-high, not high, (3 - 4 on an electric stove).

Step 6: Place as many disks of dough into the pot as will fit without touching each other, there should be at least half an inch between them.

Step 7: Check them after about 20 minutes. Depending on your stove, it might take a little longer, but not more than 30 minutes. When they're golden brown and have risen nicely, they're done.

Make 'em, bake 'em and eat 'em!

MICROWAVE JAMBALAYA

Did you read the recipe for rice pudding? If you did, you'll know who I'm referring to when I say "three crazy Spanish guys". Well, those three crazies were at it again last night with their obnoxiously large, bubbling cauldron of rice pudding. I had finished cooking my crew's dinner earlier in the day so I didn't see the apparent spectacle they made of themselves. I can totally envision the three of them running around in figure-eights stirring and screaming at each other in Spanish, rice pudding going up the walls. They may have learned a valuable lesson this time around: water and electricity don't mix. Uh, hello? I was told that enough rice pudding bubbled over into the stove to create a short of some kind and an electrical fire. I always miss the good stuff, oh well.

The next few days - before we had a visit from a civilian to fix the stove - the microwave and the toaster became our only means of preparing our meals. One of my boys told me that a lot of facilities are microwave only, so if you're in one of them, recipes like this will be perfect for you.

Jambalaya is sort of a French/Southern rendition of the Spanish paella. I happened to spend just enough time down South in New Orleans to pick up two different styles of preparing it. The first was to sauté vegetables and meat or fish, then add raw rice and continue to cook it until the rice was lightly browned. After that, tomato product, water and seasoning were added until the rice was cooked. The second way was to sautee vegetables and again, meat or fish, then add some flour as a thickening agent, tomato product, seasoning, and water, and then fold in cooked rice at the end. Like I said, the end product using both these techniques are very similar to the way most Spanish people make their paella. I like my paella dry, but that's besides the point. I wanted my jambalaya to be different, and having only the microwave to cook it in, I knew that it would be.

This recipe is awesome for utilizing leftovers. When I refer to tomato product, a seasoned tomato product will work better than an unseasoned one. For example, when I made my microwave version, I utilized some hearty leftover tomato sauce. Canned spaghetti sauce would be better than a can of unadulterated tomato sauce or plain crushed tomatoes. They will both work fine, but you will have to check and adjust your seasoning. Leftover rice, perfect, even if it's a few days old and in the back of the fridge. Another example of my veering from tradition is that I served mine on top of rice like a stew instead of mixing the rice into the dish. It all got mixed up in people's bowls anyway, but I didn't want to serve what would end up looking like a wet paella.

Here we go.

Ingredients for 3 to 4 Viking sized portions:

4 Medium cloves of garlic, minced
2 Small onions, ¼ inch dice
5 Tablespoons oil
2 Ribs celery, split in half, then ½ inch diced
1 Green pepper, seeded, membrane removed, ½ inch dice
1 Red pepper, seeded, membrane removed, ½ inch diced
1-4 oz Can mushrooms in water
1-14 oz Kielbasa sausage (or the equivalent weight of any kind of sausage, Andouilli if you can get it), peeled, sliced in half length wise, then sliced into ¼ inch moons
12 oz Tomato product
10 oz Water
6 oz Corned beef (half a can)
1 Teaspoon oregano
1 Teaspoon salt
1 Teaspoon Adobo seasoning.

Step 1: Place the garlic, the onions and the oil in a large microwaveable bowl, stir it well and microwave for five minutes, uncovered.

Step 2: Add the celery and the peppers to the bowl, stir well, then microwave for another five minutes, uncovered.

Step 3: Chop up the corned beef and add it with the Kielbasa to the bowl and stir well. Microwave for another 5 minutes, still uncovered

You don't have to peel the Kielbasa. When pan frying Kielbasa, the skin cooks more and gets crispy, but micro-waving the skin might make it chewy.

Step 4: Add the can of mushrooms with their water, the tomato product, all the seasoning, and the 10 oz of water. Stir well, partially cover the bowl, and microwave for 5 minutes more.

Partially covering the bowl by leaving the lid about half an inch off to one side, lets some steam out and will prevent any bubbling sauce from making a mess.

Step 5: Stir well, and microwave again partially covered, for 3 more minutes.

That's it, your jambalaya's done. Total cooking time is only about 25 minutes. I had some yellow rice and beans left over from another meal that worked out perfectly. Three of us had about a cup and a half of rice each with jambalaya over the top. If you're using refrigerated rice like I did, nuke it for a minute or so first, then ladle your jambalaya on top. For that "Southern Glare" add some hot sauce if you so desire.

Lastly, if your stove works, by all means use it. Follow the above steps in the same order, just use a large heavy-bottomed pot, and note the timing will be different. Cook the vegetables until tender, meats until they are cooked through, and liquid until it becomes a flavorful sauce.

Enjoy.

SAVORY FRIED HUSH PUPPIES
Makes 8 - 10

While I was testing out some fried dough recipes in the day room yesterday, some Latins were playing dominoes on a table without a blanket for a buffer. They were making enough noise that the CO from next door came in and gave them a loud "Shush". This isn't really like a traditional 'Hush Puppy' at all, but the name came to me after the CO did his little bit. You gotta shush around here, know what I'm sayin'? Nobody knows nothin'. That reminds me of a joke: Why don't Italians like Jehovas Witnesses? .... They don't like any witnesses ...OK, like I was saying ... These hush puppies weren't light and fluffy like an oven-baked version, they were deep fried, sort of like fried dough, but they were good and went well with our feast and I'm sure they'll go well with yours too.

Ingredients:

2½ Cups pancake flour
2½ Cups flour (and extra flour for dusting work surface)
2 Cups water
1 Tablespoon salt
Oil for frying.

Step 1: Mix pancake flour, flour and salt in a large container. Use a pot, or a garbage bag if you have to.

Step 2: Slowly add the water until all dry ingredients start to come together into a dough. Don't add more water than you need. This type of dough works best after it gets to rest, so cover it and let it rest in a warm spot, by the stove or on top of the microwave, both work well -- for at least 20 minutes.

Step 3: Lightly sprinkle some of the extra flour onto your work surface and knead the dough gently into a ball. Do not knead for more than two minutes or you will overwork the dough.

Step 4: Break dough off into whatever size biscuits you desire.

Step 5: Heat sufficient oil in a pan so that you will be able to submerge your dough balls halfway into the oil. When one side is golden brown, flip them over, and fry the other side until it too is golden brown.

Step 6: Place them on towels or a paper bag to absorb the excess oil.

Step 7: When the biscuits are cool enough to eat, serve warm with plenty of butter.

QUICK & EASY ALMOST BAKED BEANS
For 4 healthy servings

Sure, if someone's sending you packages and you want some baked beans, they can send them to you. However, if you don't receive baked beans in a package and you suddenly find yourself craving some, I have the solution. Luckily, at my commissary they sell everything we need for this project. Here we have three types of canned beans to choose from: black beans, kidney beans, and vegetarian beans. They're all the same price and will all work well for this dish. I know black baked beans might sound a little funny, but they will come out just as good, so if that's what you have, use them, they'll be fine. Vegetarian beans come in a sweet sauce that will work the best and they look authentic. I thought it might be counter-productive using vegetarian beans in a recipe that has bacon, but that's up to you. Hopefully you're not a vegetarian but if you are, use the vegetarian beans and just omit the bacon. As a side dish these beans went great over yellow rice with octopus and mushrooms, and for our entrée we had honey mustard extra-crispy Jack Mack. The beans and the Mack complemented each other well.

Ingredients:

2 Cans beans (any kind, your choice)
10 Tablespoons Ketchup
1 Teaspoon garlic powder
½ Teaspoon Adobo seasoning
2 Tablespoons yellow mustard

¼ Teaspoon salt
2 Tablespoons oil
3 Tablespoons honey
3 Slices turkey bacon, diced small
½ Small onion, diced small
2 Tablespoons sugar.

Step 1: Place oil in a small sauce-pot on medium-low heat (2-3).

Step 2: Add the diced bacon and cook until just starting to get crispy, about 4 minutes.

Step 3: Add the diced onion and continue cooking until they start to get tender, about another 4 minutes.

Step 4: Add all the other ingredients and let simmer for 10-15 minutes, and you're done!

These beans are good on toast, over rice, or even just by themselves.

ROAST BEEF DUMPLINGS

My 300 pound buddy Yum Yum will do almost anything for a Viking-sized bowl of food. I'm a chef and he's fat, gee, I wonder what attracts him to my cube. I don't need help cooking, nor do I need help doing my dishes, so other than payment, unless you're chipping in food, I'm not going to feed you. Yum Yum is always hungry and never has anything to chip in, I like him enough to feel bad and let's face it I'm making food that's gotta be ten times better than what he was eating on the street. I told Yum Yum one day when he asked me what was on the menu, that if he gave me ideas for my cook book that I would let him in. That meant he (1) came up with a good idea, (2) helped me cook, (3) did all the dishes anyway, and (4) shut up while we worked. I didn't want to hear how it was going to be done, I wanted to tell him what was going to be done, and how. I quoted Ralph Cramden, I said "I'm the Admiral and you're nothing, remember that."

Every once in a while Yum Yum would come up with a worthwhile idea. Of course I had to create my own measurements and technique, but he usually came up with dishes that I wouldn't have thought of, like this one. This is just another example of how versatile my all-purpose dough recipe is. The dough for these dumplings is exactly the same dough recipe I use for my Strombolis, pizzas and patties. Two to one flour to pancake mix. Once this dough is rolled out as thin as you can get it, you could fill it with anything, seal off the dough, then boil them and you've got dumplings. Today we're gonna stuff them with roast beef, fondly referred to here as "Roast Beast".

This recipe is really easy to make and on a cold day is better than a hot bowl of stew. I took the roast beast out of its gravy to make our filling, then turned the gravy into a decent brown sauce by adding a packet of seasoning from a beef ramen soup, some water and flour. As always the technique here is what's important, you can make these dumplings with any kind of filling and whatever sauce you want.

I served our beef dumplings on top of roast-garlic mashed potatoes, see my Thanksgiving/Holiday Menu in the index, and a side of canned corn heated up with butter. On a cold day these are better than biscuits and gravy.

This recipe makes 38 golf ball size dumplings. We split them three ways, if you count Yum Yum as two people, then we split them four ways. If there are only two of you, split this recipe in half if you're starving, or just make a quarter of the recipe. The mix and the dough both freeze fine, so you can make up a batch and just roll out as many balls as you want to eat right away. Make patties out of the rest and fry them another day.

Ingredients for the Dough:

1 Cup flour
½ Cup pancake mix
1 Teaspoon each of salt, garlic powder and Adobo seasoning
Extra flour for dusting your work surface and rolling
Enough cold water just to form a dough.

Step 1: Put the cup of flour, the pancake mix and the seasonings in a large pot or bowl.

Step 2: Add a tablespoon of cold water at a time while you mix with your hand, wear a glove if you can get one. Keep adding the rest of the water a little at a time and continue mixing until the dough comes together. If you don't need all the water, don't use it When you can pick up the dough ball in one large piece and there is no flour mix left on the sides of the pot, you have added enough water.

Step 3: Lift the dough out of the pot, lightly dust it with some of your dusting flour, cover and let the dough rest in the refrigerator for at least 30 minutes.

> **Note:** *Again, remember, if you refrigerate your dough for longer than an hour, like overnight, cover lightly with plastic wrap or tie tightly in two plastic bags.*

Now make your filling and sauce.

Ingredients for the Roast Beef Filling:

2 Small onions, chopped fine
2-12 oz Cans roast beef in gravy
½ Teaspoon garlic powder
½ Teaspoon salt
Pinch of oregano
2 Tablespoons oil.

Step 1: Sauté the onion in the oil on medium heat until just starting to get tender, 3-4 minutes.

Step 2: Remove beef chunks from the gravy (reserve gravy for the sauce) and add them to the onions. Add the seasoning and cook until the excess liquid has evaporated, about 5–7 minutes. Break up the chunks with a spoon as you stir the meat while it cooks. Remove from heat and set aside to cool.

Ingredients for the Sauce:

Reserved gravy from the roast beef
1 Package beef seasoning from a ramen soup
½ Teaspoon instant coffee grounds
1 oz Flour
½ Teaspoon sugar

½ Teaspoon Adobo seasoning
4 Tablespoons butter
10 oz Water.

Step 1: In a small sauce-pot place the reserved gravy, the beef seasoning, the coffee, the sugar, the Adobo and half the water. Let come to a simmer on a low heat.

Step 2: Slowly, stir the leftover water into the flour forming a paste, then just pour in the rest of the water.

Step 3: Add the flour water to the pot and bring back to a simmer for at least 5 minutes.

Step 4: Add the butter, one tablespoon at a time, stirring constantly to incorporate the butter (this is known as emulsifying).

Step 5: Check your seasoning, if the sauce has boiled too hard and become thick, just add a little more water.

Assembling and cooking the Dumplings:

Step 1: On a well-floured work surface roll out the dumpling dough into small thin rounds, about 1½ inches each in diameter. Place 1 tablespoon of beef filling in the center. Wet half of the edge of the dumpling with cold water, then seal it closed. If you can make them round they will resemble American dumplings, but any shape will work.

Step 2: Bring a large pot of well-salted water to a boil. I always taste my cooking water before I use it. What you start with is what you end up with, i.e., if your pasta water tastes good, so will your pasta.

Step 3: Place 7 or 8 dumplings at a time into the boiling water, then place the lid on the pot. They should float in 3 or 4 minutes, then let them boil for another 2–3 minutes, until tender. They will swell up to the size of golf balls.

Step 4: Remove the dumplings one or two at a time and place them right in the pot with the sauce. Bring sauce back to a simmer, then serve with sauce over mashed or boiled potatoes and your favorite vegetables, or just eat them as is.

WINGS & THINGS

Everyone likes chicken wings when they're hot and spicy, so finger lickin' good. The chicken wings they sell at our commissary are pre-cooked and rolled in a dry spice mix. They're pretty bland and anyone who knows anything (this company's cooks excluded) about chicken wings knows they are always deep-fried when served and eaten as crispy wings. If you want to make soup out of those that come in the box fine, but if you want some kind of hot wings they are definitely going to need re-cooking and an accompanying sauce for dipping.

Just out of curiosity I tried following the directions on the box and they were horrible. All fatty and nasty. I almost wrote a letter to the company (whose name I won't mention to protect the guilty). Anyway, there are hundreds of ways to serve wings but here they all start off the same way. First you must dredge the wings in flour and fry them on both sides until they are crispy. When this first step is completed, the second step is also always going to be the same, and that's to place the sauce in a pan and bring it to a boil. Add the fried wings and flip them around in the pan until fully coated. Then serve.

Here are some great wing sauces for you to work with. Of course, as always, don't be shy, add or subtract any ingredients you like or dislike, Try adding your favorite dry herbs and spices to the flour mix before you dredge the chicken. Get creative people, then let some happy, full neighbor do the dishes.

WING SAUCE RECIPE #1
Sweet Soy Orange Glaze

Ingredients:

½ Cup honey
¼ Cup soy sauce
¼ Cup orange juice
4 Cloves garlic, minced
¼ Small onion, diced very small (Brunoise)
2 Jalapenos, chopped fine

⅛ Tablespoon black pepper (if you have it)
2 Tablespoons oil
2 Tablespoons butter.

Step 1: Place oil in a small pot with the diced onions, and on a low to medium heat (2 - 3). Cook until tender, about 3 minutes.

Step 2: Add the garlic and cook until it starts to brown.

Step 3: Add all the other ingredients.

Step 4: Let sauce simmer until it has reduced by about one third and looks a little thick.

> *A sure fire way to see if this sauce has reduced enough to be called a glaze, is to do the spoon test. Dip a spoon into the sauce then remove it. If the sauce coats the back of the spoon enough so that when you run your finger down the center it leaves a path or stripe with sauce on both sides, it's done, and we'll call it a glaze.*

Step 5: On a low heat, place the re-fried wings and enough glaze to coat them in a pan. Keep flipping the wings over for a couple of minutes until they're well coated, then serve hot.

> *Don't forget, if the wings they sell at your commissary aren't fried, they're just baked or boiled, so you need to cook them. When your wings are at room temperature they should have enough moisture on the outside to make flour stick. Instead of having to make a batter just dredge the room temperature wings in enough flour to coat them. Sear them off in a little oil until golden brown, then follow step 5 of this recipe.*

WING SAUCE RECIPE #2
Onion BBQ Picanté Glaze

Ingredients:

1 Cup Ketchup
¼ Cup yellow mustard
¾ Cup orange juice
1 Tablespoon Demon Cave Hot Sauce (see Index for recipe) or any
    hot sauce you have available
1 Clove garlic, minced
½ Medium onion, small dice
2 Tablespoons honey
1 Jalapeno, small dice
1 Tablespoon oil.

Step 1: Put the oil, the garlic and the onion in a small sauce pot on low heat, (low -1). Place a plate or a lid on the pot and sweat it (sautee until the onions are translucent and soft).

Step 2: Place all the other ingredients in the pot, raise the heat and bring the mixture to a boil, then reduce the heat back to low -1, just so the mixture simmers gently.

Step 3: Follow the steps from the previous recipe to turn the mixture into a glaze. When your glaze is done ...

Step 4: Follow Step 5 from the previous recipe.

Enjoy.

Chapter 7

DESSERTS & SWEET THINGS

Fudge Cookie Things
Chocolate Frosted Doughnuts
Doughnut Balls
Rice Pudding
Jailhouse Chocolate Brownies
Brownie Ice Cream Sandwiches
Chocolate Cheesecake with Chocolate Chip Cookie Pie Crust
Cookie Pie Crust
New York Style Peanut Butter & Jelly Cheesecake
Canned Fruit Cheesecake
Canned Pie-Filling Cheesecake
About Fruit Cheesecakes
Fresh Hard Fruit Cheesecake
Fresh Soft & Ripe Fruit Cheesecake
Banana Milk Shake
Peppermint Milk Shake
Peanut Butter Punch
Black & White Frozen Tiramisu
Two or Three Layer Cake With Fruit Glaze/Fruit Tart
Two or Three Layer Almond Joy Cake
Pineapple Upside Down Cake
Chocolate Cream Cheese Icing
Lemon Coconut Crème Caramel
Apple Pot Pie
All About Making Fudge
Chocolate Peanut Butter Fudge
Coffee Fudge
Chocolate Coconut Fudge
Candied Apples
Snickers Chocolate Peanut Cookies
Sweet Pies and Turnovers
Apple Pie Filling

Everybody goes to the mess hall for the cake and chocolate milk, and takes the white bread back to their dorms. Certainly they don't go for the large slice of liver which is so terribly overcooked that it's hard to chew, and leaves stringy veins stuck between your teeth.

So, my advice? Don't go to the mess hall on liver day to get the dessert, make your own, it's a lot safer and you end up with a lot more of it.

FUDGE COOKIE THINGS
For 24 cookie things

I was just messing around with the microwave one day when I came up with these. They're softer than cookies and a little harder than fudge, so I figured I'd just call them fudge cookies. Whatever you want to call them, they're good.

E-dorm, my new dorm, is an R-SAT program (Residential Substance Abuse Treatment) and is so boring. There is absolutely nothing going on. All the other dorms have a lot of activities, and stuff to do. They rarely even turn on the television here, so to stop myself from going crazy, I found myself spending more time in the kitchen. Even when I wasn't hungry I would cook just to help pass the time. Cooking became my rec. This was one of those times. I took some chocolate bars, some cookies, marshmallows, peanut butter and milk, and went to work.

At first I thought, well, all of these things can be eaten by themselves, right? It seemed a little crazy, I was going to make cookies using cookies. Or maybe I was going to make chocolates out of chocolate bars that could just be eaten as is. This was more fun, and the combination of all the ingredients came out much better than any of them eaten alone. The choice at the commissary store is so limited that by combining some of them, I actually added variety to the list of things we could eat. I had originally envisioned a chocolate the size of a cookie, all bubbly-looking and packed with chocolate chip pieces and miniature marshmallows. However, after excessive micro-waving and stirring, the broken cookie pieces ended up getting mashed into a sort of chocolaty paste. Unsure what my end product was going to be like, I figured at this stage anything goes, so I threw in a small handful of miniature marshmallows and put my mixture back in the nuker.

Stir, stir, stir, right? Now I've got what looked like a ball of chocolate cookie dough. I still wanted cookie pieces in my mix so I crumbled up three more cookies and threw them in, and gently folded the mixture until it looked evenly incorporated. Well, now the marshmallows were totally melted in and I had not achieved the bubbly look I had originally been going for, so in went another handful. The mix was still warm so the marshmallows started melting into my mix again, but this time they didn't melt all the way, they left cool-looking white patches of goo. I think at this point some of the cocoa butter from the chocolate bars started to separate out because I had an oily liquid starting to form on the bottom of my mixing bowl. Don't fret. I just transferred my dough ball to a fresh bowl with some paper towels on the bottom. Then I spread out a garbage bag on a table and started plucking small pieces of dough off my ball and pressing them down on the table into cookie shapes. More liquid started to appear under the fudge cookie things, so after they were all shaped I lined a container with more paper towels, then patted each one dry before putting them away.

Okay. If you eat them at this stage while they're at room temperature they are soft like fudge. If you refrigerate them they become firmer, like a cookie, but they stay pliable. If you freeze them they get hard. It's up to you how you want to eat them. I dunked them at all three stages in hot coffee, wow! I could market these babies. I didn't figure out how much they cost to make, so I didn't know what to charge for 'em, but I had plenty of offers, 2 stamps for three or four sounded reasonable. I assume they will last a long time refrigerated, but trust me, they won't be around long enough to find out.

Ingredients for two-dozen Fudge Cookie Things:

5 Hershey's bars with almonds (1.45 oz each)
3 Heaping tablespoons peanut butter
3 Tablespoons milk
8 Chocolate chip cookies
2 Palms-full miniature marshmallows.

Step 1: Break up the chocolate bars in a microwavable bowl. Crumble in 5 of the 8 cookies. Add the peanut butter, the milk and one palmful of the marshmallows.

Step 2: Depending on the power level of your microwave the melting time may vary. So I suggest nuking your bowl of goodies at 10-15 second intervals until it is all combined and looks like a ball of dough, stirring after each nuke. 4 or 5 times should do it. When it all comes together, crumble the last three cookies and fold them in, and add the last palmful of marshmallows.

Step 3: Transfer your dough ball to a napkin-lined bowl to absorb any excess cocoa butter released from the chocolate.

Step 4: Line a table with a garbage bag and break off pieces of dough and press them down onto the table, forming flat cookie shapes. The larger the chunks of dough you break off, the larger your fudge cookie things will be.

Step 5: After they're all pressed out, dab each side of each cookie with a dry napkin and place them in another container, again lined with a dry napkin or towel. Refrigerate for at least 30 minutes for best results. If you can't wait, just eat 'em!

CHOCOLATE FROSTED DOUGHNUTS

So many people here talk excitedly about going home and having all these recipes and techniques that they will be able to recreate. After spending enough time in places like this, I guess I can see breaking regular routines difficult for some people. I've heard people say that when they got home they still showered half clothed, only to be confronted by their wives or girlfriends asking "Uh, honey is there a reason you're showering in your boxers and T-shirt?" Of course the only response is "Oh shit ..."

Cooking with pancake mix has become an every day occurrence here. Between myself and my compadres, we go through about three large boxes a week. Honestly, I have never in my life before coming to prison bought a box of pancake mix. If I wanted pancakes (which I never did) I always had eggs and flour in the house, so for friends

I could make them from scratch. Here I seem to be sprinkling it in everything. I even perfected an Indian bread called naan with it, that another chef and I had spent a week trying to make in a three-star restaurant in midtown, to no avail. My jailhouse version came out better with pancake mix and burnt butter (ghee), than our street version did using "real ingredients" like baking powder. It's listed here under onion bread if you'd like to try it out.

Anyway, when I get home there are a few things I would like to make for my friends and family using pancake mix, just as a result of my pure amazement that it works so well. I feel like a magician, a sort of alchemist turning lead into sponge cake. I can't wait to show my friend the chef my onion bread, or to make these doughnuts for my mom and dad. It's going to feel strange being on the street and going into a supermarket and buying pancake mix to make things I figured out in prison, I wonder what a box of pancake mix will cost me at my local grocer.

This prison is like a day camp, so my memories of my experience so far will be fond ones, of me and my buddies passing the time baking and cooking. I can just see myself in a chain supermarket holding up a box of pancake mix and laughing, thinking about who's out and who's not and what they might be cooking.

This recipe took me three tries. I kept changing the ratio of flour to pancake mix until on my last try, I realized that pancake mix (my new staple) worked best on its own. That's right, pancake mix and water. That's it. Only two ingredients to make pretty-close-to-the-real-thing doughnuts. Alright, you are also going to need oil to fry them in and whatever toppings you can procure. I had leftover chocolate frosting from one of my many cake adventures, and of course I always have chocolate chip cookies on hand for making cheesecake crusts. Well, that was easy. When my doughnuts had a chance to cool slightly I spread some chocolate frosting on one side then pressed them into crushed cookies - awesome.

They were great fresh and hot out of the pan. The next day they were still edible but were reminiscent of real, week-old doughnuts which are okay for dunking in hot coffee, or great if you're having a sugar imbalance and need to level off your blood sugar. My advice -- make 'em and eat 'em and smile.

Ingredients:

Pancake mix
Water
Oil (for frying)
Chocolate frosting
Crushed cookies.

Step 1: Add just enough cold water, a little at a time, to however much pancake mix you start off with. Stir or knead mix into a ball of dough that easily comes away from the sides of the bowl. The dough ball should be supple and soft to the touch, but not at all sticky or tacky. If you add too much water just add more pancake flour. If it's too dry add more water. Like I said, adding only a little water at a time is important because if you keep going back and forth remedying, you may end up with enough dough to open a doughnut factory, and have a stiff over-worked product.

Step 2: Rolling out your doughnuts is also very easy. Take a ball of dough about the size of a ping pong ball, and using both hands roll it back and forth, constantly pressing outward until you have a snake-like piece of dough, just a little thicker than a Bic ballpoint pen. Press the two ends together and voila, you now have doughnuts ready to be fried. Any shape will still taste the same, but I figured if I was going to make doughnuts they should be the right shape.

Step 3: Place enough oil in a pot so that you can submerge three or four doughnuts at a time. Get the oil hot enough so that when you drop a small piece of dough into the oil it sizzles and turns golden brown in about two minutes. If the dough gets dark brown and crispy too fast, that means your oil is too hot. Cool the oil down then test it again.

Step 4: When the oil is just right, at about number 3 on an electric stove, carefully place three or four doughnuts in the oil, and using a spoon or fork flip them over every 20 seconds or so until they're golden brown.

Step 5: Place the doughnuts on towels or a paper bag to absorb the excess oil.

Step 6: By the time you've finished frying your last doughnut, the first one should be cool, but warm enough to frost with your icing. (See index for chocolate icing).

Step 7: Frost 'em, press 'em into cookie crumbs, and eat' em.

Got milk?

DOUGHNUT BALLS

On my first trip to "the Box" - a Maximum Security Facility (I didn't know then that I would be returning), I met "Greg", my first real cell mate. Appropriately enough, Greg had been sent to the Box for a stabbing incident. I was in the Box because I had used the microwave oven! It's a long story. If you're curious about this fiasco, and many others, you can read all about them in my biography.

Anyway, the Box Maximum Security Facility has two sides, the main and the annex. It's a maximum facility but the annex is dormitory style, while the main is more widely-known as "The Projects" or "The Hood". The outside yard on the main side is split up into weight pits known as courts. The courts are segregated by nationality, so Greg, being Italian and white, hung out and cooked on the Italian court. I know, you're thinking, "cooking in a weight pit", well they use handball courts too but that's where he cooked. Just like Harlem in the old days. These guys are all standing outside around 55 gallon drum fires except that they're frying Jack Mack and making doughnuts. It's hard to believe right? The facility stocks the courts with chopped wood, supplies cut down metal drums, and gives them metal grates to place on top to make grills. Pots of oil go on top for frying, or pots of water for rice, you get the idea. It sounds a little dangerous to me, having inmates with pots of hot oil and firey logs out in the yard.

Greg and I started comparing our culinary notes, he went on and on describing the most awful sounding stuff. I listened politely until he finally hit upon one that sounded worthy of my trying. I am reluctant to believe a large percentage of what I hear from inmates. Greg told me he made these doughnut balls (like Munchkins) and sold them to the CO's for $5 a dozen. He told me the cops would give him cash, put money in his account, or trade him packs of cigarettes. I don't know about all that, I wasn't there. For like 2 or 3 bucks you can buy a large box of those Munchkins from Dunkin Doughnuts, so I took his story with a grain of salt then made the doughnuts as soon as I got back to my facility.

This recipe is as cheap as it gets, all you have to buy is the oil and borrow a little flour, the other ingredients - bread and sugar - come right out of the chow hall. Of course if you want to be fancy pants about it you can buy some icing or melt some chocolate to dip them in. You could try stuffing them with jelly if you're really ambitious.

Don't be discouraged when I tell you this recipe sounds easy but takes some practice. If the bread is packed too loosely it will fall apart, if it's packed too tightly the doughnut balls will come out dense and heavy. If the oil is too hot they will brown on the outside before they get a chance to cook on the inside. Like I said, it's going to take some practice to master your technique. It took me a few tries but I got it and so will you.

Greg told me he couldn't remember how many packets of sugar he used per how many slices of white bread, so I made it easy. Every morning for breakfast we are each given four slices of white bread, it's supposed to be toast but it never is, and six packets of granulated sugar, so that's what I used. I melted some chocolate in the microwave at 15 second intervals so as not to burn it, then glazed 'em up. If you don't have any chocolate bars to melt you might want to add more sugar to yours, taste one and see.

Ingredients:

White bread, crust removed
Sugar
Oil for frying
A little cold water
A couple of tablespoons of flour.

Step 1: Press together the crust-less bread and the sugar and mold it into small balls. Press them together only enough so that they come together into a dough.

Step 2: Lightly brush each ball with water - just enough to make the flour adhere in the next step. Be careful here, too much water will render dense doughnut balls.

Step 3: Roll your damp doughnut balls in just enough flour to coat them.

Step 4: Fry them in hot oil (325 degrees) until lightly browned on all sides. Roll them around with a spoon.

> *If you add too many balls to the frying oil at one time, the temperature of the oil will drop dramatically, so don't cook too many at the same time.*

> *Test the oil temperature with a small piece of dough. If the oil is not hot enough, the doughnut balls will absorb the oil and create a heavy, dense product.*

Step 5: Remove the browned doughnut balls from the oil, and place them on some paper towels or a paper bag that will absorb any excess oil. Sprinkle them with more sugar while they're hot so the sugar sticks, or glaze them with whatever you have.

Lastly, if you can get $5 a dozen from a starving CO, by all means go for it. Nobody offered me anything but stamps, and I took 'em!

RICE PUDDING

I must admit I'm not the biggest fan of anything I consider to still be in its larval stage. Oatmeal, Wheatina, Farina, cornmeal, rice pudding and tapioca pudding to me, are all like the inside of a tomato, sort of slimy and not very palatable. Wheatina is by far the worst of them all, come on, who on earth thought it would be a good idea to overcook a grain until it's like mush and then throw some birdseeds in it. How wonderful, a breakfast cereal that gets caught in your teeth - not quite my cup of tea. At my facility one of these items is served four days out of every week, so unless you cook breakfast for yourself or don't mind starving, they are difficult to avoid.

When they served us Farina it was usually accompanied by coffee cake with a decent crumb topping. Okay, the coffee cake was worth going to the mess hall for, but once I was there I would get hungry looking at everybody chowing down. One day I saw someone crumble their coffee cake into their Farina so I tried it. With six packs of sugar and three or four pats of butter it wasn't so bad. It was still mushy, but the chunks of cake added enough texture to make it palatable as long as I didn't add all the cake at once so it disintegrated. I made that mistake once and ended up back where I started with a big bowl of mush. Hey, a lot of people who grew up eating that type of food love it. I am an egg sandwich and potato breakfast kind of guy, gimme a bagel with an egg and I'm good to go.

Anyway, on this occasion when I put all my coffee cake into my Farina, I took one bite, frowned and stopped dead in my tracks. I looked up at a buddy of mine who used to work in the mess hall. He started laughing because I must have looked like I was looking for somewhere to spit it out. Still laughing he says: "I guess you won't like tomorrow's chow then." After forcing myself to swallow I asked him "Why?" I wouldn't have gone to the mess hall anyway for the next day's breakfast as it was corn meal, I'd rather have the "alternate", starvation. He told me that the reason they always had cornmeal a day or two after they served coffee cake or corn bread was because they recycled it and served it again. Oh yes, they scrape off the topping and add some hot water, BAM! Hot cornmeal. Mmm, yummy. I never went back to the mess hall for breakfast, thank goodness I have money in my account to buy food.

Well, one day I was in the kitchen in E-dorm and three Spanish guys I knew were stirring up a huge cauldron of bubbling pudding. I'll admit it smelled nice, sweet and cinnamony, but it was going everywhere. Talk about kitchen comedy, these three guys were screaming at each other like the Spanish version of the Three Stooges, hands flying, doing figure eights around each other. My Spanish is pretty good but I couldn't understand a word of what they were saying. One guy was skimming the pot, one guy was using a face-cloth to sop up what was overflowing, and the third guy was wiping what was dripping down the wall behind the stove. This is why the metal behind the stove is called the "back splash". I couldn't help but watch, fascinated, they made my day.

When all was said and done, I was impressed that the end product of all that craziness was pretty good. They were, of course, making rice pudding. My mother loves rice pudding as do many people. On the street rice pudding is more of a technique than just a recipe where eggs, gelatin and even marshmallows are carefully incorporated as thickening agents. Not having any of these "thickening" ingredients or any technique for that matter, I was impressed that they managed to concoct a thick, creamy, sweet rice pudding more than worthy of note. I refined the process and cut down on the ingredient amounts so it could be made without going all over the place. Everyone in the dorm loved their rice pudding so they tended to make a lot at once. Perhaps two large pots would have been more appropriate than cramming all their ingredients into one pot, literally having it go everywhere. If I had a video of them going at it and showed it on a fast speed I could easily win $10,000.

This one-pot rice pudding recipe will yield about six large bowls.

Ingredients:

6 Cups water
½ lb Raw rice
1 Tablespoon cinnamon
1 Cup sugar (8 oz)
½ Teaspoon salt
7 oz Coconut milk (half a large can)
3 Tablespoons butter or margarine.
3-5 oz Cans evaporated milk, (if you have only one large 12 oz can
   of evaporated milk, use it, it will be fine)

Step 1: In a large pot bring the 6 cups of water to a boil.

Step 2: Add the rice, the cinnamon, the sugar and the salt and bring back to a boil.

Step 3: Add the coconut milk and let boil for 10 minutes.

Step 4: Add one can (5 oz) evaporated milk and the butter or margerine. Let boil for another 10 minutes.

Step 5: Add another can (5 oz) evaporated milk and let boil for another 10 minutes.

Step 6: Now add the last can (5 oz) of evaporated milk and bring back to a boil.

Step 7: Lower the heat to about 2 on an electric stove and let the mixture reduce slowly for another 15 minutes or so, stirring every couple of minutes.

That's it, it's done. If you like your rice pudding thicker than that, let it cook a little longer to reduce more.

You can serve your rice pudding either hot or cold. Get creative. Don't be afraid. If you like chocolate throw in a chocolate bar and have "chocolate rice pudding", peanut butter, honey, whatever you like. How about an Almond Joy bar for chocolate coconut flavor. Go for it.

JAILHOUSE CHOCOLATE BROWNIES

They say third time's a charm. Well it was in this case. My first two attempts at making brownies were complete failures. Both of my batches burned on the bottom before the top solidified, one was too sweet the other didn't have enough flavor. It just wasn't working. No doubt the absence of baking powder and good chocolate, and not having an oven for an even heat distribution were major factors. I figured if I could bake beautiful, moist three layer cakes here, I could bake brownies right? I mean they're just brownies, it's not rocket science. I probably wouldn't have even thought of making them if the brownies they served at the mess hall weren't so horrible. It's funny where inspiration comes from sometimes. It's like when I made pizzas. The mess hall pizzas sucked wind, but having one slice gave me the taste for it, and I forged on until I had something comparable to what I was used to on the street.

Well, I was going to give up and just move on to something else, but not being used to culinary failures I had to give it another shot. My neighbor across the dorm had just enough nuts left for one more try, and didn't mind the donation in the hope that if I succeeded, my promise of half a rather large brownie was worth it. As my first two attempts were such a total failure, on my third try I not only changed the amounts of the ingredients, but I switched to a different type of chocolate and totally changed my baking technique.

At the commissary here they sell Hershey's bars with almonds. I was going to wait until my next commissary buy day to purchase a couple more Hershey's bars (1.45 oz each), and hold onto the donated nuts and then try again. Well that week happened to be the week of the Jewish holiday Succoth, sort of like Harvest Festival. When I went down to see the Rabbi for services with the few other Jewish inmates that Wednesday, lo and behold he gave us each a 3 oz bar of bitter sweet kosher chocolate. God works in mysterious ways, right? Having been a pastry chef I understood the chemical difference in chocolate types, such as the varying amount of cocoa butter and dairy product content, so my first instinct was to attribute my success to using a better quality chocolate. However, after pondering this for a while, I came to the conclusion that it's the technique that made the difference, not the chocolate. I know being locked up can leave resources scarce and money tight, but your motto must be "If at first you don't succeed, try, try again". So, if your commissary only sells 1.45 oz bars of Hershey's chocolate, use 'em.

Basically, I believe that cooking is an art, and that baking is a science. When baking and working with breads, you must use the precise amounts of leavening agents such as yeast and baking powder, otherwise you can drastically alter the outcome of the finished products: cakes deflate and fall, breads turn into piles of bubbling goo, and so on. Fortunately, this brownie recipe omits the use of baking powder, I say fortunately because its not allowed, not because I didn't want to use it!

Other than having a heavy-bottomed rice pot to bake in, the next most important pieces of equipment (which by now should be in your collection of cooking supplies) are either a really wide can (like one from a 16 oz ham), or 3 or 4 tuna fish cans with the tops and bottoms removed. From here on, these cans are going to be referred to as "risers" or "flame deflectors". Even though the stovetops in jail aren't gas and there is no flame, placing a good flame deflector directly on the burner and then placing your pot on top of it will prevent the pot from direct contact with the heat source. By evenly distributing the heat to your pot you will have a similar effect (with the lid on) as an oven would have on your baked brownie. It is very important to follow my mixing method explicitly. The order of ingredients and timing should not be altered when attempting this recipe, other methods 'might' work, but I 'know' this one does.

Okay, with all that said here is the recipe for a 12 inch round by 1½ inch high chocolate brownie. I don't recommend doubling this recipe to make it thicker. You can try to if you like, it might work, but if I want more, I make two. I don't want to take the chance of it burning on the bottom before it's done on the top.

Ingredients:

6 Tablespoons butter
3 oz Chocolate
5 oz Sugar
2 Eggs or 4 oz EggBeaters
½ Cup flour (4 oz)
½ Cup chopped nuts (4 oz), any unsalted nuts will be good
Pinch salt
2 Additional tablespoons butter, plus 2 additional tablespoons flour, to grease and flour the pot.

Step 1: Place the butter and the chocolate in a small sauce-pot on low heat, and stir until melted. Be careful not to burn the chocolate.

Step 2: Add the sugar and continue to stir until the sugar has melted and the mixture does not feel grainy to the touch. Now add the salt.

Step 3: Remove the sauce-pot from the heat and let stand for a couple of minutes.

Step 4: Crush the nuts. I placed them in a clean handkerchief in small batches, and smashed them with a pot. That worked well, but of course you can crush them using whatever method you want.

Step 5: Next, we're going to stir the eggs or EggBeaters into the chocolate mix. The mix should be warm but not piping hot, you don't want to scramble the eggs into the mix. If the eggs cook throw them out and start over. So be careful, stir fast.

Step 6: Now stir in the flour in one-thirds. Scrape the bottom and sides of the pot well, making sure the flour is well incorporated.

Step 7: To complete the brownie mix stir in ¾ of the crushed nuts, reserving about a quarter to sprinkle on top.

Step 8: Take one tablespoon of the excess butter and smear it around the bottom of your rice pot and about 2 inches up the sides. Place the pot in the refrigerator or the freezer for about 2 minutes or just until the butter gets hard. Using the other tablespoon of reserved butter repeat this process forming two layers of butter in the pot. Place about 2 tablespoons of flour in the pot and shake it around coating the pot with the flour then tap out the excess.

Step 9: Pour the brownie mix into the prepared pot and sprinkle the leftover nuts on top.

Step 10: Place your flame deflector on the burner on low. Put the lid on the pot and place the pot on the flame deflector.

Step 11: In 55 minutes remove the pot from the stove and let cool with the lid on for ten minutes. A fork will not come out clean so don't bother trying to test it, it will be done, I promise.

Step 12: Let cool completely before you pop it out of the pot. Using a plastic knife or a hard spatula, scrape around the perimeter of the pot. No plastic knife? Gently use the handle of a plastic fork or spoon. Place a plate on top of the brownie then turn the whole deal upside down. Shake it if you have to and the Brownie should pop out onto your plate. This might seem like a lot of work but it's not really. After making this once you'll see it's easy and only takes about 10-15 minutes to prepare. Waiting for it to cook is the hardest part.

Step 13: Flip the brownie over again onto another plate so it's nuts side up, and serve.

I wish I had some whipped cream but let me tell you *a la mode* works just as well, try a dollop of your favorite ice cream.

Wanna kick it up a notch? Pour a little warm chocolate or caramel sauce on top, or on the plate before you serve. Wow. I'd give what kingdom I have left for a little powdered sugar!

Got some time to kill? Ha ha! Try making these brownies into ice cream sandwiches, they're awesome, see below.

BROWNIE ICE CREAM SANDWICHES

Press some semi-soft ice cream between two slabs of Jailhouse Chocolate Brownie, (see recipe) and refreeze. That's it, you're done. Delicious!

CHOCOLATE CHEESECAKE IN CHOCOLATE CHIP COOKIE PIE CRUST

Holy cow, these cheesecakes came out so good I almost couldn't believe it. We don't have ovens here, so at first it was hard to believe that everyone made cheesecakes without using a water bath. I think if I tried to make a cheesecake in any of the NYC restaurants I worked in without using a water bath, I would have been fired on the spot. Well, no worry there, I can't get fired from this place. Jailhouse cheesecakes come out really good, but even though they have the flavor of cheesecake, the consistency is more like frozen pudding. I see some guys here using eggs in their recipes even though they don't bake their finished product. Stirring EggBeaters into cream cheese and milk in a pot and getting it hot is close, but not close enough. Even those guys end up freezing their end product, which is still reminiscent of a frozen pudding. I say this because after being offered and trying a few different cheesecakes here, I started hiding small pieces in my cube and letting them come up to room temperature. Invariably they all reverted back to a jiggling mass, no longer resembling cheesecake consistency.

This recipe tastes great but must be served very cold so it stays hard. I had a couple of Hershey's chocolate bars, so I threw them in. The chocolate melts into the mix, but after cooling and re-solidifying I believe it helps these cheesecakes maintain their consistency. They don't have to be served frozen, but I recommend freezing them right out the gate to give them a jump start, you'll see when you read the directions. If you're looking for a cheesecake that has that NYC style consistency like "Junior's" in Brooklyn, try the other cheesecakes in this cookbook. I figured out what to do to take oven-less cheesecakes to the next level, but for an easy and quick cheesecake fix, this recipe is pretty good. You can use any cookies, I used chocolate chip cookies for this chocolate cheesecake.

OK, enough talk, let's make cake.

Ingredients for Chocolate Chip Pie Crust, or other pie crust:

32 Chocolate chip cookies
(For other pie crusts, use plain cookies or your favorites)
10 oz Granulated sugar
14 Tablespoons butter or margarine.

Step 1: Place all the cookies in a large Tupperware bowl or a pot. Using something like a spice container or a jar of peanut butter, (jail-house mortar and pestle), grind the cookies into crumbs.

Step 2: Melt 12 of the 14 tablespoons of butter or margarine and add it to the cookie crumbs. Mash and stir this cookie butter mix with a large spoon until it becomes a paste. When you squeeze some in your hand it should hold its shape without crumbling. If it seems really wet add a few more cookies. If it doesn't hold its shape and is too dry, add a little more butter or margarine until its moldable like clay, but remember, not too wet!

This next step will vary depending on your containers. Any round Tupperware bowl will work. Pie shell containers are awesome if you can get them. If you have six small cereal bowls that's fine, and two huge Viking bowls will also work. I suggest pressing the cookie crust into whatever size bowls you have, going only about 1½ to 2 inches up the sides. When you pour the mix into your shells, go only ¾ of the way up the shell. A small edge should be visible so that the slices you cut later will look nice. And don't worry, the amount of cookie crust called for in this recipe should make the perfect number of shells -- no matter what size you make them -- to accommodate the amount of filling.

Step 3: Using the last two tablespoons of butter, lightly grease the insides and sides of your bowls.

Step 4: Press the cookie crumb mix into the greased bowls, making your cookie crust about ⅛ of an inch thick. Only go 1½ to 2 inches up the sides of the bowls, but keep the thickness at about ⅛ of an inch.

Step 5: Freeze the shells for at least 15 minutes. If you put them in the freezer while you make the mix, they will be nice and firm by the time the mix is ready.

Ingredients for Chocolate Cheesecake Filling:

2-8 oz Packages cream cheese
2.5 oz Evaporated milk (half a small can)
2-1.45 oz Hershey's chocolate bars

> *To make this next step faster and easier, you can, if you like, microwave the two blocks of cream cheese in 15 second intervals until they are very soft. Don't burn them, when they are soft, transfer them to a small pot. Of course you can just put them straight into the pot, but it will take a little longer to stir out all the cream cheese lumps.*

Step 6: Place the cream cheese, the milk, the sugar and the two chocolate bars in a small pot. Put the pot on a low heat and stir vigorously until the sugar and chocolate have melted and there are no visible lumps of cream cheese. Let mix cool until it is at room temperature.

Step 7: Pour mix into frozen shells leaving about ⅛ of an inch of crust visible (don't fill crusts all the way to the top).

Step 8: This is the jump start. Place cheesecakes in the freezer for 20 - 30 minutes or until they don't jiggle when you give them a shake. When they're a little firm, transfer them to the refrigerator for at least one hour.

Step 9: Cut and serve with hot coffee!

NEW YORK STYLE
PEANUT BUTTER & JELLY CHEESECAKE

Any baker worth his weight in salt knows that cheesecakes need to be cooked in a water-bath to create that moist, light, New York-style texture. We used to fill huge roasting pans with cheesecakes in water to steam-bake them. Well there weren't any ovens in any of the New York State correctional facilities I visited. Certainly there weren't any roasting pans. As usual I made it happen, but this time I even impressed myself. There goes that vain-chef-chip thing again. I made my cheesecakes in a pot on the stove with enough water to recreate a steam-bath, and they came out great.

I was very happy with the chocolate cheesecake I made while I was in C-dorm. It was creamy and delicious with an awesome chocolate chip crust. However, truth be told, it lacked that authentic New York style cheesecake consistency. Without having eggs cooked into the mix to help it solidify, I attributed its hardening and its dense texture to the chocolate that was melted into it and of course to the fact it was frozen.

Well, when I returned from my short stint in the Box, a buddy of mine who was still in F-dorm asked me if I would make him a cheesecake for his birthday. Having conquered the chocolate cheesecake I said with confidence "No problem, one chocolate cheesecake coming up." To my surprise, his response was that he wasn't that fond of chocolate and would I make him some other flavor. I told him "Sure", and jotted down the date.

OK, now I wasn't going to be able to use the chocolate (who doesn't like chocolate?) as my solidifier. This meant I had to go with an authentic style, using eggs and a water bath (which I will explain later). Without an oven I had to bake all my cheesecakes in a pot but that was not a problem. If you have an oven by all means place your pie tin in a baking dish with a little water, and bake it at 350-375 degrees for 20 minutes, or until a fork pressed all the way into the center of the cake comes out clean. Using eggs and baking it are really the keys to creating the correct texture. Since I perfected this recipe I have had lots of people say to me: "Well I use eggs and I still have to freeze my cakes because they don't firm up." For a small consulting fee I set them all straight. They all made the same simple mistake. People here seem to think if they put eggs in their mix and get it warm or hot it will magically get hard. Wrong. The eggs have to be cooked, not just warmed or heated. See, when eggs cook they get hard. Imagine scrambled eggs, they're hard right? Not liquid. They have not just been warmed through, they have been cooked.

The first cheesecake recipe and technique I have described in this book, like I said, is really good but at room temperature it's more like pudding. When it's frozen it's hard and even though the flavor is there, it's more like frozen cheesecake pudding. When trying to replicate real NYC cheesecakes, there is another problem which presents itself. The flavoring used on the street is vanilla extract and lemon juice. Most vanilla extract is made from bourbon, yeah, right, they might let that in through the package room! We need a flavor, and really any one will do.

Using this new and improved cheesecake recipe and technique, the flavor can easily be adjusted. If peanut butter isn't your thing, use whatever is. A few people who had originally turned their noses up at my peanut butter and jelly concept now ordered them on the regular for 12 stamps a piece (they cost just over 4 stamps each to make when you make three at a time). I make three at a time using two 8 oz packets of cream cheese, which is what I suggest. When you make this recipe, which takes one 8 oz packet of cream cheese, you will end up with enough mix for about one and a half 9 inch cakes, so just make one large one and one small one. For three 8 to 10 inch cakes, double this recipe. If you have metal pie tins use them, if not plastic bowls will work fine.

So, using a water bath means putting the container with the cheesecake mixture into a large shallow pan of warm water which gently cooks the cake. This method is used to cook delicate dishes like custards and cheesecakes so they don't curdle or crack. You can use your water bath on the stove-top or in the oven.

To make a water bath I clean two very thin cans like 4 oz octopus or 4 oz calamari cans. When clean, place the cans in a large enough pot so that the bowl or pie tin can sit on top of them while allowing enough room for the pot lid to still fit on the pot. Once you have your equipment ready for baking, the rest is easy.

The first list of ingredients is for one large and one small peanut butter & jelly cheesecake. You don't have to cook all the mix, if you like, just make one large cake, and refrigerate or freeze the rest of the mix for another time.

The second list of ingredients is for three peanut butter & jelly cheesecakes, (so you can make them for sale), it doubles everything except the peanut butter which requires only an extra tablespoon.

Ingredients for one large and one small Peanut Butter & Jelly Cheesecake:

1-8 oz Package cream cheese
2.5 oz Evaporated milk (half a can)
¾ Cup of sugar
2 Tablespoons peanut butter (or other flavoring)
4 oz Eggbeaters (half container), or two eggs
Pinch salt
And ingredients for Cookie Pie Crust, see Index.

Ingredients for three Peanut Butter & Jelly Cheese Cakes:

1-8 oz Packages cream cheese
5 oz Evaporated milk (one can)
1.5 Cups sugar
5 Tablespoons peanut butter
8 oz EggBeaters (one container) or 4 eggs
Pinch salt.
And ingredients for Cookie Pie Crust, see Index.

This is really easy:

Step 1: Make your crusts and freeze them for at least 5 minutes, follow the crust recipe for Chocolate Cheesecake. (See index).

Step 2: Put the milk, the sugar, the salt and the peanut butter into a small pot on a low heat.

Step 3: Microwave your cream cheese for 10-15 seconds for as many times as it takes to get it very soft (almost liquefied).

Step 4: Add the cream cheese to the pot and stir well until almost no lumps can be seen.

Step 5: Place the eggs or EggBeaters into a large bowl. Slowly, very slowly, while stirring constantly, pour the hot cream cheese mixture into the eggs, remember, stir constantly. This is called tempering.

> *Don't pour the hot cream cheese mix into the eggs too fast, this might scramble the eggs, cooking them prematurely and creating more lumps.*

> *Don't worry if you still see cream cheese lumps, because as you stir the hot mix into the eggs it will thin and the lumps will be easier to stir out.*

Step 6: Using your water bath, place your large pot on a medium heat with your thin cans inside. Any thin can will work, such as a tuna can, but remember the deeper your pot, the larger your can should be. Your pie tin or plastic bowl must sit above the water you are going to pour into the pot. So, once your cans are in the pot, pour some water into the cans to stop them from floating, then add more water to the pot, pouring only half way up the outside of your cans.

Can you picture this? A large pot with "clean" thin cans inside. Water inside the cans and enough in the pot to come half way up the cans inside the pot.

Step 7: Pour the cheesecake mix into the shell or shells leaving a quarter inch of crust visible. Don't fill the crusts all the way to the top, they are going to rise slightly and you don't want your mix going over the edge. Basically, these cheesecakes are being steamed. When they first come out the crusts will be a little soft but by the time they cool they will be nice and hard, trust me!

Step 8: Place the cheesecakes on top of the cans that are inside the pot. Bring the water to a simmer, a very gentle boil, not a hard boil because hard boiling water will rise up and we don't want water to get into the cheesecake. Place the lid on the pot and turn the heat down to low.

Step 9: Let the cakes steam for between 15 and 20 minutes.

Step 10: After 15 minutes, if a fork pressed into the center (all the way down) comes out clean, it's done. If necessary, steam it for another few minutes.

Step 11: Using clean paper towels lightly dab the tops to absorb any excess water or moisture from the top of your cake.

Step 12: Cool and let chill refrigerated 30-45 minutes.

Step 13: Spread a thin layer of your favorite flavor jelly on top and serve.

If you happen to have a can of fruit in syrup or you can "get" some kind of fruit stuff from the mess hall, make this recipe without the peanut butter and just spread the fruit on when it's chilled. Like, uh, cherry cheesecake!

ABOUT FRUIT CHEESECAKES

All my fruit cheesecakes come out great. I follow the recipe for the peanut butter and jelly cheesecake except that I leave out the peanut butter, supplement fruit juice for half of the milk ,and obviously don't top it with the jelly. We're going to make our own topping. If I was on the street and wanted to make fruit cheesecakes I would use fruit extracts for my flavoring. Like I have said before, for authentic New York style cheesecakes we would need vanilla extract and of course cream cheese. For example, if I wanted to make a pineapple cheesecake I would add pineapple extract, a drop at a time, until my mix tasted nice and pineappley. Extracts "on the street" are available in every flavor imaginable.

We can reduce fruit juices until they are concentrated and become strong syrups, which won't have the potency of extracts but will still be very good. People here at my facility have commissioned me to make fruit cheesecakes of every variety of fruit they could lay their hands on. I have come up with two easy ways to make fruit cheesecakes that will work for any kind you want to make. The type of fruit is not important, it's the method that makes the cake "righteous".

As far as I'm concerned, for our purpose there are two types of fruit cheesecakes, the fresh fruit variety and the canned fruit variety. We'll start with the canned fruit variety. OK, there are two types of canned fruit, one comes in a thick jelly-like syrup which is ready to go as a topping, and the other comes in sweetened fruit juice which is sometimes referred to as syrup, but it's not as thick as say jelly and must be reduced.

OK, I'm going to give you some examples of excellent fruit cheesecakes that can be made with any types of fruit product you have available. If I want to make my pineapple cheesecake without extract, here's what I do.

CANNED FRUIT CHEESECAKE
With Fruit Glaze

This procedure will work for any canned fruit that comes in sweetened juice -- cherries, pears, whatever, I promise.

Step 1: Make your crusts and freeze them for at least 5 minutes, follow the recipe for Cookie Pie Crust, (See index).

Step 2: I open a can of pineapple, chunks or rings, it doesn't matter. Canned pineapple comes in sweetened juice, so first I pour off half the juice in the can and substitute the missing half with evaporated milk, so the can contains half juice and half milk. For example, for two cheesecakes the recipe calls for one 5 oz can evaporated milk. Use only half a can (2.5 oz) and use half a can's worth (2.5 oz) of pineapple juice. Get it? We substituted half of the juice with the appropriate amount of milk.

Step 3: Place the remaining juice in a small pot with two tablespoons of sugar (no matter how much juice you have left). Put it on the heat and let the juice reduce with the sugar, stirring occasionally, until it's very thick. This is going to be our fruit glaze. When it's done, just set it aside until later. If it gets too thick add a little water. Right before using it, you may have to heat it slightly to loosen it up.

Step 4: Follow the procedure for the PB&J Cheesecake. Like I said, obviously we're not going to add peanut butter right? This is a pine apple cheesecake. Place a few chunks of pineapple on the bottom of the crust, cut the rings into chunks if you have to.

Step 5: Pour your mix over the chunks and bake in a water bath as previously instructed.

Step 6: After the cheesecakes have cooked and chilled to at least room temperature, top them with more pineapple chunks or rings, then spread your pineapple glaze over the top and it will both look and taste "bangin'"!

CANNED PIE- FILLING FRUIT CHEESECAKE

Now for canned fruit that comes in that gooey, jelly-like substance. It's also really easy.

Step 1: Make your crusts and freeze them for at least 5 minutes, follow the recipe for Cookie Pie Crust, (See index).

Step 2: Open the can of fruit and following the recipe and procedure for the PB&J Cheesecake (leaving out the peanut butter and the jelly) add one tablespoon at a time of the fruit mix to the cream cheese mix, but I don't recommend more than 4 tablespoons, until it has enough flavor from the fruit.

Step 3: Follow the directions for cooking the PB&J Cheesecake recipe.

Step 4: When the cheesecake is cooled to at least room temperature, spread plenty of the fruit mix on top and you're done.

FRESH HARD FRUIT CHEESECAKE

This is more complicated because all fruits have different textures, some have juice, some are sweet, some tart, etc. Any fruit can be utilized. Hard fruits like apples and pears need to be cooked until tender before they're used. Soft fruits like mangos or bananas don't need to be pre-cooked. Taste your fruit before you start, to check for sweetness. It's very important that your fruit is sweet and tastes like what it's supposed to. We will still need to make a glaze for the top, so we are going to have to make a syrup. Here's what you do for hard fruits, like let's say a baked cinnamon apple cheesecake -- sounds good right? Note for one cheesecake you only need one apple.

Step 1: Make your crusts and freeze them for at least 5 minutes, follow the recipe for Cookie Pie Crust, (See index).

Step 2: Peel and core the apple. I suggest cutting your apple from top to bottom into quarters, then peeling and coring it after cutting it, so you'll have four large pieces all the same shape. Slice the wedges into ¼ inch thick slices. Taste one, is it tart? Is it sweet? Sautee the apple slices in sugar and cinnamon with a little butter, until they're just turning brown and are slightly soft. If the apple is tart add a little more sugar.

Step 3: Place the apple peel and any apple scraps in a small pot with just enough water to cover them. If you happen to have apple juice, use it instead of water. Add two tablespoons of sugar and reduce this on a low heat until it becomes a nice apple glaze. Strain it and set it aside.

Step 4: Now follow steps 1 through 5 for the Pineapple Cheesecake under the section "Canned Fruit Cheesecakes". Pour some apple mix on the crust and add your glaze/syrup. When it's cooked, top with more apples and glaze. Just like in the pineapple recipe. Cinnamon apple cheesecakes, woo woo. This will work for any hard or unripe fruit. Don't have or like cinnamon? Leave it out and call it a baked apple cheesecake.

FRESH SOFT & RIPE FRUIT CHEESECAKE

Step 1: Make your crusts and freeze them for at least 5 minutes, follow the recipe for Cookie Pie Crust, (See index).

Step 2: For softer ripe fruits let's say mango for example, you would peel the fruit and make some nice appropriate-sized slices. Again taste it, make sure it's sweet, if not either find a sweet one or add two extra tablespoons of sugar to your glaze.

Step 3: After you have enough nice slices to top your cheesecakes, and a little extra to put inside the cake, take the leftover fruit with the skin and pit removed, and place it in a pot. Cover with water and two tablespoons of sugar (4 if it's very tart) and reduce the water on a low heat until it's a nice thick syrup. Never use the peels or pits of soft fruits in syrup, they're bitter, for example mangos, kiwis, bananas etc.

Step 4: Now you have fruit and syrup once again. Follow the instructions for the Pineapple Cheesecake. The process will be the same. Remember, if your glaze/syrup-glaze is difficult to spread when cool, just heat it slightly until it's runny. Use a paper towel to brush the glaze over the whole surface of your cheesecake and fruit.

After you have made a few of each type you will see they're all very easy. Taste everything as you go, taste your glaze, even taste the fruit from the cans.

Now make cake!

BANANA MILK SHAKE

While on Rikers Island, a buddy of mine in the cell next door came up to me and asked if I had a banana to contribute for a milk shake. He said he had everything else but was short one banana. Luckily I had saved my banana from lunch and was more than willing to contribute it for my first cooking lesson in prison. It was not my last.

If available, which it wasn't to me at that time, one 6 oz scoop of vanilla ice cream or your favorite flavor would make this even better. We made it without ice cream and I could not believe how good it was. It was thick, cold and delicious, the way a banana shake should be, but made without a blender.

Ingredients:

3 Ripe bananas
9 Packets sugar
1 Pint cold milk.

Step 1: Place all the ingredients in an empty soda bottle and shake until the bananas have macerated.

Step 2: When you've finished shaking, place the soda bottle under cold water to chill it. I would recommend refrigerating for an hour, or until cold

PEPPERMINT MILK SHAKE
Makes 3 delicious, frothy milk shakes

Ingredients:

1-16 oz Container vanilla ice cream
6 or 7 Peppermint candies (crushed into powder, instructions below)
2-5 oz Cans evaporated milk.

Step 1: Place 6 peppermint candies in a plastic bag and place the bag inside a Tupperware container. Using an unopened can of food, crush the peppermints into a powder. If you're a huge peppermint fan use 7.

Step 2: Place powdered peppermint and evaporated milk in a large empty soda bottle or any container that is large enough to hold 26 oz of liquid and still be shaken. Shake for 2-3 minutes, then add the ice cream and shake like crazy until the consistency of a thick milk shake.

Drink!

PEANUT BUTTER PUNCH

Peanut Punch, that's what my new neighbor called it anyway. I changed the name appropriately to Peanut Butter Punch because after all, he uses peanut butter not fresh peanuts. I never really gave much thought to the term "milk shake" before I came to jail. In actuality the only times I have ever seen a milk shake being shaken has been behind the wall, or in this case, if you want to be technical, behind the fence. Everywhere, from county jails like Rikers Island to the maxest of maxes up North, people incorporate various liquids, flavors and of course something cold into large enough containers to be able to "shake" them vigorously. After a good shaking they all end up with a nice thick milk shake creation of their very own.

But think about it, when have you ever seen anyone on the street ever shake a milk shake? Perhaps there was some shaking machine used 100 years ago from which the term may have derived, but I've never seen one. These days when you make or buy a milk shake they are made in what's known as an "immersion blender". At home people use regular blenders and certainly commercial establishments that sell thousands of shakes daily have their own industrial strength machines, but I assure you shakes are never shaken. This whole concept is ironic when making this recipe because although this drink is shaken as vigorously as all other jailhouse shakes, this one doesn't get very thick. This is why it's called a punch.

"Abdullah", my neighbor, is a Muslim, and during the 30 days of Ramadan he would only eat after sundown, actually after his religious services were over. Inevitably Abdullah never got to eat before 10.30 pm. The mess hall makes up brown bags of food for the Muslims to take back to their dorms with them to eat later. Unfortunately for them the kitchens in the dorms close around 10 pm. Abdullah was given six little packets of peanut butter and two half pints of milk along with an interesting assortment of breakfast items. I would have withered away from starvation, having to live on what he was given, it must have been difficult. Perhaps he was supposed to suffer for 30 days. I wonder if anyone else noticed the parody between being given little boxes of cereal and hard boiled eggs, essentially breakfast to breakfast. Abdullah made these peanut butter punches and would eat a few slices of cheese every evening, which obviously sustained him. He had a contract with one of our other neighbors who would purchase his eggs and cereal every day so he wasn't living on much. Maybe that says something about the nutritional value of this recipe. Remember its not a shake, so don't expect a milk shake consistency. It's thicker than regular milk but it's a punch and it's delicious and easy.

Ingredients for one large Punch:

2 Half pints milk, one frozen and one room temperature
7 Large tablespoons sugar
5 Large tablespoons peanut butter

4 oz or enough hot water to liquefy the peanut butter and the sugar. Use the water out of the hot water machine if you have one, the water temperature should be about 190 degrees.

Step 1: Place the peanut butter, the sugar and just enough hot water in a jug, and stir until all of the sugar has dissolved and the peanut butter is a stir-able liquid.

Step 2: Peel the carton away from the frozen pint of milk and cram it into the jar.

Step 3: Pour the room temperature milk into the jar.

Step 4: Screw the jar lid on tight, and shake like crazy.

Now is the time to adjust the flavor to your own taste. If you like it sweeter or more peanut-buttery, add what you feel it needs. There is going to be a large chunk of ice milk floating around but that's what you want. That ice chunk will keep your punch cold while you drink it. Of course if you want a more traditional style milk shake use some ice cream, but I enjoy this as a punch. If you're working out and using supplements like protein powder made from egg whites, this drink is perfect. Put your daily dosage of whey or egg white supplement right in with the punch.

Now don't be shy, be creative, got a soft banana? Throw it in and shake it baby!

BLACK & WHITE FROZEN TIRAMISU

I love tiramisu. Traditionally, it's made by soaking ladyfingers in espresso, and wedging them into a pan. A generous layer of Italian pastry cream is spread on top of the soaked ladyfingers, (delicate sponge cookies, see glossary). These layers are alternated until whatever sized pan being used is almost full, and then it's topped with more pastry cream and a sprinkling of cinnamon. Sounds good, right? Well let's see... in jail we didn't have Mascarpone (Italian cream cheese), nor would anyone have even heard of it if I asked, and I certainly couldn't get a whisk. No spices were allowed in for fear of drug smuggling, so no cinnamon, and last they don't sell ladyfingers at commissary. I could have had some ladyfingers sent to me in a package from home, but I figured if I'm going to improvise everything else why not just make do with what I've got. Isn't that what this cookbook is supposed to be about anyway? Yes. Another question: If I didn't have any of the ingredients to make what I wanted why wouldn't I just make something else? Good question also. Answer: I like a challenge and I like Tiramisu. It was that simple. After going over a commissary sheet I discovered that it could be done, and 'Mock Tiramisu' is a great summer dessert! Okay, okay, it's really more like an ice cream cake, but it's my recipe, and I can call it whatever I want!

Ingredients:

1 Box Doughnut Sticks
1 Box Chocolate Swiss Rolls
2 Pints ice cream (your favorite flavors or whatever flavors they sell at your facility)
1 Bag instant coffee
Hot water.

Step 1: First of all survey the kitchen area, if it's too hot, work in your cube or cell. That's what I did. I got a garbage bag from the CO, spread it out on top of my locker and went to work.

Step 2: For this dessert you can use any shape or size Tupperware container with a lid. I wanted to make mine rectangular so I hunted around my dorm until I found one large enough to make a big Tiramisu. If you're gonna be a bear, be a grizzly!!!

Step 3: Make some very strong coffee, like espresso. Start with about 3 cups. When the coffee is very bitter and you wouldn't drink it, add another spoon of coffee Set aside and let cool to room temperature.

Step 4: Using a plastic fork push 4 sets of evenly spaced holes along the doughnut stix and the Swiss rolls. This is professionally known as 'docking'.

Step 5: Stir both of the ice creams separately until soft enough to spread. Don't melt the ice cream all the way or when it refreezes it will have a strange consistency. Spoon enough of one type of ice cream into your container and spread it all over the bottom and sides. Place the container in the freezer for 5 minutes.

Step 6: Soak the doughnut stix one at a time in the strong coffee. Totally submerge them for exactly 2 seconds. No more, no less. Place them in the container, wedging them in lightly creating your first layer.

Step 7: Pour ice cream over that layer until covered.

Step 8: Repeat this process alternating with Swiss Rolls, ice cream and Doughnut Stix until the container is full. Your last layer should be ice cream. Because your Swiss Rolls are black and the doughnut sticks are white, when alternated we will get a black and white effect.

Step 9: Place the lid on your container and wrap it tightly in a garbage bag and freeze it over-night.

Step 10: To un-mold your Tiramisu simply rub your hands around the sides and the bottom of the container slightly melting the outer ice cream. Put a plate on top then flip it over. Lift off the bowl and Voila!

You will know if you soaked the Doughnut Stix for the right amount of time if, when you cut a slice, you can still see some of the white of the cake where the coffee hasn't soaked all the way through. It will look as good as it tastes with the circular swirls of the chocolate Swiss Rolls and their cream showing. I guess basically this is an ice cream cake, but I'm the boss right? So this is my version of a black and white frozen tiramisu.

On the street most people would garnish a cake like this to make it more attractive. Covering it with thin slices of a candy bar like a Snickers bar will work, or if you have cookies, crush them up and press them to the sides and the top. Coconut shavings would also be a good idea, but let's keep reality in check. Just eat them!

TWO OR THREE LAYER CAKE WITH FRUIT GLAZE/FRUIT TART

I heard people had baked cakes in prison but I had never seen it done. Apple turnovers are big inside because we get apples at chow and since they're in abundance and free I see them frequently. Guys in my dorm make what they refer to as Dutch ovens. I'm sure other people make better Dutch ovens than the ones I'm seeing here. . My buddy Joe makes pretty good turnovers but his Dutch oven technique needs work. He puts three tuna cans on the burner then a pot on top of that, upside down. On top of the upside down pot goes another pot, also upside down, to keep the heat in. This balancing act is quite the performance. I would just as soon deep-fry them, they come out okay.

One day I noticed that there was "*moist and delicious*" Duncan Hines Yellow Cake mix on our commissary list. A cake with no oven? Scoffing at the concept and laughing to myself, I knew I had to try it. I ordered two boxes and had awesome success on the first try.

I was going to use hollow cans under a pot as heat deflectors and start my own juggling act, then thought better of it. I figured if I used a heavy-bottomed rice pot on a low heat I could just cook it right in the pot. The directions on the box - '350 degrees for 35 to 40 minutes' - instantly became useless. How am I supposed to gauge the internal temperature of a rice pot without a thermometer? I realized that if I tried to bake anything for that long in a dry pot I would definitely burn the bottom and perhaps the sides. The remedy? Only cook half the cake at a time. Not only did this dividing of the batter, and baking it half at a time prevent it from burning -- by cutting the cooking time down to only 15 to 20 minutes per cake layer -- but BAM! I now I had two, even, perfect layers. I love it when a plan comes together. You can read the instructions on the box if you like, but by no means follow them. Trust me, follow mine and it'll come out fine. The technique is what's important here.

Ingredients for one fruit filled, Two or Three-Layer Cake:

1 Box (1lb 2.25 oz) Duncan Hines cake mix
2 Tablespoons butter or margarine
2 Tablespoons flour
2 Cups cold water
8 oz EggBeaters or 4 eggs
Icing or frosting of your choice (if you like to frost).

Step 1: In a large bowl mix the cold water and the whole box of cake mix.

Step 2: Take a couple of large spoonfuls of that mix and place it in a small microwavable bowl and nuke it for 20 to 30 seconds. Stir well to incorporate.

Step 3: Return the batter to the large bowl with the rest of the batter and the EggBeaters. Stir very well until there are few or no visible lumps.

Step 4: Using one tablespoon of the butter or margarine, grease the bottom and sides of a heavy-bottomed rice pot. Dust the inside of the pot with one tablespoon of the flour. Shake the pot around to evenly spread out the flour then turn it upside down and shake out any excess flour.

Step 5 for a **Two Layer Cake**: pour half the cake-mix batter into the rice pot and place it on a very low heat (2-3), with the lid on, until the lid feels hot to the touch, 3-4 minutes. Then lower the heat to low (1) for another 10-15 minutes. When the center of the cake is slightly firm to the touch and spongy, it's done.

Step 5A for a **Three Layer Cake**: divide your batter into three even portions, and cook them following Step 5 above, except 8-10 minutes should be enough time for each layer to cook.

Step 6: Let it cool for at least five minutes before you try to take it out of the pot. When the cake cools slightly it will come away from the side of the pot easily. So, to remove it, gently place a plate or a lid from a bowl on the cake, turn the pot upside down so the plate is on the bottom, and the cake will pop right out onto the plate.

Wash and dry the pot before you bake the other layers. Of course if you have two pots, or three, you can bake all your layers at the same time! If not, follow steps 4 and 5 again.

Once you have your two or three layers, you can top each layer individually with the following delicious fruit glaze, which will give you two or three tart-like fruit cake layers. I called them tarts, but they are really cake layers.

Ingredients for Fruit Glaze:

1-15 oz Can Fruit Cocktail
4 oz Water
4 oz Sugar
4 oz Strawberry jelly.

Step 1: In a pot, bring the fruit cocktail, the sugar and the water to a boil. Let stand until cool.

Step 2: Separate all of the liquid from the fruit.

Step 3: Mash the fruit with the jelly, using a fork, until well mixed.

Step 4: Use the liquid to brush all sides of your cake layers, this will make them very moist and delicious.

Step 5: Spread the fruit and jelly mixture liberally between the layers.

For a tart, spread half the glaze on top of only one layer.

TWO OR THREE LAYER
ALMOND JOY CAKE

So remember my advice, don't go to the mess-hall on liver day just to get the cake, make your own. Here's a great recipe for a cake with a bit of a coconut flare because I added a couple of Almond Joy bars to it. If coconut isn't your thing, you can substitute two other kinds of candy bars , or just leave them out altogether.

The steps for this cake are very similar to the Fruit Glaze cake, except we're going to add Almond Joy candy bars and a chocolate cream cheese icing.

It was my buddy Sal's birthday so I went all out. I made a chocolate cream cheese icing, then dusted the outside with crushed chocolate chip cookies. Look for the chocolate icing in the index. You could use this icing in-between your layers as a filling if you like, or you can just top it with ice cream. Again, it's the technique that is important here. The recipe I have created uses candy bars. They aren't necessary, but if you have any, throw them in, it's a really good thing.

Ingredients for one Two Layer Almond Joy Cake:

1 Box (1lb 2.25 oz) Duncan Hines cake mix
2 Almond Joy chocolate bars
2 Tablespoons butter or margarine
2 Tablespoons flour
2 Cups cold water
8 oz EggBeaters or 4 eggs.

Step 1: In a large bowl mix the cold water and the whole box of cake mix.

Step 2: Take a couple of large spoonfuls of that mix and place it in a small microwavable bowl with the two Almond Joy chocolate bars, and nuke it for 20 to 30 seconds. Stir well to incorporate.

Step 3: Return the batter and chocolate bar mixture back to the large bowl with the rest of the batter and the EggBeaters. Stir very well until there are few or no visible lumps.

Step 4: Using one tablespoon of the butter or margarine, grease the bottom and sides of a heavy-bottomed rice pot. Dust the inside of the pot with one tablespoon of the flour. Shake the pot around to evenly spread out the flour then turn it upside down to remove any excess flour.

Step 5: for a **Two Layer Cake**, pour half the cake-mix batter into the rice pot, and place the pot on a very low heat (2-3) with the lid on until the lid feels hot to the touch, 3-4 minutes. Then lower the heat to low (1) for another 10-15 minutes.

Step 5A: for a **Three Layer Cake,** divide your batter into three even portions, and cook them following Step 5 above, except 8-10 minutes should be enough time for each layer to cook.

Step 6: When the center of the cake is slightly firm to the touch and spongy, it's done. Let it cool for at least five minutes before you try to take it out of the pot. When the cake cools slightly it comes away from the sides of the pot easily.

Step 7: Now put a lid (from a bowl) or a plate on the cake, and turn it upside down. This will pop the cake right out.

Wash and dry the pot before you bake the other half. Of course if you have two pots, bake both halves at the same time. If not, follow steps 4 and 5 again. Remember to wash out your pot between layers and don't forget to re-butter and flour the pot before you start again.

Ice your cake layers, (see index for chocolate cream cheese icing), decorate and serve.

PINEAPPLE UPSIDE DOWN CAKE

So this isn't really a pineapple turnover, although the cake layers do get turned over, but it's really just a pineapple cake. This is another variation on the two-layer fruitcake, with a slight difference. If you wanted to turn this into a real turnover you could very easily, see index for Sweet Pies and Turnovers.

Just place pineapple slices around the bottom of your rice pot then pour in the batter. After it's cooked and you pop it out of the pot, your cake will have nice rings of pineapple around the outside. Follow the directions for the fruitcake mixture and follow the same timing. Here's how I did it.

Step 1: I know that a 16-oz bean can is two cups, so I use one bean can of water (2 cups) when I make my cake mix. Here, we're going to substitute pineapple juice for some of the water. This recipe requires one can of pineapple rings in juice (20 oz). Take the rings out of the can and pour the juice into your measuring can. If you can't get any more pineapple juice from the mess hall or your commissary, just fill the 16 oz can the rest of the way with water to make your two cups of liquid.

Step 2: Now, after your first layer has cooked for 10-12 minutes on low heat, take five pineapple rings and microwave them until they are very hot, about 30 seconds.

Step 3: Carefully float the five hot pineapple rings into the cooking batter. Replace the lid and let that layer of cake finish cooking (another 8-10 minutes or so).

Step 4: Repeat this process with the other half of the batter and the other five pineapple rings.

Note: *Remember to wash out your pot between layers and don't forget to re-butter and flour the pot before you start again. This will give you two nice layers of cake with pineapple rings in them. If you have access to more pineapple juice use some to brush on each layer to make the layers even more moist. If not, use some "simple syrup" (even amounts of sugar and water brought to a boil), 2 oz of either pineapple juice or simple syrup will be enough.*

Step 5: When the cake layers are cool, ice one of them and sandwich the two layers together. Spread your icing over the rest of the cake and serve.

I like the chocolate icing with this cake, but if you have a favorite, use it. If you don't believe me, try dipping a piece of pineapple into melted chocolate, it's a delicious combination.

Note: *If you decide to place the pineapple rings in the bottom of your pot to create the more authentic version, (a) yes you still need to flour and butter the bottom of the pot, and (b) when the cake is cool, ice only the sides so you don't hide the nice golden brown rings of pineapple.*

That's it.

CHOCOLATE CREAM CHEESE ICING

Okay, I finally tried the generic brand of icing they sell at my commissary and it wasn't that bad. I still like mine better, and admittedly mine is a little more expensive. If you're selling slices of cake and are in competition with another jailhouse baker who uses the store bought brand, try this recipe. You may or may not be able to turn a 3 stamp slice of cake into a 5 stamp'er, but you will probably be able to scoop up a few more customers from the competition.

I took a box and a third of cake mix and cooked it in three batches. That gave me three even layers. Follow the baking instructions for Two Layer Almond Joy Cake (see index). When my three layers were cool, I brushed them each with 'simple syrup', which is made with even amounts of sugar and water brought to a boil. This will ensure that your cake is moist. Next I spread a nice amount of this icing on each layer and stacked them up. It looked like a huge hamburger and at first I was a little discouraged. However, after icing the whole cake and refrigerating it for 30 minutes, I took it out of the fridge and iced it again. Once the icing was nice and even on all sides I pressed crushed chocolate chip cookies evenly around the sides and it looked great. I didn't put any cookie crumbs on the top so it looked kind of cool. I refrigerated it for another hour before I cut into it. Three layer chocolate cake, easy as pie. Just kidding!

This recipe made almost the perfect amount of icing for three layers. If you are only making two layers go ahead and just make it all. Press the excess icing between cookies and freeze them, they come out great. If you are baking one large cake and not making layers, only make half this recipe. Oh yeah, the only straight up chocolate bars we have here are Hershey's with almonds. I recommend picking out the almonds and eating them. That's up to you.

Ingredients:

5–1.45 oz Hershey's Bars
8 oz Cream cheese (one block)
2 oz Warm water
8 oz Sugar (one cup).

Step 1: Place all ingredients into a microwavable bowl. Nuke for 10 seconds at a time, stirring each time until smooth. That's it.

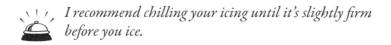 *I recommend chilling your icing until it's slightly firm before you ice.*

LEMON COCONUT CRÈME CARAMEL

You ask what is crème caramel? It's like flan. You ask what's flan? Hmm, crème caramel and flan are like custard. They're both thicker than pudding or custard. This baked dessert is wonderful any time of day, a chilled molded dessert made of custard with loose caramel dripping down the sides. This is so easy to make the only extra equipment you're going to need is 5 tuna fish cans (6 oz each), cleaned and dried, and a riser (three tuna cans with the tops and bottoms removed, or one wide can – such as that from a 16 oz Dak ham. You really can use any size can you want. I would advise against using tall cans, but any deep, wide cans will work).

This recipe will yield you 30 oz of crème caramel mix so make sure your cans will accommodate at least 30 oz. Basically, we are going to pour liquid caramel into the bottom of our molds and spin them around, coating the sides. Use a towel if you need to, the metal cans will get hot. When the sugar reaches a caramel stage it will be over 320 degrees. That's hot, so be careful. Need a visual? Boiling water is only 212 degrees. OK, once your caramel coated cans are cool we're going to fill them almost all the way to the top with our coconut lemon crème then bake them in a water bath for 20 to 25 minutes, or until a plastic fork or spoon handle inserted at the center touches the bottom of the can and comes out clean. Use a paperclip if you don't have a plastic knife, or anything you can slide in and out without ruining it, think something thin. When they cool they will be perfect. The top should feel slightly solidified. After chilling them for at least another half an hour they will be ready to un-mold.

Here's what you do. Fill a large bowl half way up with hot water, submerge the crème caramel containers as far as you can without getting water inside them. Holding them at the very top with your finger tips count to 30 then pull them out. Using a towel, dry off the cans then place a plate on top and flip them over. Gently raise up the can, and your crème caramel should slide right out. If it doesn't, submerge it again for another 30 seconds, dry and flip again. If that still doesn't work, run the handle of a plastic fork or spoon - or anything you can slide down the side of the can - along the inside edge, that'll definitely do it. Mine came right out first time, no problem.

The Spanish guys here in my new dorm love this one, and if you like coconut and lemon and caramel you will love it too. Yeah I got moved again, now I'm in G-dorm. When I came back from the Box I was put in C-dorm, but it was only a matter of time. All inmates whose "program" is working inside grounds get to go to G-dorm. They like to have us all housed together, it's easier for counting purposes at 5:00 am when we have to go out to shovel snow. Even after shoveling for two hours I ate a chilled crème caramel, with a hot coffee of course. Try 'em, you'll like 'em.

Ingredients for Five, 6 oz Crème Caramels:

1 Can coconut milk (13.5 oz)
5 Tablespoons lemon juice (4 if you have a real lemon)
9 Tablespoons sugar
1 Container EggBeaters (8 oz) or 4 fresh eggs
Additional quarter cup granulated sugar to line five tuna fish cans.

Step 1: Get your five tuna fish cans (6 oz each) cleaned and dried.

Step 2: Place the quarter cup of sugar in a stainless steel, non-reactive pot (a pot that will not react with acids or brines; the most common are glass, stainless steel and enamel), a non-stick pan will work fine too. Put the pot or pan on a low heat, like 1 or 2, shaking it constantly, mixing the sugar that's cooking on the bottom with the sugar on the top. When all the sugar has melted it will start to turn a nice amber color. Don't burn it, remove pan from the heat. If it smells burnt throw it away and start again because it will taste bitter. Placing the pan in some cool water will stop it cooking, but then the sugar will be hard to get out and you'll have to heat the pan again.

Step 3: Pour the sugar into each can covering the bottom, and swirl the cans so you get sugar about half way up the sides. Set your caramel cans aside to cool while you make your coconut mix.

Step 4: Place the coconut milk, the lemon juice, and the sugar in a pan and heat until the sugar dissolves. It doesn't have to boil.

Step 5: Next, we're going to slowly pour the hot liquid into the Egg-Beaters while whisking with a fork. Go slowly, this is called tempering, and the higher the temperature of the coconut mix the slower you should pour it into the eggs and the harder you should whisk. If your mix is really hot let it cool down some, you don't want to scramble the eggs.

Step 6: Place a wide hollow can or three smaller hollow cans on the stove top, to act as your riser. Place a large (wide) spaghetti pot on the riser(s), and put about one inch of hot water in the pot and bring it to a boil.

Step 7: Fill each caramel can with coconut mix almost all the way to the top.

Step 8: Lower the heat under the large pots of water down to a simmer, and gently place as many crème caramels into the pot as will fit. Make sure the water only comes about half way up the cans (not any higher).

Step 9: Now be careful with the lid. You must leave the lid slightly off to one side to release the excess steam. However, you have to avoid water dripping off the edge of the lid back into the pot, so it must be carefully redirected. To do this you must be meticulous about placing the lid, the water dripping off the lid must go back into the simmering water, not into one of the crème caramels.

Step 10: After 20-30 minutes they should be done. Stick the handle of a plastic fork or spoon in the center until it touches the bottom of the can. If it comes out clean, they're ready. As before, use anything you can slide in and out without ruining it, think something thin. Chill for at least 30 minutes before serving.

Step 11: To serve: submerge each can individually in hot water for about 30 seconds, making sure the water doesn't go over the top of the can. Dry can, flip onto plate and eat.

These are as good as any I've ever had on the street, actually better.

APPLE POT PIE

It's amazing to me what I have been able to accomplish in a kitchen without an oven. My cakes rise perfectly, my brownies are out of this world, and the peanut butter and jelly cheesecakes are awesome. With all these accomplishments why should I be leery of trying to bake pies? Well, I'm not. As I talk to more and more inmates here who have been in other facilities, I'm finding out that this facility is not like most other prisons, it's run more like a reception house. Apparently other correctional facilities have ovens and are far more lenient as to what they allow in through the package room. Guys tell me that they were allowed to have cake pans, pie tins, and all sorts of other gastronomic tools on their previous bids.

I made an apple pie in a large rice pot just like I did with my cakes and brownies. Making apple pies is the most economical dessert you can make in jail. Again you ask why? We've been over that. Save apples from the mess hall, they are free. Now all you need is flour, butter and sugar. I have a buddy who takes a class here called "food service". He frequently brings spices back to the dorm, so I have cinnamon. If you don't have cinnamon, it will still be good. I even saw a guy sneak out apple crumb dessert from the mess hall every week and freeze it until he had enough to add cinnamon flavor to his apples. Whatever works. This dough recipe will make one pie shell and top. If you don't want to make a top, this recipe will make two pies.

Ingredients for the Dough:

1½ Cups all purpose flour and more for dusting your work surface
    and the pot
½ Teaspoon salt
2 Heaping tablespoons sugar
1 Stick butter and two tablespoons more for greasing (remember, 1
    stick = 8 tablespoons)
12 Tablespoons cold water.

Step 1: In a large enough bowl mix all your dry ingredients (salt, sugar and flour).

Step 2: Cut the butter into very small pieces and chill until firm. Add the small pieces of butter to the flour one tablespoon at a time.

Step 3: Using a thick plastic fork mash each cut-up tablespoon of butter into the flour mix. The idea here is to mash and stir each tablespoon of butter until it is incorporated into the flour mix so that you no longer see any butter. Lots of people like to incorporate their butter until the mashed butter resembles little peas. Not here. We want this flour mix to look like sand, so keep mashing.

Step 4: When all 8 tablespoons (one stick) of butter have been incorporated and your mix looks like sand, start adding the cold water, about two tablespoons at a time. At this point discard the plastic fork and start kneading with your hand. With one hand squeeze the dough gently as if you were giving a massage. Using the other hand drizzle in the cold water. Don't use all the water if you don't need to. (Remember, the tablespoon measure is actually a large plastic teaspoon, so it's not a teaspoon and it's not a tablespoon either). When the dough comes cleanly and easily away from the sides of the bowl, stop adding water.

Step 5: Let dough rest for at least 15 minutes, preferably covered with a damp cloth.

> **Note:** *If you refrigerate your dough for longer than an hour, like overnight, cover lightly with plastic wrap or tie tightly in two plastic bags. Let it come back to room temperature before you use it.*

This is a good time to prepare your filling. See index for Apple Pie Filling.

Step 6: When your filling is ready, split the dough in half. On a plastic bag-covered work surface sprinkle a little flour. Roll out the first half of the dough to a thickness of about ⅛ of an inch.

Step 7: Prepare your baking pot by generously buttering the bottom and the sides (at least 3 inches up the sides). Chill the pot in the refrigerator or freezer for two minutes, then butter again using the last tablespoon of butter. Take about two tablespoons of your dusting flour and shake it all over the pot, flouring everywhere you just spread the butter.

Step 8: Using the lid from the same pot as a stencil, place it on top of the rolled out dough and cut around it. Since the tops to heavy bottomed rice pots are larger than the can bottoms, this will give you the perfect sized pie shell.

Step 9: Place dough inside pot and make sure the dough comes at least 1½ inches up the sides of the pot.

Step 10: Pour in your favorite filling to the top of the dough.

Step 11: Roll out the other half of the dough to the same ⅛ inch, follow the same cutting procedure from Step 8 and place it on top of the pie filling.

Step 12: Using the fork, poke holes in the pie top (this is called "docking") to release steam.

Step 13: Using a paper towel or your finger if you have to (a pastry brush would be nice), spread a thin layer of egg wash or simple syrup on top. Remember to always wash your hands after handling egg whites or yolks.

> **Note:** *Egg Wash - One tablespoon of sugar mixed with one table-spoon EggBeaters. Stir until sugar has dissolved.*

> **Note:** *Simple Syrup - This is just water and sugar mixed in equal parts. It's usually brought to a boil to melt the sugar, but for this project, stirring in warm water until the sugar is dissolved will be fine. A tablespoon of each will be enough for one pie.*

> **Note:** *I must emphasize again, if using your fingers to spread egg-wash, remember to wash your hands afterwards.*

Step 14: As risers/flame deflectors, place on your burner three tuna cans with the tops and bottoms removed, or one wide can – such as a 16 oz Dak ham can -- and turn the heat to #1. Place your pot pie on top of your risers. Do not put the lid all the way on the pot, leave a tiny space for steam to escape so the top of your pie will cook. Let cook for 30 minutes. Lower the heat to low and let cook for another 30 minutes.

Step 15: Let cool, then serve right out of the pot. The first slice might be difficult to wedge out, but after that all the other slices should come out beautifully. Serve a la mode (with ice cream).

If you're on the street or have access to pie tins and an oven, well, lucky you. Go ahead and Bake pies at 375 degrees for 15-20 minutes or until golden brown on top.

Pies are best baked in the center of the oven on a middle rack. But then they would just be delicious apple pies, and not my special apple pot pies wouldn't they?

ALL ABOUT MAKING FUDGE

Fudge is a soft, rich candy made of sugar, butter and flavoring. My buddy wanted chocolate fudge but he only had one Hershey's chocolate bar, so I suggested we add peanut butter and said "It will probably be like a Reese's Peanut Butter Cup" and it was. This recipe is extremely easy with or without using a thermometer. The sugar mixture needs to be cooked to what is known as a softball stage, which is 234 to 238 degrees. It's called the softball stage because when the cooked sugar mix is dripped into cold water it forms soft balls. Some fudge recipes took only five minutes to reach the softball stage after it came to a boil because I used a large pot. The smaller the pot the longer it will take to cook, because there will be less surface area in contact with the heat from the stove. When its ready you will notice the bubbles of the boiling liquid suddenly get very small and become an even size. I suggest testing a few times at various stages until you can do it by eye (unless you have a thermometer).

Get a small cup and fill it half way with very cold water. After the mixture has boiled for two or three minutes on a medium heat, using a spoon, drizzle a couple of drops into the cold water. Wait a few seconds then feel the mixture, it will be really, really soft, just a little harder than syrup. After about five minutes repeat this process. When the cooled droplets are firm but can still be squashed, that's a soft ball. If the drops of sugar mixture in the cold water are not firm yet, just let it continue to cook, testing it every few minutes until it is. It should be firm, but malleable. If the droplets are very hard the sugar mixture has reached a hardball stage and is overcooked, try again!

So to recap., basically, the softball stage is when the mixture has boiled long enough so that a small amount drizzled into cold water becomes firm. This will take around 15 to 25 minutes depending on the size of your pot and the heat of your stove. If when a little is drizzled into the cold water it seems to be taking a long time to get firm, don't worry, it will eventually happen. Keep a fresh cup of cold water by the stove and continue to check it. When some of the mixture dripped into the cold water feels hard and firm but not yet solid, it's ready.

CHOCOLATE PEANUT BUTTER FUDGE

I am baffled at how few guys in my dorm know what fudge is. Only two out of the forty guys in my dorm who I offered a piece of fudge to, knew what it was. Where did all these guys live before they came to jail, outer space? One of my friends asked me if I could make fudge and I said sure, so counting my friend and myself, it's safe to say only about four of us out of 60 had heard of fudge!

This recipe will yield, I'm guessing, about two pounds of fudge, maybe a little more.

Ingredients:

2 Cups sugar. If you have brown sugar and white sugar, use one cup of each, if not, all white is fine.
2 Tablespoons butter
Pinch of salt
½ Cup milk, (4 oz). Any milk will work, evaporated, condensed, coconut, regular, Vitamin D
1 Hershey's chocolate bar or 1.5 oz chocolate
1 Teaspoon vanilla, if you have it. If not, it's OK
6 oz Peanut butter -- ⅓ of an 18 oz jar
1½ Cups unsalted nuts (any kind) optional.

Step 1: Place all ingredients except the peanut butter in a small, clean pot.

Step 2: Bring mixture to a boil then lower the heat to the lowest setting. Only stir it until it is boiling then leave it alone. Do not stir after it boils!

Step 3: Bring the mixture to a soft ball stage, about 240 degrees. You can tell if the temperature is right by doing the drip test. Drizzle a little bit (only a few drops) into a shallow cup of cold water. When the drizzled mixture in the cold water gets a little solid to the touch, not hard, just a little solid, this is a soft ball. It may take five or even ten tries, don't be discouraged, just be patient and keep testing it every few minutes.

Step 4: Using only a tiny bit of butter, grease a bowl or large dish or tray, whatever you have. When you're done greasing you should have used so little butter that you can't see it on the bottom or sides of your container. (No visible white streaks or lumps of butter). This is the container you're going to use to actually cool the fudge in and store it.

Step 5: When the mixture is at the soft ball stage, remove pot from stove and stir in the peanut butter. Pour mixture immediately into a large bowl then stir until the mixture looses its sheen and becomes dull looking. If you're going to add some unsalted nuts, now is the time to stir them in.

Step 6: Pour the fudge mixture into your greased container and let it cool. Do not put a lid on the fudge or cover it until it's cooled to at least room temperature. If you cover it while it's hot, steam will be trapped inside and drip into the fudge.

When cooled, cut and eat!

COFFEE FUDGE

If you read the Chocolate Peanut Butter Fudge recipe, you will know how shocked I was to learn that few of my cohorts here knew what fudge is. Well, believe me they all know what fudge is now, and they want more.

I have a buddy here who is kind of a sugar junkie and loves fudge. Everyone seems to have a jail name, like Gutter, or just letters like E&P. Some people are called by their last name, like me, and some end up going by a rendition of either their first or last name. So for all intents and purposes my friend the sugar junkie will be known as Dribble, a rendition of his last name.

My mom sent me some recipes off the Internet and a couple of cookbooks that were hard to work with because of the lack of required ingredients. Substitution became a challenge and inevitably fun. In general I find baking to be a science. A pinch of this or a dash of that in cooking and most pastry work may be fine, but too little baking soda or too much yeast and you're in trouble.

Dribble was hangin' out in my cube reminiscing about our previous batch of chocolate fudge and flipping through a cookbook my mom had just sent me. Being the fudge junkie he is, when he saw a recipe for coffee fudge his eyes lit up and he said "Hey, can we make this?" almost yelling at me. He asks "What's cream of tartar? What happens if we just leave this out?" I read the recipe and indeed it called for ⅛ of a teaspoon of cream of tartar. Cream of tartar is one of those ingredients that turns baking into a science and we didn't have any. I remembered someone telling me once, I think, that you could substitute lemon juice for cream of tartar, or was it tartaric acid, a substance used in sugar work? I couldn't honestly remember but I forged on confidently, exclaiming "No problem, a drop of lemon will work just fine", not really sure, but we never let 'em see us sweat, right?

I made the recipe with a few slight adjustments and accidentally dripped three drops of the fake lemon juice into my mix instead of one. Showing no sign of my mess-up I looked over at Dribble who was rubbing his hands together and licking his lips in anticipation, and said "There, that ought to do it", hoping it would. This recipe took almost 8 to 10 minutes longer to get to the soft ball stage than the chocolate fudge did, and Dribble got nervous. He said "You know the last time I tried to make fudge at home I just ended up with syrup." He almost made me nervous because it was taking a while, they say a watched pot never boils.

Well, we paced back and forth in front of this little pot, watching it and testing it until it got to the soft ball stage. Like I said in the chocolate version of this recipe (which I suggest you read) if you have a candy thermometer, great, if not don't worry, I'm going to show you how to test for the soft ball stage without a thermometer.

When the coffee fudge mixture reached approximately 240 degrees, I put the pot into a bowl of cold water for about two minutes. Next I scraped the coffee mixture into a dry bowl and told Dribble to beat it with a spoon. I left the kitchen for only two or three minutes and Dribble was standing there sulking, stirring the bowl. He said "See, syrup". I said "I told you to beat it, not stir it" and proceeded to show him what I meant. You have to beat the mixture by hand and move the bowl around the table to cool spots while incorporating air into the mix. Don't fret like Dribble. Suddenly it will just harden up and you will have fudge. You must be patient when you follow my instructions on how to test for soft ball, don't be discouraged, it takes a while. My first few tests were complete let-downs. I thought I could eye a soft ball stage, but when I tested it by dripping some of my mix into cool water it just dissolved. Now I've got Dribble dancing around totally nervous behind me saying "See, see I told you." Be patient, it will harden up. One minute it dissolves, the next it starts to solidify, then a few more minutes and the coffee mix when cooled in the cold water becomes firm to the touch but still malleable. That's when it's ready. You must be patient at both stages, the cooking and the beating, so just chill out and wait. It's worth it. Do you know how much fudge costs on the street? A lot, I mean a lot, it's expensive.

Ingredients, for about 2 pounds of Coffee Fudge:

I Cup strong coffee
2 Cups sugar
1 Tablespoon butter
1 Tablespoon evaporated milk or cream
1 Large pinch of salt
3 Drops lemon juice or ⅛ teaspoon cream of tartar
1 Good shake cinnamon - optional
1 Hershey's chocolate bar with almonds - optional
1 Handful unsalted nuts, crushed – optional.

 For the strong coffee I used 3 tablespoons of instant coffee mixed with 1 cup (8 oz) of water.

 For the two cups of sugar, if you have brown sugar and white sugar use one cup of each. If you only have white sugar, it will be fine.

 Cream is the best, but I used evaporated milk and it worked fine. Freeze the rest in a plastic jug until you make a cheesecake or something else.

 You don't need to add the chocolate bar or the nuts or even the cinnamon. They are all optional. A fudge purist wouldn't add them, but I think it's much better with them and I recommend using them if they are available.

Step 1: Bring the cup of strong coffee (8 oz) to a boil in a small, heavy-bottomed pot.

Step 2: Take the pot off the stove and add everything except the cinnamon, the chocolate bar and the nuts.

Step 3: Put the pot back on the stove and bring to a boil again.

Step 4: Lower the heat to just above low, about #2 on an electric range.

Step 5: Bring to a soft ball stage, about 240 degrees.

Step 6: Boil the mixture for about five minutes, then drizzle a little bit (only a few drops) into a shallow cup of cold water. This may take five or even ten tries. Don't be discouraged, just be patient, and keep testing it every few minutes. When the drizzled mixture in the cold water finally gets a little solid to the touch, not hard, just a little solid, this is a soft ball.

Step 7: Remove the pot from the stove and submerge it about halfway in a bowl of cold water. Let it sit for about three minutes.

Step 8: Scrape out the mixture into a large dry bowl and add the cinnamon.

Step 9: Beat mixture with a large spoon incorporating air and moving the bowl around to cool spots on the table.

Step 10: When the fudge turns a light brown and starts to harden, add the crushed nuts and the crushed chocolate bar. Stir until incorporated.

Step 11: Scoop the fudge into a lightly buttered bowl and let it cool to at least room temperature without a lid. You can refrigerate it to cool it, but again, don't put a lid on it or it will steam and water will drip into your fudge.

Step 12: That's it. Serve with ice cream or just cut and eat as is.

CHOCOLATE COCONUT FUDGE

By the time I'm done with this guy Dribble, he's gonna be able to open up his own fudge shop. I told him to be careful when choosing his location. Location, location, location, right? Obviously an area where people know what fudge is would be a good idea. We had little tiny pieces that we gave out as samples to entice customers. It caught on after a while. Dribble was getting three stamps for six little pieces the size of mini candy bars, not bad considering we made about two pounds each time for under two dollars.

I told him if he wanted to open a shop one day and keep his store's rent down, and if it was in an out-of-the-way area, he would just have to hire a couple of cute little honeys to stand on the corner handing out samples like he did, but the honeys would wear skimpy shorts. Who would ever think someone would find their calling in here of all places.

As Dribble and I became better friends and I saw his enthusiasm for "Food Arts", I gave him some valuable advice that anyone can benefit from, namely that in the United States the government is easily swayed into giving up the bucks for continuing education. "Culinary Arts" is a biggie.

At my correctional facility they have a food service course. When you see the course through to completion you get a state certified food handlers' certificate. They learn stuff some of which might be useful in the real world, but people take the course because they have to meet a vocational quota that aids them in various ways toward being released.

Anyway, I told Dribble if he took the course and acquired that certificate he would be eligible to receive both grants and loans from the government for those continuing their education. Alternatively, an inexpensive six-month course at some culinary academy or accredited school would provide the same benefit upon completion. Good cooking schools can run well over $40,000 before room and board, so if he wanted to consider becoming a chef he could move on with free money.

Take a course, what the hell, it beats being a thief which he says was his last profession, and since he's here, I gather that didn't work out so well. While under my tutelage in E-dorm he's learned a hell of a lot more than he would in that food service course, but I can't give him a certificate, only food to eat, potatoes to peel, pots to wash, and knowledge.

Here's another fudge. We doubled up this time in the hopes that I wouldn't have to make more for a few days. I don't have a scale (the police took all my scales), but this made a lot of fudge. I recommend having two bowls about 9 inches in circumference each, to let it set in. You're also going to need a slightly larger pot than the one I used to make the other batches, so get a medium sized pot (at least 3 quarts). This way you can avoid making a mess with all the bubbling sugar.

Ingredients:

1-13 ½ oz Can coconut milk
2-13 ½ oz Coconut milk cans full of sugar (just under 4 cups)
¾ Cup powdered hot cocoa mix
4 Level tablespoons butter
Pinch salt
1 Almond Joy candy bar.

This Recipe comes out smooth and delicious, but if you like a little crunch you can always add some unsalted nuts, two handfuls rough chopped (smashed with a can of Mack) will work.

Step 1: Bring the coconut milk to a boil in a medium, heavy-bottomed pot.

> **Note:** *Keep your coconut milk cans, they are your measuring cups. While the coconut milk is heating, rinse out the can from the coconut milk and dry it. You should note that in making fudge we always use twice the amount of sugar to the amount of liquid. Instead of trying to measure out 27 ounces of sugar, your coconut milk-can becomes your measuring cup, and two cans equals 27 ounces of sugar.*

Step 2: Remove the pot from the stove and add the two cans of sugar. Stir well until dissolved.

Step 3: Add the cocoa powder and place the pot back on the stove on medium heat, about #5 on an electric range.

Step 4: Bring this mixture to a soft ball stage. If you have a candy thermometer this will be just under 240 degrees. Without a thermometer test for the soft ball stage by performing the drip test: Drizzle just a few drops of the mixture (only a few drops) into a shallow cup of cold water. When the drizzled mixture in the cold water gets a little firm to the touch, not hard, just a little solid, this is a soft ball. It may take five or even ten tries, don't be discouraged, just be patient and keep testing it every few minutes.

Step 5: When you have achieved a softball stage, remove the pot from the stove and submerge it in a large bowl of cold water, this will stop the cooking process. When there are no more bubbles forming on top of the fudge mixture, let it sit for two minutes more in the water. This will bring the temperature of the fudge mixture to around 130 degrees.

Step 6: Remove pot from cold water and stir in the butter and the Almond Joy bar. If you're going to add the two handfuls of nuts, now is the time.

Step 7: Now beat mixture, incorporating air until it starts to harden up, 5-7 minutes.

Step 8: Lightly butter two plastic bowls and spoon the fudge out of the pot into the bowls.

Step 9: Refrigerate uncovered, until cool and solidified.

> **Note:** *At my facility they won't let me receive coconut shavings. If I had them, I would have used a cupful (pan toasted until lightly brown) instead of the Almond Joy bar. Also, I had only one Almond Joy bar, but if you have three or four, you can try adding them to get more coconut flavor.*

CANDIED APPLES

I guess apples must be really cheap up North. We get bananas here once a month for breakfast, but apples seem to come around more like three times a week. We get lots of canned fruit, but if you avoid breakfast here like the plague, as I do, the only fresh fruit your gonna see are apples. Yeah, we're allowed to have fresh fruit sent in by mail, but hey, the apples are free. Consequently I have lots of apple recipes that are all good. I don't want to bore you with apples, but this is what we have to work with, so bear with me.

Candied apples, apples and sugar, that's it. The first few times you caramelize sugar it's going to look weird and you might get worried that something's wrong. Don't fret, that's normal. Now sugar burns pretty easily, so if you have a lot of sugar in a pot you have to keep it moving by either agitating (swirling) the pot or stirring it. It could burn on the bottom before anything happens to the top. The only sign will be billowing smoke suddenly coming out of the sugar. That would be garbage, throw it out. After placing your sugar in a small sauce-pot on a medium-to-low flame, you can't take your eyes off it. You should swirl the pot around every minute or so. When the sugar on the bottom of the pan starts to liquefy and you swirl the pot, here's what happens: the melted sugar rises to the top, cooling quickly and forms lumps with the uncooked sugar. This is fine if you have a spoon that won't melt, like a wooden spoon, so you can mash out the lumps or just keep swirling. We only have plastic spoons which are fine for quick mashing, so in and out. The sugar will be about 300 degrees, so don't leave your plastic spoon in the sugar. If your spoon comes out a toothpick, your sugar is now garbage, throw it out.

Professionals tend to keep a large bowl of cold water on the side of the stove to dip their pot into. It's an in and out thing. Not seconds, literally in and out. This will stop the sugar from cooking any further than the point that it's at. I do not do this, but if your sugar starts to get dark it might get bitter, so this technique is a good idea for beginners. When my sugar reaches a nice amber hue, even if there are still some lumps, I pull it off the stove and swirl it around on a cool metal counter (remember it's 300 degrees, so be very careful, boiling water is only 212 degrees). Sometimes I go back and forth from the counter to the stove until all the lumps have dissolved.

The apples they serve here at Chez Demon Cave aren't very big. They're not crabapples, but they're not nice big apples. I guess I should refer to them as small apples. Just over an ounce of melted sugar will coat one of these small apples. So for six "small" apples you're going to need about 8 oz of sugar (one cup). If you run out of sugar you can just add more to the pot and let it melt, it will work fine. Been there, done that. Make sure your apples are at room temperature, this is pretty important. If your apples are cold too much sugar will stick to them and they will be hard to eat, been there and done that too!

I knew nobody in my dorm had any, but for fun I thought I would go around asking everyone if they had any Popsicle sticks. No luck there, but if you have any lying around here's your chance to get rid of them. Alternatively, plastic forks will work fine. If you happen to have a piece of tinfoil, great, if not you're gonna need a few crushed up cookies. After you stick the apples with the forks, and have swirled them around (only once) in the melted sugar, you're going to have to put them down. If you have tinfoil just put them down with the forks sticking straight up. If you don't have tinfoil crush up 6 - 8 cookies into a layer of cookie crumbs on a flat surface, like a plate or lid. Do not try to use a plastic bag for your cookie crumbs, any sugar that leaks through will melt the plastic bag. Again, place the candied apples down onto the cookie crumbs with the forks sticking straight up. When they cool the tops will be flat (look familiar?), and covered with cookie crumbs!

Ingredients:

6 Small apples, washed, dried and at room temperature.
8 oz White granulated sugar
6-8 Crushed cookies.
Tin foil, or a plate or lid.

Step 1: Stick your forks into the bottoms of the apples.

Step 2: Place the crushed cookies (cookie crumbs) on a flat surface, like tinfoil, or a plate or lid.

Step 3: Swirl sugar in a clean, dry pot until it is a nice, even, reddish caramel color.

Step 4: Dip apples in the melted sugar and swirl only once.

Step 5: Place apples on crushed cookies, fork side sticking up and let cool.

That's it. You're done, get at least three stamps each for 'em. If you feel like experimenting, once your sugar is a nice amber caramel color, you can add a little Cherry Cool Aid for flavor and additional color.

How about caramel apples? At the same melted amber stage try adding a little cream. A tablespoon at a time will make the pot bubble and go a little crazy, but that's good. After it settles down drip a little on something to let it cool. If it still gets hard, taste it. It will taste like caramel because that's what it is. Too much cream will prevent the sugar from hardening, so only add a little at a time. Good luck!

SNICKERS CHOCOLATE PEANUT COOKIES
Makes 30 cookies

I'm going to lay this on you right out the gate, so you won't be disappointed. I finally had some baking powder smuggled out of the mess hall. Yes, I paid ten stamps ($3.70) for a spice container full, that's .75 oz or about 20 grams. While I was at it, since I'd found a connect, I bought black pepper, red pepper, more cinnamon and some vanilla extract. Needless to say with all my new "special" products I have come up with a whole slew of new recipes. I realize you may not have access to all this wonderful contraband, so I'm only going to add a few recipes, like this one, to the book.

These cookies came out so slammin' that I couldn't leave them out. I was flipping through some old Gourmet Magazines my mother had sent me, and after seeing a few cookie recipes the idea started to rent space in my brain. So I went for it. Some of the guys saw me attempting a few different methods of cooking this recipe, and they were all in disbelief that someone was attempting to bake cookies in jail. Well, I conquered making brownies in three tries, and that was before I had baking powder. I knew I could do it and I did. After experimenting with about half a dozen cooking methods, it turned out that the simplest one I tried was the one that worked.

You're going to need a non-stick frying pan with a tight fitting lid. The lid from my neighbor's rice pot happened to fit my frying pan perfectly. Of course like I mentioned earlier, a little baking powder will have to be procured.

Ingredients for 30 Cookies:

1 Stick, less one tablespoon, butter (a little less than half a cup), at room temperature.
¾ Cup sugar (6 oz)
1 Teaspoon vanilla (optional, if you have it)

1 Egg (or 2 oz EggBeaters, ¼ container)
½ Teaspoon baking powder
½ Teaspoon salt
1 Cup flour (do not add all at once as you may not need it all)
2-2 oz Snickers bars, chopped very small
1½ Tablespoons hot cocoa mix.

This is very easy.

Step 1: Beat the room temperature butter with the sugar until well mixed and the butter turns a little lighter in color.

Step 2: Mix in the EggBeaters (or fresh egg) and the vanilla extract (if you have any).

Step 3: Stir in the baking powder, cocoa, and salt, and slowly add just enough flour until your dough reaches a cookie dough consistency, not so dry that it's crumbly, but it shouldn't feel moist or tacky to the touch. Mix very well.

Step 4: Stir in the chopped up Snickers bars.

Step 5: Cover and chill mixture in the refrigerator for about 20 minutes, or until firm enough to form half-tablespoon size balls.

Step 6: Place your non-stick pan on an empty, upside down can with holes poked in it, and place on a burner set to medium heat (4-6).

Step 7: Place balls of cookie dough in the pan leaving enough space between them so they can spread out without melting into each other and becoming one large mass. Or you can just make huge cookies.

Step 8: Place the tight fitting lid on the pan and in 10 - 15 minutes your cookies should be done.

Step 9: Let the bottom of the pan cool slightly before you try to spatula out your cookies. If you're impatient like me, use a cold wet towel to cool down the bottom of the pan. If you happen to have a bowl large enough to partially submerge your pan in that's great. Fill the bowl with cold water, dip the pan into it and its instantly cool.

Step 10: Wipe out any cookie bits left in the pan and continue baking.

Note: *If you're at home: (A) Use half a cup of white sugar and a quarter cup dark brown sugar. (B) Use about 4 oz of chocolate chunks and a handful of unsalted peanuts. (C) Lastly, bake on a cookie sheet at 350 degrees for about 10-15 minutes.*

They are great warm and soft, and just as good the next day dunked in coffee or milk.

SWEET PIES & TURNOVERS
Makes one covered pie or ten nice sized pockets

This dough would be great for an apple pie, it's light and flakey. However, without having any metal pie tins I had to stick with making little pockets or turnovers. This whole Dutch oven thing seems like way too much trouble for cooking any of the recipes I've come up with thus far for my cookbook. At my facility they no longer allow pies and cakes from companies like Entenmanns in through the package room. When they did, the leftover aluminum pans apparently made great pie tins. I can see that. I've seen a couple of guys making their turnovers in their versions of Dutch ovens, but I didn't think all the dramatics were really necessary. A non-stick pan and some flour worked just fine for me, but this light dough will be good cooked in your version of a Dutch oven, sautéed in a little oil or butter, or even deep-fried. The microwave is definitely a no-no. I made cinnamon apple pockets and threw one in the microwave. The result was a mess. Get this, a heavy plastic plate that I use for nuking food all the time with no problems was ruined in 30 seconds in the microwave because the sugar got so hot it burned and melted my plate as it oozed out of the popped open pocket. Yeah, you know, smoke, burning plastic – so don't microwave apple pockets.

Here's my dough recipe, fill at will. Good luck.

Ingredients: one covered Pie or about 10 nice size Pockets:

2 Cups flour
Pinch salt
½ Cup sugar (4 oz)
1¼ Sticks butter or margarine (6 oz, ⅔ cup)
A bowl of ice water.

Step 1: Place flour, sugar and salt in a bowl, mix well.

Step 2: Cut small pieces of butter into the flour mix, and using a fork or your fingertips, gently work the butter into the flour. After 3 or 4 minutes this mix should look like wet sand.

Step 3: Start kneading the dough with the palms of your hand, add a tablespoon of ice water at a time. About 20 tablespoons of ice water should give you a nice soft dough. It's done when it easily pulls away from the side of the bowl. If you add too much water and the dough is tacky and sticky to the touch, add enough extra flour until the dough is smooth and soft.

Step 4: Flour your work surface and roll dough out to about ⅛ of an inch thick, this sweet dough is now ready for you to fill with any dessert filling you like.

Step 5: Again, if you make small pockets (turnovers) try lightly dusting a non-stick pan with flour, and on a low-to-medium temperature (2-3) lightly bwn off all sides and the bottoms too.

Voila!

APPLE PIE FILLING
To fill one large 12" pie shell

I prepare my apple pie filling in two stages. The first stage is where I sear the peeled apple chunks to get them a little brown. The second step is where all the apple and other ingredients get to infuse, and the reduction becomes a delicious syrup.

Ingredients for Stage 1: Sauteing the Apples::

6 Apples peeled, cored and chopped into 1 inch pieces
3 Tablespoons oil
3 Tablespoons butter
3 Tablespoons sugar
3 Tablespoons cinnamon.

Ingredients for Stage 2: delicious Apple Syrup:

2 oz Water
4 Tablespoons honey
1 Tablespoon lemon juice
2 More teaspoons cinnamon.

Step 1: If you place too many pieces in the sauté pan at one time they won't sear, they will begin to boil and steam. We're not making applesauce, so use high heat and don't overcrowd your pan.

Step 2: In a pot or pan, on a medium-to-high heat, melt 1 tablespoon of the butter in 1 tablespoon of the oil. Add ⅓ of the apples, 1 table-spoon of the sugar, and one teaspoon of the cinnamon. Stir and toss until lightly browned on all sides, 3-4 minutes.

Step 3: Repeat this process 3 times until all the apples are seared.

Step 4: Place all the apples and any liquid produced into a large pot with the 2 oz water, 4 tablespoons honey, 1 Tablespoon lemon juice, and 2 more teaspoons cinnamon. In only 2 or 3 minutes on a medium heat, all the ingredients should combine to give you a nice syrup. The apples should still be a little firm, they will cook the rest of the way in your pie.

Chapter 8

HOLIDAY MENU

Thanksgiving, Christmas, Easter

Pineapple Glazed Baked Ham

BBQ Fried Chicken

Roast Garlic Whipped Potatoes

Candied Yams

Caramelized Onion & Corn Stuffing

Apple-Orange-Cranberry Sauce

Cookie Crusted Pumpkin Pie

Two Layer Cake

HOLIDAY MENU

Just because we're in prison doesn't mean we shouldn't enjoy a nice, bountiful Thanksgiving, Christmas or Easter meal. At this Thanksgiving meal, the only two things that are missing are whipped cream for the pumpkin pie, and of course, a huge roasted turkey. I didn't include a regular vegetable because we didn't have one. If you have the fixings for a nice green salad or some fresh green beans or asparagus, by all means make them. It goes without saying that this menu is perfect for any holiday celebration.

After Thanksgiving I wrote my mother:

"I hope you all had a happy Thanksgiving and that my little dog (a 46 pound Black Lab/Greyhound mix) didn't eat too much turkey and gravy, I know he got a bowl! Thanks to you I had the best meal I've had here so far. I think having fresh vegetables beats everything else. In terms of food, I think loading me up twice a month with fresh produce would be a good idea: peppers, garlic, potatoes, cucumbers, lettuce, and any veggies on sale, whatever's cheap, broccoli, squash. Not zucchini, yellow or green, more like butternut or spaghetti squash, and fresh corn. Healthy stuff is preferable to canned goods.

"Five of us pooled our resources and came up with the menu: Glazed Ham, BBQ Chicken, Garlic Mashed Potatoes, Candied Marshmallow Yams, Corn, Peas, Turkey Gravy and Cranberry Sauce. And Cherry Cheesecake, Pumpkin Pie, and Chocolate Cake.

"We took a large table and spread our goodies out on a sheet for a tablecloth. We took a second table and laid it out for eating. We said grace, it was very nice. I had to orchestrate kitchen time and pot usage with others in the dorm, but it worked out fine. There's a big black guy here who I made friends with on Day One, of course he's a 'cook' on the street, and he fed about 15 people Mac 'n cheese and chicken and other stuff, no comparison, but they had a nice meal too. He asked me to make him two of my famous three layer cakes.

"It's funny, people are talking about my cooking all over the place here. I hear stories daily from the gym and the yard and the school building about my pies and cakes. People are asking for recipes. They need this book!"

OK, stove space around the holidays can be tight, so I advise cooking some things up to two days in advance. Make the mashed potatoes, the cranberry sauce, the cake, the pumpkin pie, the BBQ sauce, and the stuffing ahead of time, and the majority of your work will be done. On Thanksgiving Day all you'll have to do is fry the chicken, bake the ham and re-heat the rest of your meal in the microwave.

The following recipes combined will feed five people comfortably, and you should still have some leftovers for the next day. We will assemble this later on, but it's really important to read the whole recipe before you start cooking, so you will know what items you can make in advance, and also so you can make sure you have all the ingredients for every component of this really good holiday meal.

PINEAPPLE GLAZED BAKED HAM

Ingredients:

2-16 oz Cans of ham
3 Tablespoons honey
2 Tablespoons sugar
1-16 oz Can pineapple rings, and their juice
1 Teaspoon cinnamon
1 Teaspoon lemon juice
Pinch of salt.

Step 1: Drain the liquid from the pineapple rings into a large pot. Add the sugar, the honey and the lemon juice and the salt. Put the pot on the stove and heat the mixture until it reduces by half.

Step 2: Lower the heat to the lowest setting. Slice each ham into 10 slices and place them in the simmering liquid.

Step 3: Place the pineapple rings around the top of the ham slices and sprinkle the cinnamon on top of them.

Step 4: Place the lid on top of the pot leaving it slightly askew, so some steam will escape. When the liquid turns into a golden brown syrup it's ready to serve.

Step 5: Just place the whole pot on the table.

BBQ FRIED CHICKEN:

Ingredients:

1½ Boxes frozen fried chicken (12 pieces)
Oil for re-crisping in frying pan later
BBQ Sauce, *see recipe for Tangy BBQ Sauce.* This BBQ sauce tastes
   best after it has had a few days to sit so the flavors marry. Make
   this up to a week in advance and leave it in your locker. You can
   refrigerate it if you want to but it's not necessary.

ROAST GARLIC WHIPPED POTATOES:

Ingredients:

3 Pounds potatoes, peeled and cut into small pieces. (Keep the
   potatoes in water while peeling and cutting so they don't turn
   brown).
1 Small head of garlic, peeled. All the peeled cloves should be the
   same size for even cooking, so if some of them are larger than
   others, cut them down so they all pretty much match.
1-5 oz Can evaporated milk
1 Stick butter or margarine
3 Tablespoons of the oil from the roasted garlic (see later)
Salt to taste.

*Even if I had one, I find trying to peel potatoes with a
plastic knife virtually impossible, and using the "cutter"
the COs provide wastes a lot of potato. By the way, in the real
world that "cutter" is known as a bench scraper, and it's used
for making and cutting dough on a table. So, get yourself a*

nice new green scrubby pad, and under running water scrub away all the potato skin. See? Perfectly peeled potatoes and zero waste. I learned this trick doing a "stagie" (working for free) at another famous high-end NYC restaurant. The pastry chef there uses green scrubby pads to gently smooth out the lines left on pears and apples after peeling them so they look perfect. Nice trick, huh?

Step 1: Peel and dice the potatoes. Place them in a pot large enough to allow you to add more than two inches of cold water above the potatoes. Add two tablespoons of salt and place on high heat.

Step 2: Place the peeled garlic cloves (all the same size) in a small pot and cover with cooking oil. Cook cloves on the lowest heat possible, stirring occasionally until they turn very soft and are a nice golden brown. This may take a while but it will happen. The extra-plus item here is that after removing the garlic you end up with awesome garlic oil. Use this for anything, it's delicious. We're going to add 3 table-spoons of it to the potatoes later.

Step 3: When the potatoes are tender enough for you to easily press a plastic fork through one of the pieces, they're done. Strain out the water and leave them in the pot.

If the garlic is not golden brown yet, leave the potatoes covered so they stay warm, until the garlic is ready, and do something else. If the garlic is soft and golden brown go on to Step 4.

Step 4: To the pot add the butter or margarine, the 5 oz of milk, the garlic, 3 tablespoons of the garlic oil, and a little salt. Using a large spoon mix like crazy. As we don't have whisks, 'whipping' the po-tatoes with a spoon will have to do, we can still call them "whipped potatoes". Once they're smooth, check your seasoning and add more salt or butter to your liking.

The trick to making these potatoes up to two days in advance, is cooling them down, <u>uncovered</u>, before you refrigerate them. If you cover them while they're hot they will go sour, so make sure they're cool before you cover and refrigerate them.

CANDIED YAMS

They sell canned yams at the commissary at Franklin where I happened to be this Thanksgiving. Simple and easy, true enough, but if you have fresh yams do it from scratch.

Ingredients:

3-16 oz Cans cooked yams, plus half the liquid from one can
2 Tablespoons honey
2 Tablespoons sugar
½ Stick butter or margarine
Pinch of salt
1 Teaspoon cinnamon.

This is a five-minute deal, so it can be done on Thanksgiving Day. You can have everything ready in a bowl ahead of time if you like, but it's really not necessary.

Step 1: Drain the liquid out of two and a half cans of yams.

Step 2: Empty all 3 cans of yams, and half of the liquid from one can, into a large bowl.

Step 3: Top the yams with all the other ingredients then microwave in 30 second intervals, gently stirring until the yams are heated through and the butter and other ingredients have come together into a nice sweet sauce. If you have stove space, of course this can be done in a small pot, but the 'nuker' works just fine. I'm serious about being gentle, if you stir these yams too aggressively you will end up with mashed yams. The end product should be nice looking pieces of yam with a thick, rich, brown glaze.

CARAMELIZED ONION & CORN STUFFING

Some facilities like Franklin sell stovetop stuffing, but our commissary was sold out. I guess lots of people planned ahead and the commissary didn't anticipate seasonal items being popular at certain times of the year.

This stuffing recipe is really easy and much better than anything you can buy in a box anyway. If you have never cooked with eggs before don't worry, this will be great. The eggs bring all the ingredients together and make them firm. If you need a visual, think flan, frittata, quiche.

Ingredients:

2 Medium onions, sliced
3 Large cloves of garlic, minced
1-4 oz Can mushrooms, drained
1-15 oz Can corn, with its liquid
8 Slices bread, toasted
1 Packet of chicken seasoning from a ramen noodle soup
1-5 oz Can evaporated milk
5 oz Eggs (half container of eggbeaters, or 3 fresh eggs, lightly beaten)
1 Teaspoon each salt, Adobo seasoning, garlic powder and oregano
1 Tablespoon sugar
Oil for cooking.

Step 1: In a pan with very hot oil, fry the sliced onions in batches. Don't overcrowd your pan or they won't get nice and golden brown (caramelized). Add the garlic to the last batch of onions and cook until it turns brown. Place in a bowl and set aside.

Step 2: Fry the drained mushrooms in a little oil until they start to brown and get a little crispy. Add to bowl with the onions and garlic.

Step 3: Still using the same pan, add the corn and its liquid, the sugar and all of the seasonings. On a medium heat let the corn and seasonings simmer for 3–5 minutes or until the liquid has reduced by half, then add it all to the onion, garlic, and mushroom mixture in the bowl. Crumble the 8 slices of toast into the vegetable mixture and stir well to coat all the toast.

Our toaster was out of commission because some brain surgeon thought it would be a good idea to butter the bread before toasting it. Hellooo, where did he think the butter was going to go?

Apparently, this is the second time this has happened in our dorm. Well, we shall overcome. I had to take a thin flat can (a sardine can) and poke lots of holes in it with the "cutter" from the CO. I placed the can upside down right on one of the burners which I turned on to medium heat. I placed our bread slices right on the can and this worked fine as an improvised toaster. You need to toast each side of all 8 slices. If you burn them don't use them, it will make the stuffing taste bitter. Make extra toast, bread from the mess hall is free, so have extra on hand just in case.

Step 4: Pour the eggs and milk into the bowl with the vegetable and toast mixture, and stir well to incorporate everything.

Step 5: Microwave the stuffing mix in the bowl in 15 to 20 second intervals. Every 15 to 20 seconds feel the top of the stuffing. When it's lightly firm it's done, about two minutes should do it, depending on how powerful your microwave is. Don't cook it for two minutes straight, cook it for 15 to 20 seconds at a time, testing its firmness at the center with your hand.

Note: *If your microwave doesn't spin (ours didn't) give it a quarter turn at each cooking interval.*

The stuffing can be prepared up to two days in advance, but remember, it has dairy in it and is perishable. You must cool this stuffing down to at least room temperature before you cover it and place it in the refrigerator, or it may go sour on you. "Remember the rule, don't cover 'til cool"!

APPLE-ORANGE-CRANBERRY SAUCE

Last year my mom sent me a couple of bags of fresh cranberries, which was nice. This year I happened to have one 16 oz can of cranberry sauce so I simply converted it into a gourmet dish that nobody would ever know was out of a can. I guess the secrets out now, huh?

Ingredients:

1-16 oz Can cranberry sauce
1 Medium apple, (peeled and diced small) (from the mess hall)
2 Oranges (or 2, 3 oz cans of mandarin orange segments in juice)
1 Tablespoon sugar
2 Teaspoons lemon juice
2 Tablespoons honey.

Step 1: Peel and dice the apple and place it in a small bowl with just enough cold water to cover it, and 1 teaspoon of the lemon juice (this will stop it from discoloring).

Step 2: Section the two oranges and set aside the segments from half of one orange until later. Do this segmenting over a small pot or on a plate so you don't lose any of the orange juice. After sectioning the oranges, squeeze the pieces from the one and a half oranges to yield as much of the juice as you can. If you use cans of oranges, just separate the juice from the orange segments.

Step 3: Place the orange juice, the sugar, 1 tablespoon of lemon juice and the honey in a small pot. Cook over medium heat just until the liquid has reduced by half.

Step 4: Empty the can of cranberry sauce into the pot with the reduced juice and stir until it's well mixed. Bring cranberry mix just up to a simmer and remove from the heat. Let stand for five minutes.

Step 5: Drain the acid water from the apples and discard it. Gently fold the apples and the orange slices into the warm cranberry mix.

Note: *If you want it to look fancy, reserve some of the orange slices, and after you have poured the cranberry sauce into the bowl you're* *going to serve it in, place the orange slices on top of the cranberry sauce decoratively. When it's cool cover it and refrigerate until you serve your meal. Remember, it is important to cool this down before you cover it, just to be safe.*

TWO COOKIE CRUSTED PUMPKIN PIES

At Franklin Correctional they won't let us receive the spiced-up pumpkin pie mix that comes in a can. We are allowed to have pumpkin puree though, and that worked just fine. Instead of making pie dough, since I had some cookies in my locker, I made a cookie crust (see recipe for cookie crust under cheese cakes).

For the filling I followed the directions on the back of the pumpkin puree can. The only change was that I added a little more sugar as I was out of vanilla extract. I found that when following the recipe on the back of the pumpkin puree can, I ended up with enough mix to make two pies. The recipe says it yields one 9" pie. Perhaps the pie shell I have is not 9"? It looks like 9"and I made two pies, so prepare to make two pies, they're so good you'll be happy you did.

And oh yeah, before I forget, don't try to freeze pumpkin or yam or sweet potato pies. They go weird. Wrapped well and refrigerated they all keep well for at least a week. Again, do not freeze them.

Ingredients:

2 Cookie crust pie shells
1-15 oz Can pumpkin puree
12 oz Can evaporated milk (Carnation comes in 12 oz cans)
2 Eggs or 4 oz EggBeaters (half a container)
Pinch of salt
1 Teaspoon cinnamon
1 Cup sugar

Step 1: Make two pie shells and freeze. (See Index for cookie pie crust recipe.)

Step 2: Mix together all the other ingredients.

Step 3: Pour the mix into one pie shell.

Step 4: Put two clean, small cans (like octopus or sardine cans) inside a large pot, with enough boiling water to almost reach the pie tin.

Step 5: Place the filled pie shell on top of the cans in the pot, place the lid on the pot, and steam until firm, 20-30 minutes, and the handle of a plastic fork or spoon comes out clean after being carefully inserted dead center. As usual, use a paperclip if you don't have a plastic knife, or anything you can slide in and out without ruining it, think something thin.

Step 6: Chill in the refrigerator for at least one hour before serving. Overnight is better.

> **Note:** *If you're really daring, you can bake these pies in an improvised Dutch oven, but be careful not to burn the bottoms.*

HOLIDAY TWO LAYER CAKE

For a good selection of cakes, just go to the desert section in this book. There are plenty of goodies to choose from. Basically, there are two reasons my cakes come out so moist and delicious:

First, I never try to cook a whole box of cake mix at once in a pot. The bottom will inevitably end up being a little dry before the top and center are done. In an oven it would be different. Bake half of the cake mix at a time. This not only gives you a moister product, but will yield you two even layers of cake and will decrease your overall cooking time by one third.

Second, I always brush each layer with some sort of syrup before applying the icing. Basic syrup is 50-50 sugar and water brought to a boil. You can of course adjust this with any flavoring you like, such as jelly or juice.

Now, on Thanksgiving Day...

All you have left to do, besides reheating and serving, is to re-crisp the chicken in a frying pan and slather it with BBQ sauce, and bake the ham.

That's it. Serve everything hot except the desserts and the cranberry sauce.

How's that for a GREAT HOLIDAY in jail?

HAPPY HOLIDAY!

Alphabetical Recipe Index

C

F

G

S

T

GLOSSARY
Dictionary of terms you might find helpful

A LA MODE: Pie a la mode refers to pie (usually apple pie) served with a scoop of ice cream (usually vanilla) on top.

AL DENTE: Describes pasta and (less commonly) rice that has been cooked so as to be firm but not hard. "Al dente" also describes vegetables that are cooked to the "tender crisp" phase - still offering resistance to the bite, but cooked through.

BAIN MARIE: Also called a Water Bath. A container with food is placed in another container with simmering water. This method is used for making custards, melting chocolate and other foods which require slow and gentle cooking.

BAM!: What TV Chef Emeril Lagasse says when ramping it up a notch with a special ingredient known only to the chef.

BÉCHAMEL SAUCE: A white sauce made by heating milk and stirring butter and flour into it.

BEURRE MONTE/MOUNTING SAUCE: Butter whisked into a small amount of boiling water and used as a sauce or as an ingredient in other sauces. It's good for poaching, and for resting cooked meat. Make this butter near the time it will be used and keep it in a warm place, but under 190 degrees to keep its consistency. It can also be refrigerated and used later.

BOUQUET GARNI: A bunch of mixed herbs tied together and dropped into stews and soups. Sometimes the herbs are placed in a small square of cheesecloth to prevent them disintegrating into the broth.

BRACIOLE: Thin slices of beef pan fried in their juice.

BRAISE: To slow cook a food in a covered pot until tender.

BRUNOISE: Diced very small. Usually vegetables. The food item is first julienned (sliced thinly lengthwise) and then turned 90° and diced again, producing small cubes of a consistent size.

BUBBLE, PLEXIGLASS: Plexiglass dome shielding area where correctional officers sit on guard duty.

BUNKY/BUNKIE: Cell mate.

BUTTERFLY: Making a slit down the middle of a piece of meat, chicken or fish, and opening it leaving both halves attached.

CARAMELIZING: Browning food quickly at high temperatures.

CARAMELIZED ONIONS: Chopped or sliced onions are sauteed in oil and/ or butter over a medium heat and stirred constantly until they turn a nice brown. In the professional kitchen, the onions are sauteed in butter in a large frying pan over medium-high heat for 8 to 10 minutes or until golden, while stirring frequently.

CARAMELIZED SUGAR: The melting of sugar at high temperatures, followed by foaming (boiling). At this stage saccharose (sugar) decomposes into glucose and fructose. Sugar is placed in a hot, non-stick pot on a medium to high heat, and stirred constantly while it slowly melts into caramel.

CARBONARA: Pasta sauce usually containing eggs, minced bacon or ham, grated cheese, and seasonings. From the Latin carbon, charcoal, as in charcoal grill.

CHILLIQUILLA: Mexican casserole, similar to lasagne.

CLARIFIED BUTTER/GHEE: Unsalted butter cooked until oil and milk solids separate. Used in French and Indian cooking.

CO/C.O. Correctional Officer

COOKIE SHAPER/COOKIE PUNCHER/COOKIE CUTTER: A clean, empty can (size of your choice), edge dusted with flour to prevent sticking, used to punch out disks of dough for biscuits and cookies.

CREAM OF TARTAR: A kind of salt best known for helping stabilize and give more volume to beaten egg whites and to produce the creamier texture in sugary desserts. White vinegar or lemon juice can be used as a substitute.

CREMA: Cream.

CRIMPING: A method of sealing/closing the edges of a pie or other food item requiring a filling to be secured inside, e.g., pasta ravioli, turnovers, and empanadas; a ruffle created by pinching together the edges of the lower crust and the upper crust between thumb and forefinger, or pressing the tines of a fork around the edges.

DEGLAZE: To add a small amount of liquid to the juices left in a pan after Sautéing foods, often wine, to create a thick glaze.

DOCKING: To pierce, (make holes) usually in pastry, before baking or soaking, to allow steam or liquids to penetrate.

DOUBLE BOILER: See Bain Marie.

DOWN-LOW/ON THE DL: Down-low or on the down low is a slang phrase, often used to refer to something that is secret or hidden, it's between us, nobody has to know.

DRIP TEST: A method of testing fudge to see if it has reached a soft ball stage, (just under 240 degrees using a candy thermometer). A few drops of mixture are drizzled into a shallow cup of cold water. The soft ball stage is reached when the fudge cools in the cold water and remains firm to the touch, still malleable but not hard.

EGG WASH: One tablespoon sugar mixed with one tablespoon EggBeaters. Stir until sugar has dissolved. Used to brush on pies and pastry, makes a seal and a nice shine.

ÉTOUFFÉE: A Cajun dish typically served with shellfish or chicken over rice, similar to gumbo, very popular in New Orleans In French, the word "étouffée" means, literally, "smothered" or "suffocated". The usual staple of an étouffée is seafood such as crawfish, shrimp, or crab meat. Chicken or a combination of chicken and seafood are also popular.

FARMER CHEESE: Like cottage cheese that has been pressed to remove the liquid. It should be sufficiently firm to slice and crumble.

FLAME DEFLECTOR/RISER/POT RISER: A can, washed thoroughly, with the top and the bottom removed, and placed on the heat source under the pot or pan so the heat is deflected, allowing for slower cooking.

FLAUTAS: Rolled and filled tortillas.

FRA DIAVOLO: 'Brother Diavolo'. Spicy sauce for pasta and seafood.

GHEE: A fat made of clarified butter, used in Indian and Egyptian cuisine. Unsalted butter is simmered until all water has boiled off and protein has settled to the bottom. The cooked and clarified butter is spooned off to avoid disturbing the milk solids on the bottom of the pan. Unlike butter, ghee can be stored for extended periods without refrigeration, provided it is kept in an airtight container to prevent oxidation and remains moisture-free.

GUISO: Spanish for stew.

GUMBO: A thick stew or soup originating in Louisiana, and found across the Gulf Coast of the United States and the US South. It consists primarily of a strong stock, meat and/or shellfish. It is thickened with 'filé powder' which is made from the sassafras leaf (not flour), and celery, bell pepper and onion. The soup is traditionally served by placing the rice in the center of the bowl on top of the gumbo.

HUSH PUPPY: This Southern specialty is a small cornmeal dumpling flavored with chopped scallions, deep-fried and served hot. Served as a traditional accompaniment for fried catfish. It is said that to stop hungry dogs begging for food, cooks tossed scraps of the fried batter to the pets while saying "Hush, puppy!

IMUSA: Brand of aluminum cooking pots. Prison friendly, they are molded aluminum with no screws and non-removable handles. Check your facility for rules on sizes.

JAMBALAYA: A Louisiana specialty, traditionally made in one pot, with meats, sausages and vegetables, and rice added to the pot later in the cooking process.

JULIENNE: Cutting food into thin strips (Julienned).

KNEAD: Part of the process of preparing bread and pastry. The dough is placed on a floured surface and pressed and stretched with the heel of the hand; it is folded over and rotated and the process is repeated for about ten minutes until the dough is slightly elastic and smooth. If the dough were baked without kneading, the ingredients would not mix very well and the resulting bread would be very weak and full of large air pockets.

KNOB: A "dollop", heaped teaspoon, usually refers to a piece of butter.

LADYFINGERS: Light, delicate sponge biscuits, round ended, half inch thick, four inches long, light and crispy. Among the oldest of French pastries.

LASAGNE: Very wide, flat pasta strips. Usually baked with layers of sauce, ground meat, and cheese.

MACERATE: To let food, usually fruit, soak in liquid to absorb flavor. Fruits are usually soaked in liqueurs.

MACK: Mackerel, also called Jack Mack.

MARRY: Usually the bringing together of flavors, when flavors meld together.

MASCARPONE: A triple-cream cheese made from crème fraîche, manufactured with tartaric acid or citric acid or lemon juice. Sometimes buttermilk is added. It is milky-white in color, and spreads easily.

MEDALLION: Usually a small round piece of meat or chicken.

MISE EN PLACE: To have all your ingredients ready before you start cooking.

MOLÉ: A popular, Mexican chocolate-flavored sauce.

NAN/NAAN: A round, Indian and Middle Eastern flatbread made of white flour.

NON-REACTIVE POT: A pot made of a product that doesn't deteriorate when acids or brines are put in it, e.g., glass, stainless steel, enamel, and nonstick.

PARBOIL: To partially cook in boiling water. The cooking is completed by some other method.

PASTRY RING: See Ring Mold.

PB&J: Peanut Butter and Jelly.

PECHE: Fish.

PICANTE: Spicy sauce, typically containing tomatoes, onions, peppers and vinegar.

PIZZAIOLA: An Italian sauce made with tomatoes, usually served on steak - Steak Pizzaiola.

POT RISER: See riser.

PUNCHER: See cookie shaper.

PUTANESCA: "...the way a whore would make it" a reference to the hot, spicy flavor and smell.

QUESADILLA: Corn or wheat tortilla stuffed with cheese. Literal translation from Spanish "Little Cheesy Thing".

RATATOUILLE: A French dish which translated means a stirred, chunky stew. 'Rata' is slang from the French Army meaning 'chunky stew', and 'touiller' which means 'to stir'.

REC: Recreation time.

RECTANGLE/OBLONG: Four sided square, longer than it is wide.

RENDER: Remove excess fat, usually from meat, by slow-cooking it in a skillet.

RING MOLD: Easy to make. A large, hollow can, such as that from a sardine or ham can, washed and dried thoroughly, with the top and bottom removed. Used to fill with cake mix or soft foods to set them into a round molded shape, such as puddings and Jell-Os. When the contents are ready, the ring mold is removed and the contents will hold their shape.

RISER/POT RISER/FLAME DEFLECTOR: Two types, both easy to make, are placed under pots to deflect heat. Allows slower cooking and prevents burning. You can use a ring mold described above, OR you can punch holes in both ends of a can large enough to support your heavy pot. Place riser on the heat and place cooking pot on top of riser.

ROLLING PIN: The best is a full can of soda, without ridged edges. (Ridged edges tear the dough).

ROLLING SURFACE: For rolling out dough, or other activities requiring a clean, non-stick, non-slip surface. Tear off a large enough piece of a clean garbage bag to cover the intended work surface. Don't try to work with a whole garbage bag. Sprinkle a little water on the intended work surface, spread it around, then wipe it off with a towel, but leave it damp. Place the piece of garbage bag on the damp surface, and with a dry towel smooth out the bag, pressing out any air pockets. The bag will stick to the work surface. If it doesn't stick, you have used either too much or too little water under the bag. Tape can be used instead of water, but water is free and works better.

ROUX: A mixture of flour and fat cooked together and used as a thickening.

SAUTÉ/SAUTÉE: To fry lightly in fat, in a shallow open pan.

SEARING/PAN SEARING: To brown/sear all sides of the surface of the food (usually meat, poultry or fish) quickly over high heat without covering, so that a caramelized crust forms.

SHEETER: Machine for rolling very large sheets of dough.

SHU: Special Housing Unit/The 'Box'. 24-hour lockdown for prisoners who "misbehave".

SIMMER: After bringing liquid to a boil, lower the heat so it continues to boil slowly and gently.

SIMPLE SYRUP: Equal parts water and sugar usually brought to a boil to melt the sugar, but may also be made by stirring the sugar in warm water until it has dissolved. Can be brushed on cake to moisten and sweeten.

SKIMMING: Removing fat and foam from the top of a boiling pot of cooking food.

SOFFRITO: A combination of onions, red peppers and garlic, diced small, and cooked in a little oil until just starting to become tender. Used as a flavor starter.

SOFTBALL STAGE: A term given to sugar and fudge mixes when they reach the right consistency. Usually determined by performing a 'Drip Test' where the mixture is dripped into cold water and forms a soft ball.

SOFT PEAKS: Soft beaten egg whites, the peaks will softly flop over.

STIFF PEAKS: Egg whites beaten until stiff, the peaks will stay upright.

SPREAD: A "feast" of inmate-invented culinary specialities! Particularly on holidays, inmates pool their food to make a meal. Anything edible goes in, canned fish, jerky, tamales, fried chicken, roast beef, tortillas, canned ham, pickles, fried foods, potato chips, peanut butter, bread etc. It's all put into a common container such as a large plastic garbage bag or a large topless one gallon jug. and heated. Garbage bags can be suspended in hot water to heat, while jugs are heated with 'stingers' (immersion heaters).

STROMBOLLI: An island off the North East coast of Sicily. Gives its name to bread dough baked with stuffing (usually cheese & peppers).

SWEATING: Sautéing with the lid on, usually onions alone, or onions with carrots and celery (known as the Holy Trinity).

TEMPERING: Time- and temperature-sensitive process that allows the crystals in chocolate to be distributed and suspended evenly throughout the final product. Correctly tempered chocolate yields a bright, crisp, and shiny chocolate, while incorrectly tempered chocolate produces a streaky and dull product.

TEMPURA: Japanese, lightly battered and fried vegetables or seafood.

TIRAMISU: Dessert cake infused with liquid such as coffee or rum, layered with rich cheese filling and topped with grated or powdered chocolate.

TORTILLA: Flat, unleavened bread made from finely ground corn or wheat flour.

TRIANGLE: A three sided square, with all three sides of equal length.

TUILLE: A tube shaped, crunchy cookie that has been wrapped around a tubular shaped object immediately after being removed from the oven, while it is still hot and soft. When it cools it assumes the shape of what it has been wrapped around.

UNLEAVENED: Made without yeast or any other leavening (rising) agent.

WATER BATH: See Bain Marie.

WEIGHTS & MEASURES:
    1 stick butter or margarine = 8 oz
    3 small teaspoons = 1 large tablespoon
    A 15 oz or 16 oz can = approximately 2 cups

ZEST: The outer skin of citrus fruits like lemons, limes, oranges and grapefruits. Usually refers to the grated skin, used for flavoring.

Made in the USA
Las Vegas, NV
19 September 2023

77844887R00144